Lynne Segal is Anniversary Professor of Psychology and Gender Studies at Birkbeck College, University of London. Migrating from Australia to Britain in 1970, just when the women's liberation movement kicked off, she made her name as a feminist activist, writer and scholar. She has published widely across the spectrum of sexual politics, gender concerns and broader issues of social justice, most recently in support of Israeli–Palestinian peace initiatives.

Making Trouble

LIFE AND POLITICS

Lynne Segal

A complete catalogue record of this book can be obtained
from the British Library on request

The right of Lynne Segal to be identified as the author of
this work has been asserted by her in accordance with the
Copyright, Designs and Patents Act 1988

First published in 2007 by Serpent's Tail,
an imprint of Profile Books Ltd
3A Exmouth House
Pine Street
Exmouth Market
London EC1R 0JH
www.serpentstail.com

ISBN 978 1 85242 937 9

Designed and typeset by Sue Lamble
Printed by Mackays of Chatham, plc

10 9 8 7 6 5 4 3 2 1

Contents

For Agnes, unexpectedly,
for Eamonn, as promised,
for Zim, from the beginning

Acknowledgements

It's nice but not so easy to express my gratitude to
the many people who have helped me with this
book over the last six years. They have done so in such
differing but necessary ways, from keeping memories alive
and making me laugh, to assessing the Zeitgeist and
correcting commas. First up, I am very grateful to my
publisher, Pete Ayrton, not only for making this book
possible but also for his always helpful editing and commentary,
even when we disagreed. It is the greatest pleasure that
I was able, once again, to have Ruthie Petrie as my editor; her
insights into the world we shared in the Seventies were often
invaluable. I could say much the same about other old
friends who read many of my drafts and responded so
generously to my queries about the life and legacies of our
shared political dreams, especially Marsha Rowe, Sarah
Benton, Sheila Rowbotham, Cora Kaplan, Barbara Taylor,
Catherine Hall, Sally Alexander, Mandy Merck and Barbara
Ehrenreich.

Other feminists inspired me with their own political
reappraisals of the last three decades, Sue O'Sullivan, Denise
Riley, Jill Nichols, Michèle Roberts, Gillian Slovo, Irene
Bruegel, Jenny Taylor, Susannah Radstone, Virginia Blain,
Kate Soper, Cynthia Cockburn, Wendy Hollway, Janet Rée,

Nira Yuval Davis, Janet Sayers, Gaby Charing, Paula Nicholson, Ursula Huws, Mary Kennedy and Rachel Moore. Men too were generous with their comments, especially my friends Peter Osborne, Alan Sinfield, Bill Schwarz, Stuart Hall, John Fletcher, Ralph Edney, Chris Whitbread, Steve Skaith, and James Swinson, plus others who sent me their thoughts, Jonathan Rutherford, Julian Wood and Bruce Robbins.

The Australian sociologist, Raewyn Connell, is another friend whose rigorous attention to gender matters, especially in the global domain, usefully challenge my own more parochial tendencies. Roelof Smilde was invaluable in his extensive commentary on my memories of the Libertarian milieu in Sydney, I am most grateful for the work he put into reading and editing this chapter.

One way or another I am indebted to other very old friends from the Sixties, Jan Allen, Peter Kingston, Anthony Wallace, Tony Skillen, Ian Bedford, Ross Poole, and Roseanne Bonney. Going further back, I want to thank my sister and brother, Barbara and Graeme, those necessary commentators on the place we started out from, while my son Zim was the essential ingredient helping me to move onwards into a very different future.

My new Israeli friends Uri and Mirjam Hadar have given me precious sustenance over the last three years; also, of course, Misha, and his uncle Arnon Hadar as well. I have enjoyed the friendship of others in that troubling land, my young friend Daniel Tsal and, bridging his generation and mine, Sigal Goodlin. Helping me work out how we might try to assist those working against impossible odds to bring peace to that region, I am hugely indebted to Richard Kuper and Irene Bruegel, as well as others who work tirelessly in Jews for Justice for Palestinians. I was also assisted in my thoughts on Israel and the paradoxical nature of Jewishness by Moshe Machover, Brian Klug, Anthony Bale, Daniel Monk, Oren Yiftachel, Eli Zaretsky, as well as the encouragement and inspiration of Judith Butler.

Others whose love, wit and wisdom kept my writing going, especially in the early years when I was unsure whether I would continue include Peter Osborne, Paddy Maynes, Katherine Johnson, Mehmet-Ali Dikerdem, Bill Schwarz, Sarah Chapman, Alan Sinfield, Loretta Loach, Nel Druce. Rachel Calder, Norma McArthur and Mary McIntosh were essential supports in the early days of writing, while Éamonn McKeown was there for the duration, one way and another offering his love and wicked humour, as well as his elegant editing skills in the final months of writing. More recently Marina Warner and Nick Davidson have given me warmth, advice and encouragement. My colleague Stephen Frosh was supportive throughout, reading at once everything I sent to him, while others at Birkbeck, especially Maria Aristodemou and more recently, Lisa Baraitser, have become valuable friends, and Patricia Kelly was always generous with technical assistance. My copy-editor, Catherine Best, was excellent at ridding me of some of those unnecessary commas. Siobhan Culhane helped me keep mice and other nasty things at bay.

Who have I forgotten? My dearest friend Agnes Bolsø is of course on my mind, with her physical grace, generosity of spirit and gentle political intransigence. And now I would like to begin again, thanking all those who keep me going day to day, but the task is invidious, so I can only hope you know who you are, and repeat my gratitude.

Prologue

This is not a memoir. At least, it is not simply a personal reckoning of my life so far. That would mean recording all its hopes, ambitions, triumphs, loves, friendships, dreams, and more, always much more, sketched out for you alongside its fears, failures, follies, heartaches, rivalries, disappointments, with who knows what, never named or acknowledged, hiding in the shadows. No, this is not a memoir. For any one sequential tale I might unfold, including the political life and times I mainly dwell upon in these pages, could be rolled right back in again, to be replaced by another set of narratives. Nevertheless, the personal reflections that mean most to me, which provide a certain temporal continuity and help sustain those attachments to others so necessary for our sense of self, often take me to places that are also political. They transcend the segregation between the personal and the political. That barrier is always breached when we hear voices we have not heard before, people speaking more confidently, sometimes for the very first time, framing things differently, as they insert themselves, usually precariously, into burbling public arenas where they were not evident before. For better or for worse, it was listening out for such voices that often brought me to life, drawing me into identifications and belongings that would give me the most lasting sense of who I was and what I wanted, negotiating my way through the pitfalls of life.

An expat in London, I have now lived most of my days far from my birthplace in Sydney. It is not a move I regret, though things did not begin auspiciously, when I arrived, all suitcases stolen in transit, on that first day of September, 1970. Worse, the minute I landed in London, in my mid-twenties, I fell into bad company. For once I had not even gone looking for it, as I had in Sydney's bohemian Sixties. Knowing next to nobody, lost and lonely, I was urgently seeking work and a home for my infant son and myself. I was quickly installed in a job at Enfield College of Technology, and it was in this very respectable setting, via a colleague who moved into the flat I had rented in the smart end of Maida Vale, that a handful of wild young anarchists with the suitably childish name 'the Angry Brigade', appeared briefly on my doorstep.

These inept would-be insurrectionists, passionately projecting rage onto all around them (those they dreamed up with 'guns in their pockets and anger on their mind') were swiftly apprehended, having managed at the height of their fame to blow up a dustbin belonging to the then Tory home secretary, Robert Carr.[1] For this the four men and two women subsequently convicted received the harsh sentence of ten years in jail. (Today they'd probably never be released.) I was soon helping to run an appropriately anarchic crèche, created for a small band of children, my son included, whose mothers wanted to attend the trial at the Old Bailey of those arrested for conspiracy to cause explosions – the lovers, friends and, for the most part, highly critical supporters of this hapless band of revolutionaries. The location of the crèche was a notorious commune in Grosvenor Avenue, north London, famous for its lack of a door on the loo at the top of the hallway (initially merely unfinished business, rather than scatological intention to shock, so one of its founding members told me), its rejection of all rights to property (including clothing), and its supposed sexual freedom, allowing everyone to sleep with anyone they chose: wherever I lay my body, you can have it. I never lay down. But I did lose my favourite coat, hand-stitched by a Sydney friend, which was duly delivered to one of the Brigade women in Holloway prison. I began visiting Jake Prescott, the fetching working-class casualty of Angry Brigade bravado. This thoughtful and sympathetic soul, at least as I saw him, who wrote to me over the next decade from his many different places of incarceration, was described in his prison files as a 'fanatical Marxist psychopath', who could 'never settle down in civilized society'.[2] It was an odd political detour, you might think, on a journey which would lead me all the way onwards to a share in the mainstream professional status gradually more available in the post-war period for many a university-educated white woman.

However, this was the 1970s, in many ways the friendliest decade there has yet been for western women, certainly for foolhardy single young females who were also – in my case accidentally – mothers. With a little help from our friends, we triumphantly escaped the old stigma as 'fallen' or 'abandoned' women, yet we were still too few in number, still too far out from established patterns, to have found ourselves re-branded anew as the selfish, male-ejecting go-getters responsible for 'disturbing the nest'. We escaped this particular assault on single mothers, accused by new moral missionaries today of creating the 'most urgent social problem' of our time: fatherless families.[3] With or without men, independent young mothers (ideally unmarried) in the 1970s were often the early heroines, the immediate beneficiaries and, so it soon seemed, the ultimate success stories, of the early years of Women's Liberation. 'Women with children,' as Sheila Rowbotham later observed, 'were our equivalent to the Marxist proletariat ... the vanguard of the women's movement.'[4] Cheerful or tearful in all the usual combinations, everything about our lives then tended to feel significant and engaging. With all-too-absorbing political and cultural lives, lovers, children, jobs, or – earning the most respect in our topsy-turvy, anti-bourgeois appraisal – tolerable welfare assistance, our identities and belongings as feminists could hardly have been more solid. As I describe in this book, being part of a radical movement became, for a while, our life's agenda, whatever the private sorrows or public squabbles we encountered or created for ourselves along the way.

At least, that is the way I recall those times. It is how history, as I see it, shaped my particular experience of domesticity, motherhood, intimacies, job aspirations and, enduringly, political affinities. But it is far removed from the usual accounts of second-wave feminism appearing in both popular and scholarly assessments today. One of the main incentives for writing this book is knowing that even our memories, as many have said before me, are never safe from the rewritings of history. The present always reconfigures the past in terms of what comes afterwards. Yesterday's female agitators seem particularly prone to generational misunderstandings: older women's envy of youth plays a part; so does younger women's need to affirm their distinctiveness, highlighting separation from precisely those 'mothers' who might seem closest to them in confronting modernity's recycled predicaments. Older feminists must also endure the reverberations of more defensive, conservative times, seeing marketable aspects of once oppositional challenges selectively incorporated into the contemporary orthodoxy, even as notions that still contest it are thrust aside or amended.

The revised account of Women's Liberation is one in which second-wave feminists, although right to demand more equality and respect for women, are misconstrued as having been ambitious mavericks. In later variants, Seventies feminists stand accused of 'betraying' mothers, ignoring children and – of course, of course – hating men. Yet men were the very creatures so many of us spent so much of our lives working with, seeking out and loving, even as we tried, with no small measure of success, to tame and to train them out of their inherent sense of entitlement and into fully sharing the struggles and responsibilities of our personal lives.[5] Although there were passionate rows and many tensions, some men did adjust rather quickly, soon immersing themselves in domestic life and relating with genuine concern and warmth to children, including those who were not their own. As I turn back time, reviewing my personal past, I find the Women's Liberation Movement providing the first secure moorings in a world hitherto largely devoid of significant meanings, morality or goals. This was despite and also because of our ardent attempts in the 1960s to shed all the conventional trappings of competitive social ranking and respectability, which women such as I had been raised to secure. Those women who tried to change the world at the very least usually managed to change themselves. What becomes of any such 'dangerous' young radicals as they age?

Living memories

This book is one attempt to answer that question, brooding over my own backward glances, and those of others before me, who – at least for a while – tried to live with a strong sense of connectedness with and responsibility for others. Some feel such bonds through religion, others by way of more diverse loyalties, most of us – at least some of the time – on the smaller stage of family ties. Those who interest me most now, as they have hitherto, are people who grounded a significant part of their lives in their identification with oppositional politics, perpetually grappling with questions of justice, recognition and the self-serving orthodoxies of the powerful. Identities are always best seen as active and ongoing projects, which encompass the culturally freighted psychic dynamics of how we become, and try to remain, the people we are expected to be. This also includes how we variously squirm within or try to thrust aside certain antici-pations surrounding us. Passionate political identifications are prevalent when cultural shifts and ruptures encourage confrontation with old constraints, especially with the opening up of new public spaces. When successful, resist-ance often accompanies parallel acknowledgement of the injustice and suffering of others.

Such times seemed a world away from the situation in which I began thinking about this book, in the closing years of the last century. Broad-brush demographic surveys, quite as much as cultural analysts and moral pundits, corrobo-rated my sense of a startling decline in democratic participa-tion beginning in the 1980s, whether in trade unions, political parties or any other collective associations. This accompanied reports of the dramatic rise in political cynicism, evident not just in declining voting patterns, but in people's absence from any form of community organization. (Six in ten people born in the 1940s apparently belonged to at least one collective group by the time they were in their thirties, compared to less than one in ten young people born in 1970 on reaching that age.)[6]

Today, we are allowed, indeed positively encouraged, to

narrate our personal histories. It was not always so, even in my lifetime. Once, as Edmund White noted of the 1950s, that dutiful and compliant decade when he and I grew up, people felt 'a certain contempt for autobiographical fiction'.[7] Wartime survivors for the most part, it seemed, would not, could not, look back. They wanted only to face forwards to the future – to furnish homes, tend gardens, raise children destined for a better life – now that it was, finally, all quiet on the western front. Avid materialism, not introspective musing, was the mood of the 1950s. The cultural and domestic traditions of late-nineteenth-century bourgeois society were firmly, if briefly, back in place. These were enforced by continuing punitive attitudes towards divorce, 'illegitimacy', 'delinquent' children, 'problem' families, accompanying support for the death penalty and harsh regulation of all those who would not or could not conform. However, increasing distance from the multiple horrors of war (at least on our own doorstep), plus the continuing cultural shifts over the last half-century (scrambling social conventions and political convictions alike), has encouraged the turn to autobiographical narration. As the latest sanctioned means for stabilizing one's place in the world, it can provide an anchor to moor the vicissitudes of personal lives, reaching right back to childbirth.

Offering resources to facilitate self-disclosure, autobiographical services, from study guides to educational projects and courses, are currently blooming along with creative writing courses. 'In the project of finding an identity through the processes of historical identification,' Carolyn Steedman comments, 'the past is searched for something (someone, some groups, some series of events) that confirms the searcher in his or her sense of self, confirms them as they want to be, and feel in some measure that they already are.'[8] This can be absorbing, for both storytellers and their audience – at least for those who see their own lives reflected in the text. However, from the closing decades of the twentieth century, self-narration has tended to conform to a Zeitgeist largely disdainful of any broader analysis of the social and economic underpinnings of selfhood. It was just such vigorous insertion of personal lives into the political domain that had been, for a while, the distinctive hallmark of that first 'post-war' generation, but their reappraisals of everyday problems were now disappearing along with the radical movements that generated them.

Certainly, it was not tales of shared hope, but rather of individual triumph over trauma, that had popularly surfaced in the memories pouring forth at the close of the twentieth century. This was and still is a time of unprecedented interest in life stories, highlighting the importance of memory, but their nub was regularly the recognition of childhood damage, and the unfolding journey was one of solitary transcendence. As those already busy writing about the 1990s have commented, that decade saw an extraordinary flowering of cultural obsession with trauma, everywhere encouraging the *cri de cœur* of the 'walking wounded', detailing their uniquely gruesome tales, whether of sexual abuse, personal injury, parental loss or the living of one's premature dying.[9] With the dawning of the twenty-first century, an exhibition assembled by the Hayward Gallery hosting the recent artworks of twelve leading international artists, began touring the major art galleries of Britain – its title, simply, Trauma.

In another telling rendition of changed times, the German writer and feminist scholar, Frigga Haug, recalls the 'catastrophe' attending her attempt to teach a course on 'memory work' in Canada in the 1990s. She was shocked to discover that her students insisted on the need for attendant therapists and the imposition of other forms of psychological safeguards. They all thought it self-evident that 'memory work' would involve attempts 'to reveal an incestuous past, an idea that they found fascinating and horrible in equal measure'.[10] It was not what this older Marxist feminist had anticipated, nor what she had encountered a mere decade earlier. As I will try to depict, those I think of as 'my generation' (with all its attendant conceptual haziness) had early on turned to Left-wing politics to help us move beyond personal anxieties. Entering adulthood in the 1960s, our ways of thinking seemed wholly out of kilter with the settlements accepted by our mothers. Soon, as newly emerging feminists, many sought collective solutions to shared female afflictions: 'An End to Sexual Misery and Exploitation', 'Solidarity with Our Sisters', especially those in prison or mental hospitals, were just two of our early quixotic catchphrases. Little hint of such demotic grandeur attends today's fondness for self-narration, where psychological damage has become the 'secret' the world loves to divulge. But its disclosure unlocks doors leading only into private households of shame or suffering. No wider political maps are provided for locating them within regimes of male dominance (unless they happen to be in 'alien' cultures), or for underlining the brutalizing effects of poverty, insecurity, failure, disregard, disparagement, on those seen as 'losers' in our world.

Yet, even as we are encouraged to individualize at every turn, we speak only with and through the words of those with whom we manage to affiliate – reflecting back their favoured metaphors and idioms, thoughts and sentiments. In the beginning we may all come to know ourselves solely in relation to that first and primordial Other, remaining forever entangled with the inscrutable effects of her unique mother-tongue, mother-touch. But a host of others will soon enter and give meaning to our stories, hopefully for the rest of our lives, if gradually more rarely and weakly: 'we are, fortunately, never done with appropriating others', as the French psychoanalyst J. B. Pontalis comments in his own charming, fragmentary autobiographical writing.[11] In theoretical texts, we are certainly reminded often enough that human lives unfold with, and only with, the generation of stories, through the cultural modes available to us for the telling and hearing of them. It is widely known that both individually and collectively we forget far more than we remember, registering what seems important according to our milieu, cancelling out anomalies through 'the art of forgetting'.

'To be a convincing "I-witness", one must ... first become a convincing "I",' that master of critically self-aware, cultural ethnography, Clifford Geertz, noted.[12] But it is the struggle to become a convincing I which is becoming the end in itself: consummation, not prologue to witnessing. 'Ultimately there is no country but childhood's' has an elegiac pull that is hard to resist, to be sure, when we are forever haunted by that first landscape.[13] Yet it is only in the modern era that this particular notion of stories of remembered childhood would become the key to the narrative of the self.[14] In line with these new subjectivities of modernity, it is from this time too that psychoanalysis emerged and, despite all its critics, remains for many the pre-eminent marker, midwife and mender of lives.

Nevertheless, if forever shadowed by the place from where we began, alongside all that will later constrain us, it is only in the explicitly more knowing, socially recognised projects of adulthood that we continue that childhood project of self-making, and leave (or fear we may fail to leave) some imprint on the world within the spaces we pass through – whether our lives prove fulfilling or not, are valued or remain unsung. We only gain some measure of that world, or any sense at all of our footing within it, through the shared stories we can create and sustain via our ties to others. For me, and for those in my generation I was closest to, it was the bonds we forged in collective efforts not just to wrestle with the world, but also to try to change it which, for a while at least, gave us our strongest sense of ourselves.

Ruptures and renovations

Every group and allegiance has its own hostilities and conflicts, both at its heart and on its fringes. Nonetheless, it was primarily external forces – victories and accommodations, alongside defeats and disillusions – that vanquished the first and broadest sense of collective belonging in those eager women's liberationists who had hoped to build a better world to meet what we then understood of the differing needs of women everywhere. Disparities between women were not ignored in those early days, nevertheless it was a totalising commitment to a universal standpoint, so distrusted of late, that made us search for transformations that might apply to 'humanity' as a whole, to women and men alike. Our collective signs, symbols, pamphlets and speeches came fiercely adorned with 'revolutionary' images and rhetoric (in ways now plundered and twisted both in mainstream political oratory and commercial marketing), yet I know I never really expected 'revolution around the corner'. All my closest friends and companions, comrades and lovers, were attempting to create havens of mutuality and equality throughout the 1970s, hoping against hope, over many years, to achieve Rudi Dutschke's 'long march through the institutions' of power, creating change from within society by radicals forming ever more integral alliances in every part of it.[15]

In ways disappearing in the mists of time, we expressed the sentiments of the original New Left of the early 1960s, discarding the old antagonism between 'reform' and 'revolution', while seeking routes of collective participation that bypassed party structures and went beyond a defensive Labourism.[16] That too is a story I try to reassess here, wondering what has become of that conflict-ridden Left milieu from which Women's Liberation emerged, selectively incorporating even as it challenged aspects of this heritage. For sure, some people we worked alongside and interminably quarrelled with, often comrades in Leninist groups, did appear to believe that the Bolshevik model, with its strict party discipline designed for sudden revolutionary seizure of the state, was still relevant, or at least they liked to act as though they did. 'Come on, sisters, the revolution won't wait', one friend amuses us today, recalling raucous shouts as vans pulled up in Leamington Spa, ready to bus radicals into pitched battle between thickets of police and the thousands of people massed in support of a year-long strike for trade union recognition by Asian women at a small sweat shop named Grunwicks, in west London in 1977.[17] His revolution has proved a little more than patient.

It is now clear that both here and in the USA we were taken far more seriously than we deserved by the authorities of the day. Their spying, prying and MI5 filing suggest that they really did seem to fear that powerful revolutionary currents might be unleashed – although it is always hard to separate out the paranoia of the powerful, evident in their perpetual policing of dissenters, from the existence of a more genuine sense of alarm over possible threats to the existing order. Nevertheless, if most of those I knew did not anticipate rapid revolution, we did strive confidently for radical change – seeking ever-increasing equality and the gradual purging of the multiple underpinnings of systematic cultural disparagement and exploitation. The prevailing Left ambience throughout much of the 1970s, which now appears hopelessly utopian, was that we really could help to create better times for all. As it turned out, in the unintended consequences which so inescapably shadow desired victories, the world changed far faster than feminists or any other radicals had imagined, bringing some of us unforeseen power and authority, even as other women, especially lone mothers with dependents, found themselves poorer and more harried than ever, along with the disadvantaged everywhere. In hindsight, the grand hopes of feminism and the Left, at their height in the 1970s, can provide us with a benchmark for gauging not just their successes, but also the depth of their failure in relation to those women who remain on the margins three decades later.

It was the feminist dream of a common language, of shared values or goals, which began to fall apart as the Seventies drew to a close. Earlier bonds fragmented and competing feminist identities emerged. The differences between women were soon ever more sharply etched, as each distinctive collectivity of women entered the fray, impatient to change their lives and question their position on all fronts – including, especially, their status within the Women's Movement itself. Only years later, however, via poststructuralism and the shifts and fragmentations of the broader Left, would that unstructured, determinedly leader-less movement of the 1970s itself stand condemned as both totalitarian and imperialistic for its universal aspirations. In this book, however, I am less concerned with the evolution of more intricate feminist scholarship than with a broader sketching of feminist trajectories in order to gauge what remains afterwards, as high hopes decline over a lifetime.[18] What traces of the past might we be carrying, after everything changes and angry young rebels become wary older women, ageing in a leaner, meaner time: a time which more than ever before exalts only the 'new', its popular media reflecting an orthodoxy that daily disparages all it portrays as the 'old'? These are older women – the mothers, perhaps grandmothers of today's feminism – who often express regret or criticism of current developments, despite frequently displaying significant signs of power, status and authority which they do not shrink from exercising; older women who themselves sometimes have new engagements with the creation and dissemination of knowledge, skills and resources, whether in the educational, welfare or political domain.

Without consciously setting out to, I am one of the women of my generation who benefited directly from the feminist politics of my earlier years as they came to influence the world of higher education. Assisted by changing economic and ideological shifts overall, the same is true for many other women. I need to confess that I still agree with much that I thought and said decades ago, although I understand so much more about the intractable impediments to realizing the hopes they encompassed. Nonetheless, it is still hard to get the measure of the changing significance of formative political attachments, to view again the support they have offered and the frustrations they have roused, both when flourishing and when in retreat. Dissident political attachments are rarely static.

Who dares capture the consequential moment for others? The courage to protest is one thing, holding on to the diverse legacies of struggle quite another. The burning political questions around which proselytizers position themselves, wrangle and fall out at any one moment – from labelling the precise inadequacies of the Soviet Union to the assorted wrongs of marriage for women – become irrelevant, even absurd, the next. Perhaps political beliefs and feelings have always been just a little akin to fashion accessories, whether slipped on like comfortable old boots or newly acquired, like Prada footwear. But there have been eras when Left politics has seemed exciting and creative, at the centre of any dynamic life; in other times, it is viewed askance, the preserve of careerists, old fogies, the clamour of sudden eruptions of collective feeling that dissipate as the day is done. The particular nature of our convictions seems also, partly, a matter of contingency, of fortuitous twists of fate. The historian Gareth Stedman Jones recalls of his perceptions of the world when a student at Oxford in the 1960s: 'Like the rest of my generation, I assumed that being intelligent and being on the Left were synonymous', adding in sad parenthesis, that it 'came as a real shock in the 1980s and 1990s to find that cleverness had apparently become the hallmark of the Right'.[19]

Yet, however contingent our political journeys, recalling them stirs up questions of undying significance – from what it is that inspires hope in those most in need of it at any moment, to the conditions and contexts which all too easily erase awareness of surrounding cruelties, corruptions or exclusions. Noting the remarkable absence of any sense of place in his memories of growing up in Wales, until rather recently, the psychoanalytic writer, Adam Phillips, concludes that even our most personal stories are always a far broader cultural and political affair, 'often in need of new translations'.[20] Exactly so.

It is just that broader domain that I want to engage with in making sense of my own life, exploring what became of my generation of dreamers, what formed us, and where we are now, in these times when pessimism seems to pervade what remains of public life. Searching for answers I have used various resources to hand, from my own and others' historical research to fictional explorations of the twentieth century. I have looked in particular at the political reflections of those whose lives most directly touched upon my own journey, in ways I barely understood hitherto. They are the memoirs of older men or women of the Left, as well as the most immediate precursors of my form of feminism. It is my own story, reflected as best I can through the words of those necessary others who were part of it, of our journey to date from threatening young radicals to tiresome old 'crusties'. But, in the increasingly congested field of autobiographical writing, focusing upon political memories just might suggest a few new tricks for us to try out as we continue to age.

1

Strictly personal

t is all too easy, I find, to tell one's life as stand-up comedy; all too tempting to amuse with anecdotes which, in their well-rehearsed familiarity, smother self-doubt with self-display. But comic turns are not the usual mode of entry for tales of political belonging, though they might resonate well enough with a few of their less effective tendencies. Nevertheless, it was the appeal and significance of certain shared collective goals that at times helped me move beyond the needy, performing self that emerged from my childhood, forever in search of attention, warmth and affection.

Where did it begin? Of course, literally, and for most women so crucially, it starts with our mothers. That sometimes peculiar presence, the father, was usually somewhere in the background when I was a child; behind the scenes, though in my case much too obtrusive, unwelcome, redundant, disturbing. Feminist reflections still provide the only rational outlook for any shrewd woman. However, I've thought for a long time, and heard others agree, that the particular affiliations we espouse vary just a little according to which parent we were closest to, which was most admired, feared, mourned, or seemed in need of protection. As Beauvoir said, 'the great danger which threatens the infant in our culture lies in the fact that the mother to whom it is confined in all its helplessness is almost always a discontented woman'.[21] *Discontented*? This is far too weak a word to describe my mother's bitterness and scorn, reciting the litany of my father's sins.

In the beginning

My parents were both medical doctors, although my mother's training and achievements were far more distinguished; she had qualified as a surgeon – only the second woman in Australia to do so. From early on she had the busier surgery, much to my father's annoyance, and before too long she also had the higher remuneration, the greater admiration from patients and colleagues, while working hardest to secure them all. My father's habitual irritability (which I thought manifest in his strange, jumpy, nervous tics); his miscellaneous infidelity; his small cruelties, hurtful teasing, enduring selfishness, seeming incompetence; these formed the background of my childhood. PAY BY INTERCOURSE was the graffiti my mother said he made her – *made her?* – scrub off the high walls around our large and ugly suburban house, which doubled as his surgery. 'What happened to the patient?' I asked. 'He had her certified, of course,' she replied; well, of course. 'I always knew how to get a woman with an infertile husband pregnant – send her to your father,' was another of my mother's scathing asides (though no illegitimate siblings ever surfaced).

Was he really *that* bad? My sister thought so. My uncle thought so (though he too heard his sister's shocking stories). I can summon up few contrasting images of him, nor did others praise him in my hearing, to mitigate our mother's bile: 'I cried myself to sleep every night after my marriage,' she said. I tried to sleep every night, praying –

literally, to a God that I did not believe in – that my father would stop making her so unhappy, stop being so bad-tempered, stop arguing with her. Things never changed. Nor was it only through my mother's tales that I shrunk back from his way of being in the world. There was also the tenor of his strangely sadistic humour, face brightening, it seemed to me, only when he could manage to upset one of us: attempting to provoke jealousy between his children, teasingly ridiculing us before friends, trying to heighten our fears of pain before injections or other painful medications. Perhaps it was a type of humour he had known, which I just wasn't ready for. I cannot say that he had no redeeming features, no ambiguities or goodness; I can only say I did not know them. My brother is a little less critical, believing that our parents were exceptionally badly matched. In his view, our father, the oldest son of first generation, impecunious eastern European immigrants, felt rebuffed and diminished by a wife who was clearly cleverer than him, and better loved by the world, if not by him.

This wife, our mother, was the once cherished and distinguished daughter of far from wealthy but highly regarded second generation Anglo-German Jews, already at the heart of Sydney's very respectable Jewish community. My father, from a poorer background of Lithuanian Jews (then seen as more foreign, or 'oriental'), arrived in Australia in the early twentieth century. However, I learned absolutely nothing about any of this from my parents. They never spoke of their childhoods, nor of the birthplaces of our Ashkenazi forebears, in Prussia, Poland, Lithuania and Britain, although I now see the bitter tensions I was born into as perhaps, in part, condensations of some of that earlier racist friction, fear and defensiveness at a time when, unknown to me, genocidal anti-Semitism had just engulfed most of Europe.

Mother's dutiful daughters, my sister and I had no

positive feelings for our fault-finding, quarrelsome father. Unknowingly, we repeated the story of his sisters, who had despised their own father (apparently also for his philandering, and their mother's consequent bitterness), refusing to speak to or visit him, even on his deathbed. (This grandfather was another absent presence in our life, along with our maternal grandfather, who died before we could ever know him.) Today, I simply wish I had ways of fathoming what it was that made our father so completely unable to show affection for his daughters. He seemed barely able to approach us, let alone touch us; he did not visit me in hospital following my childhood asthma crises, even when spotted calling upon one of his patients within the very same building. I can only speculate on the demons that may have stalked that infant Jewish boy growing up in a family with parents who were apparently so harshly alienated from each other that they only communicated by using their children as intermediaries.

Born in Cape Town in 1904, my father arrived in the slums of Sydney in 1906 with parents who had fled persecution in eastern Europe. He made his way laboriously out of unhappy, far from respectable beginnings (about which he remained forever silent, forever ashamed) into Sydney's then still conspicuously anti-Semitic, professional middle class. His unmarried sisters remained factory workers all their working lives, another source of embarrassment to him. What is more surprising, perhaps, is that as children we learned nothing at all about our mother's background or childhood (apart from her prestigious educational accomplishments), although her much-loved father, Alfred Harris, had been a key, indeed pivotal, figure in sustaining Australia's Jewish community for most of his life.

Buried pasts

'Are we Jewish?' my brother recalls asking our non-Jewish housekeeper as a child. 'Yes, I suppose you are, dear, but you don't have to tell people,' she replied. That must have been one of the very few sentiments she shared with her arch-rival, our mother, who also thought it best, I now realize, to divest herself of any blatant signs of Jewishness. Our mother's passionate atheism, from which she never lapsed, must have helped distance her from home-grown anti-Semitism, not to mention the nightmare of Hitler's slaughter of the Jews of Europe. (No known relative of ours was killed.) With her strict rationalism, she thought that only an imbecile could believe in any God, let alone one who allowed such barbarism to befall his self-appointed chosen people. Less judgementally, I find it hard not to agree.

Many Jews thought similarly at that time. All religion is folly, Richard Wollheim recalls his father declaring angrily in Britain in the 1940s, insisting that to classify people as Jews 'had no basis in scientific fact', but was merely the first step on the way to mistreating them. As a child, Wollheim did not even know that his father was Jewish, although he later discovered that he had spent a great deal of time and money rescuing not only his own relatives, but also friends and even acquaintances from Hitler's lethal clutches.[22] In much the same way, my mother, although dutifully attending synagogue in her young life, later came to regard all religion as absurd, even evil. My parents were not the only Jews then making their homelands in 'new' worlds who came to see complete assimilation as the only answer to it all. My mother's brother expands on this view today, making me realize that, despite little blatant discrimination, anti-Semitism was a frightening threat in my parents' early life in ways it has simply never been in mine.

Indeed, till very recently, Jewish identity would remain a largely empty category. My father, feeling only shame for his impoverished past, focused instead on various recreational activities and hobbies, none of which linked him to any Jewish communities. Along with so many of the people and places she encountered, my mother, I see in retrospect, had internalised not only the intense racism of 'white' Australians, but also their disdain for 'foreign' Jews. The home-grown images etched in the psyches of every Australian child of her generation came from its best-loved fairy tales, written and beautifully illustrated by May Gibbs, in which the light and fluffy Snuggle Pot and Cuddle Pie lived forever in titillating fear and dread of the dangers threatened by scary, thick-lipped, dark and hairy, Big Bad Banksia Men.[23] My mother did not like us to spend time in the sun, not yet expressing a fear of its ultra-violet rays, but rather in thrall to light skin. My mother's more specific distance from Judaism, I now suspect, was also an aspect of her lifelong eagerness to fit in and be well-liked and acceptable, shored up by a positivistic rationality aligned with her medical studies at Sydney University and the general intellectual climate she encountered at the time. Her heroes were always the great humanists, Bertrand Russell and George Bernard Shaw. The flight from her family roots was also encouraged by my mother's shame at the emotional frailty of her own mother (my grandmother, who suffered, I heard only recently, from serious bouts of depression), as well as embarrassment at her father's relative poverty, compared with the wealthy Anglo-Jewish establishment he was part of. These wealthy Jewish families were eager to court her, so she told us, only after she graduated at the top of her year in medicine and was, briefly, a celebrity. Finally, her distance from her Jewish past was also, no doubt, amplified by her enduring marital disappointment, after a lavish Jewish wedding entered into, she said, at the behest of my grandfather when he discovered his daughter 'in bed' with the man who would become my father.

It is only after my mother's death, in my middle age, that I can grasp something of the sadness and loss in her repudiation of her own past, with its very particular and significant Jewish heritage. As an unregenerate bragger, there was much she might otherwise have been proud to affirm. In childhood she was the devoted daughter of a self-educated man, who spent almost all his life attending to Australia's Jewish community as its writer and reporter. Alfred Harris, leaving home and school at fourteen, managed with his father, Henry Harris, to set up the first successful Jewish weekly in Australia, *The Hebrew Standard*, in 1895. Against enduring odds, he edited the newspaper for almost fifty years – despite the chronic financial worries, overwork and emotional exhaustion that many thought helped to shorten his life. He is described in Australian Jewish history books as an unusually gentle, humane and selfless man, who saw his life work as preserving the spirit of orthodox religious life, while encouraging both friendship across all faiths and patriotic citizenship from Jews, in whatever countries they lived.[24] He also used his paper, from the early decades of the twentieth century, to oppose the growth of political Zionism, a project he believed to be 'unjust, dangerous to a degree, even cruel in its inevitable consequences and, after all, unattainable.'[25] Such passionate anti-Zionism would lead Australian Jewry to spurn much of my grandfather's legacy once Jewish support for Israel became hegemonic after the state's founding, in 1948. 'To live in hearts we leave behind, is not to die,' his friend and mentor, the first Australian-born prime minister, Sir Isaac Isaacs, said in his appreciation of Alfred Harris after his death in 1944: 'I say unaffectedly his passing has left a void in my life's experience beyond my power of adequate expression.'[26]

That my mother was not able to express any appreciation of her father's legacy, I now think, added to her abiding sense of inner emptiness, her failure to feel good about herself or her life, despite her considerable achievements. It was not easy being a successful professional woman in mid-twentieth-century Australia, and many women I would later meet described my mother as an inspiration to them. Nevertheless, a sense of bitter loss and futility dogged her. Whatever its intricate source, this sense of emptiness was something I too seemed to absorb from my mother, or often feared I had. It would be over fifty years before I came to reflect upon the nature or significance of my family's Jewish heritage. As ever, it was politics that finally led me back to the question of what it might mean to be a Jew, in a world where our putative ties with Israel and its continuing Zionist project seemed to matter more than ever, aligning me with the buried maternal legacy. That ambivalent Jewish identification, however, would prove just as elusive as the various other identities I have acquired or grappled with throughout my life.

Household shadows

Back in the 1960s, I had trouble accepting any of the roles that awaited me on leaving school. It was not merely that many women coming of age in the Sixties had no inspirational guides or mentors – we had the reverse: danger signs everywhere, anti-models galore. Even our mothers, and not only my mother, wanted our lives to be different from their own. Why had so many of them become bitter, or disenchanted, with their lot? It's a complex story, which I'll return to again, encompassing the aftershock and disruptions of wartime, the orchestrated charade of a supposedly 'conflict-free' peacetime, and the extraordinarily repressive nature of mid-century Australian society. I have come across its strange legacy over and over, the sham barely concealing the gloomy truth inside those Fifties families. Happy families are not all alike, but an unhappy family is certainly unhappy after its very own fashion. My mother was not a bored and frustrated housewife, unable to put her skills, training and intellect to use (like the mothers of many of my friends). She was an admired, successful, endlessly busy gynaecologist, doing a job she seemed to enjoy. Always alert for that phone call that would whisk her away from the argumentative husband, three obedient children and the working-class mistress our father had installed as 'housekeeper' (just before her marriage), it was coming home that was her problem. The phone call usually came. That was my problem. I was always happiest when she was somewhere around, at least when she was not too unhappy, and she could ignore us all as she tried to impress some – any – passing visitor, worker, or stranger. Another, better world always beckoned, where she could forget her conjugal miseries.

It beckoned to me too. 'We couldn't take you out,' the same housekeeper-cum-nursemaid told me, years later, 'you'd just toddle up to some stranger and wander off with them.' Rather sensible little steps, it might seem, when her other weird tales included leaving me most of the day alone in my cot, upstairs on the veranda, pulling threads out of my nappy; waving eagerly at those passing strangers out of the window, once I was able to stand. *Can I believe these stories? Have I imagined them? Where was my brother, only a year older?* I do know that from the beginning, in the housekeeper's eyes, I took after her rival, that mother of mine: my red hair – a sign of bad temper, she said – was the maternal lineage. The jet black locks of my brother and my sister (born fourteen months after me) were shared with our father. They were the two children with whom the housekeeper always, and quite obviously, enjoyed mutual affection, never with me. Fixated as I was on the fleeting maternal presence, I didn't seem to mind, although scolded by the housekeeper as my mother's favourite. 'Why do they say I am your favourite?' I questioned my mother (who would invariably visit me in hospital whenever I was rushed there after some bronchial crisis). I asked the question knowing, of course, and agreeing also, that only my brother, the budding 'genius', could hold that position. 'Well,' she replied, or I dreamt she did, 'you seem to need me most.'

Such were the protocols of the life I recall in this particular unhappy family. But, when not squabbling, I played contentedly enough with my younger sister. I looked forward to the evenings when my mother, in her soft, flowing dresses, put us to bed or, at the very least, arrived at the bedroom door of the girls' room, to blow us both huge, noisy kisses. I was usually happy in school, occasionally the teacher's pet, cheerful with classmates. As the children of two doctors, we were received with kindly approval most places we went. I looked up to and admired my clever brother, who was indulged by all (apart from his peers at school) as a gifted, exceptional child, allowed to say or do whatever he liked at home. For the most part, that involved staying in his room, in pyjamas, hairgrip securing his long front lock, while absorbed, apparently contentedly, in his books. In the evening, my mother spent much of her time reading my brother's homework or listening to him run through or recite by heart things he was learning – perhaps a play by Shakespeare, Russell's mathematical proofs of modal logics, a Tennyson poem. After puberty, we three children spent most of our time outside school doing homework, or at least, in my own case, often pretending to.

It afforded me much time for daydreaming, usually some mildly masochistic, erotic reverie. We did not live in the vicinity of the schools we attended, so had no local friends. At the weekend, our mother might take us to the beach, or on some longer, pleasant trek.

It was at night that my troubles often started: I found it hard to sleep, frequently wheezing and fighting for breath in bed; I was always frightened of the dark, sensing a threatening presence in the air which I felt in some mysterious way linked up with my father, in league with the housekeeper. Yet, even while confronting these bad spirits, it was the good ones emanating from my mostly absent mother that kept me sane and, so often lost in pleasurable daydreams, happy enough – despite suffering chronic asthma attacks from the age of four. 'It's because she's spoilt by her mother', 'she only puts it on to get attention', the two adults who frightened me would pronounce. These two, my father and the housekeeper, were responsible, as I saw it, for packing me off alone to the country at five, or rather, accompanied only by another of my father's mistresses (*how did I know that? I think my mother told me*) and then to boarding school for four years at eight. Neither daft diagnosis of my illness, nor the various banishments from home, made a jot of difference to my lifelong asthmatic condition. My mother too, though usually kinder, shared the view that there was something shameful in suffering from an illness that could not be cured by antibiotics: 'tell them you have bronchitis' was her instruction, an early lesson in the art of duplicity.

I was thought to be an 'oversensitive' child, far too easily disturbed by any news of road crashes or other disasters, over-reacting to books or films that were even mildly scary or sad. Ironically, though, my own daily reveries always involved my undergoing and surviving some vaguely imagined pain and humiliation in order to end up in the strong comforting arms of some older protector (who before puberty was always a female), soothing me for all I had suffered. But I could not handle any comparable representations orchestrated by anyone but myself.

The seriousness of my childhood asthma, in my adult eyes, was a strictly medical, physiological matter, involving allergic reactions, at times exacerbated by infection, not a psychosomatic expression of emotional need or anxiety. I know the many loops that can bind illness to psychic states, whatever the triggering somatic weakness, but I have never been able to trace a link between asthmatic wheezing and ongoing troubles or anxieties. Nevertheless, it is true that when gasping for breath at night, back then, I knew that if I could make it to my mother's bedside, creeping past the housekeeper's room, stealing round the near side of the double bed in which my father slept, I would begin to feel, blissfully, much better, my breathing becoming easier as I knelt quietly close to her on the far side of that bed. The relief was short-lived because, once awakened, she and I would have to dart off for the barbiturates that would sedate me. Should my father awake, I would simply be ordered angrily back to bed, with no medicine to help me breathe, or sleep.

When I was sent away from home and feeling lonely, strangers often came to my rescue – whether finding me in hospital, the countryside, boarding school (where I was sent for four years when I was eight, again supposedly to cure my asthma), or elsewhere in the wider world. I developed, I think, a special knack for making friends: my skinny body in childhood resulted in censure at home, but softer attention from elsewhere, helping to sustain a kinder world around me. I have stayed on the lookout, ever since, hopeful of finding similar strange, friendly faces, just a little way beyond hearth and home.

Searching for values

I was raised with very hazy moral principles, but four values were unambiguous in our strictly atheistic household: way out front, the importance of academic achievement, followed by visible wealth, surface conformity and a rigorous utilitarianism, the last implying that one should try, by whatever means worked, to be liked and to keep people happy. These were my mother's ideals. (My father's moral precepts, I never knew. I think I assumed he didn't have any, but that may be unfair.) Hurtful truth-telling outraged my mother. The only patient she ever ordered out of her surgery, warned never to darken her doors again, was a young pregnant woman who had been unable to conceive the baby she longed for by her much older husband. Following my mother's advice on possible solutions, her patient had taken a younger lover (fortunately not our father) and become pregnant. But instead of returning joyfully to thank her wise gynaecologist, she had gone in fear and trembling to her priest, obeying his advice to confess all to her husband. In my mother's expedient morality, this was not just 'stupid', but 'wicked', causing pain all round. I imagine now that such complete moral pragmatism tied in with, or helped obscure, the intense contradictions she faced as a lone woman trained by and later working alongside medical experts in a then crushingly male profession, notorious for its contempt for women. She sometimes mentioned the routine sexual gropings, which we now call sexual harassment, she had received as a trainee doctor from senior medical figures. These medical authorities also expressed their utter contempt for women who became pregnant outside marriage, including women, so she said, they had themselves pressurized into having sex. All moral absolutes seemed suspect when her only adult mentors were these men who exploited and despised her sex. Her own attitudes towards women were, at best, ambivalent. She was a daughter who had always apparently adored her father, and had been mainly embarrassed by her mother's struggle with depression.

In my adolescence, it was not difficult to spot the weaknesses in my mother's moral outlook: truth, virtue, goodness were empty categories, to be filled in instrumentally. The pragmatic pursuit of fleeting forms of happiness seemed her only guide as a woman, with the accumulation of money its eventual substitute. But it was a happiness that was largely beyond our ken, since she was herself, as she so often told us, extremely unhappy. I knew of no virtues, other than to condemn cruelty, but had not the least idea how to prevent it. I needed something, anything, to throw into that open chasm.

I also saw myself as, and feel I remained, yet another disappointment in my mother's life, though I watched her try in flimsy ways to hide it. Not only was I a skinny, sickly child (that weakness a little offset for her by the curly auburn hair others admired in childhood), but also I was never what she had been, the number one star pupil. She had come first in each and every subject in school, just as my brother did, after her. There was a very short scale between 'genius' and 'feeble-minded' in her cosmology, and heading up history, english or biology as I sometimes did would not necessarily save you from the latter category. Accordingly, when I arrived at Sydney University in the 1960s, it was without the least idea of what I wanted to do, or could possibly be; without any definite sense of what was right or wrong. Having studied the thoughts and deeds of my parents, heeded their talk about the lives of their patients (who would be ridiculed and condemned for conduct my parents at times indulged in themselves), I felt, in some deep but largely inexpressible way, that most people led lives based on lies, hypocrisy and cruelty.

For a while, nothing fitted my missing ethical outlook better than the type of full-frontal assault on bourgeois moral values and authoritarian institutions and practices that I discovered among a small group of anarchists I encountered at seventeen. Moreover, there was a pool of untamed men to trawl, in search of brand new relationships, at a time when the wider world was still – though not for much longer – grimly disapproving of women having sex before marriage. Australia in 1960 remained one of the most sexually censorious countries in the developed world, a place where, for example, half of all feature films coming from abroad were either rejected or significantly cut. To this day I can recall a succession of sex scandals that celebrities from 'overseas' faced when visiting its repressive shores during my childhood: the career of the famous English conductor and composer who had transformed the Sydney Symphony Orchestra into a world-class outfit, Sir Eugene Goosens, was utterly destroyed by accusations that he had imported 'banned' photographs; the world-renowned classical pianist, Claudio Arrau, had no sooner arrived in Sydney than he was arrested and charged with moral indecency, while Marlene Dietrich refused to enter the country at all, after being strip-searched at Sydney airport.[27]

Interpreting lives in terms of parental imprints, childhood landscapes and adolescent turmoil is, of course, only one way of tracing back some of the unique dynamics that might play a part in pushing a person towards politics as an anchor of identity. It seems to me that something about my childhood, in what early on became a comfortably middle-class if eccentric and deeply conflict-ridden household, helped foster awareness of an unjust world, alongside an inclination to identify with the apparently powerless –

although with little belief that much could be done to change things. However, it is the historical contingencies of time, place and other unpredictable encounters, that encompass the twists of fate that will determine our specific journeys. Understanding life backwards, the spirit of each decade I entered in my adult life appears, remarkably, in perfect harmony with my needs of the moment. I embarked upon sexual life in the Sixties, in the growing clamour for sexual liberation. I became a single mother in the Seventies, as feminism bloomed again. In the late 1980s, I began a retreat into the respectable shores of academe when, if you were lucky, you could be both paid (though increasingly poorly) and acclaimed for performing your 'oppositional' politics on university lecture circuits, at just the moment when Left and feminist activism were largely vanishing from more accessible public forums, in preparation for the dismal decade of the 1990s. But, living life forward, you see none of this, struggling to grapple with the day-to-day, whether working for change, comfortable with the present, or barely surviving.

2

My Sydney Sixties

'Someone should give you a slap', Germaine Greer said loudly to startled faces, encountering me again at a gallery in London during the summer of the year 2000. It was almost forty years after we first met, around a coffee table at Sydney University. I was always her junior in every sense, though for a while we travelled similar roads. Leaving my homeland for London at the same age, I had picked up the same principles, shared the same thoughts, frequented the same places, slept with the same men: 'I'll be seeing you/In all those old familiar places/In the pub and at the races ...', she had sung, back in the 1960s. In 1961, in precisely those strange new spaces for suburban girls to venture into, I was eagerly seeking out the men – yes, of course, it could only have been the men – who were the most visible rebels in the landscape, the Sydney 'Push'. Sharing affinities with post-war urban bohemians around the world, they were a fluctuating group of free-floating intellectuals, university lecturers, journalists, students, libertarian businessmen, dropouts, drifters and gamblers who could be found hanging out in Sydney from the late 1940s to the 1970s. As anti-utopian, pessimistic anarchists, their notoriety as radicals in the 1950s and 1960s was inseparable from their sponsorship of 'free love'. Indeed, this was the issue over which Germaine and I later clashed, when she objected to something I had written about her shift from 'erotomania to erotophobia'. In *The Female Eunuch*, Germaine had exhorted women to 'embrace the penis'; twenty years later she was, for a while, earnestly counselling women to welcome celibacy, when writing of the vicissitudes of sex and love as a post-menopausal woman, in *The Change*.[28] Today, with another volte-face, she has returned to her rhetorical roots, and is busy once again celebrating sexual allure, having discovered the charm and beauty of the Boy. But all that comes much, much later.

Sleeping around

Sex and love, more than anything else, were surely what I was searching for in those early days. But that is looking back, as a reluctantly ageing woman. Perhaps I am now also seeking at least the vicarious frisson of conjuring up that younger, sexier self, those days when there always seemed to be intimacy available, should one want it, if a solitary evening loomed. I had few resources for being alone at the time, so a need for the focused attention of others to soothe existential anxieties almost certainly lurked at the heart of the matter. Our sense of self is held together through constant patching up, continuous reconstruction, for as long as we can manage it. I watch myself still busy making and mending my own. This is why self-narration is so consoling, especially if or when the future seems to shrink, while the days speed up. Memory, as wise folk know today, following Freud, Foucault or Derrida, can be a way of inventing the past. It helps just a little if we rehearse our life stories before the suspicious eyes of family and friends, heeding their doubts, while blending in as much background detail and historical context as we can disclose and they can offer, always evoking the images which endure for us while knowing others have vanished.

I now feel it was because I lacked a moral compass of any sort that I turned to politics to make some sort of sense of things in young adulthood. There was a passionate morality in what the world saw as the immorality of the leaders of the Push. Defying the rigid surface conformity and deep conservatism of the newly domesticated post-war world we were born into, their stance was extravagantly at odds with the orders and outlook of State, Church and every other orthodoxy of bourgeois life, or so they thought. Opposing repressive institutions, refusing hint or whisper of servility, they stood for individual freedoms of every kind. Personal autonomy, seen as a mix of integrity and sexual freedom, was their morning, and certainly their evening, star. Their name, most thought, derived from the romance of the rough-living, lawbreaking men of the Sydney docks, back in the 1920s, known as 'the Push'. As satirized in a popular ballad, the 'Leader of the Push' quizzes 'the Bastard from the Bush' (who later robs the urban riff-raff): 'Would you have a "moll" to keep you – like to swear off work for good?' Well yes, I can reply, for the next generation, many would, and did, although before too long we women were to prove more cunning molls – several, in the end, abandoning the men, their demands on our bodies, and sometimes our purses, for feminism.

Indeed, it was the leading men of the Push, living off their wits and refusing all inducements for career, achievement, or even savings, who were more often weakened in the end, certainly financially, by their pursuit of a principled bohemianism. A living legend in this milieu, as a man who had never, for one day, compromised his commitment to a life of comprehensive freedom, Darcy Waters died penniless at 69 in 1997, even then still surrounded by a small group of friends and followers of all ages who lionized and supported him. In his fifties it was this drifting insolvency that enabled Darcy to publicize the fruit of his habitual fascination with the crimes of the powerful, exposing the stories he tracked down of corruption within the police, judiciary and ruling Labour Party (then in power in New South Wales) in his anti-corruption broadsheet, *Horsetalk*. That he had no assets helped to deter libel suits. Darcy, of course, never married, but the women who at various times consorted with him, or with other charismatic Push men, usually ended up choosing, or being forced into, more conventional lives. They kept their jobs, if only to support their men, or the children they might end up raising, often alone. Having learned to speak and act less submissively than other women in the pub culture of the Push, it was the women who would sometimes flourish in their careers, occasionally (at least for a while) rather prominently, like Lillian Roxon, Eva Cox, Liz Fell and Wendy Bacon. But none did so with quite the panache of Greer, and she carried it off while staying, determinedly, closer than I ever would to the mores of our first mates and mentors, the Sydney Libertarians. They were the intellectual wing of the Push, and they remained, as she would later broadcast, 'the strongest influence on my life': 'If ever, of anyone, I desired a good report, I desire it of them, my guides, philosophers and friends, the Sydney Libertarians'.[29]

But what did I yearn for, what life did I imagine for myself, hopping into bed with whoever took my fancy back in the 1960s? Oddly, I'm sure, I yearned to fall in love. But I had no idea what might come next. Marriage was certainly too flawed to mention. It embodied, in my eyes then, servile conformity to the prescriptions of an authoritarian state – rather than, as subsequently envisaged by feminists, to men. I was studying on a scholarship at Sydney University, an inevitable move for someone from my family background, with any alternative pursuit a tag of sub-normality. ('It would seem, she *hasn't* got a PhD,' I once overheard my mother say, with scornful pity, referring to a woman who had, fleetingly, had a sexual encounter with my brother, by this time already an Oxford don at the tender age of twenty-one.) But those I hung out with lived their lives as exemplary icons of freedom and rebellion: whatever the world approved, we opposed it; career ambitions were discreditable; 'opting out' of any form of sanctioned achievement was the worthier goal in our topsy-turvy world. I tied my hair up high in a wild and woolly beehive, which meant I never had to cut or comb it (a style I saw as all my own invention), and I was certainly a danger to other diners if I accidentally dipped my head forward on the occasional more conventional dates in candlelit restaurants: the vilest of odours flared up, as if in warning of my transient anarchist leanings.

Anarchism without ends

My first 'honourable' police arrest, at eighteen, was for the strange midnight spree of plastering 'DON'T VOTE' stickers all over Sydney's Central Station. Voting was compulsory in Australia. (A year or two later, the now distinguished anthropologist Michael Taussig, then one of our number, went to court to argue our principled abstentionism – despite his eloquent defence of the anarchist's need to decline to vote for others to rule over us, he received the usual fixed penalty.) Our transgression was treated with scornful condescension (we were released with a caution). But while under arrest, I was not quite so foolish as to fail to register that a recent Italian immigrant (a group then branded as wogs or dagos), entering the police station voluntarily to report the theft of his watch, was being far more roughly addressed, even ordered to stay put when –

feeling threatened – he tried to leave. It was one of many early intimations of the incapacity of our anarchist outlook to grapple adequately with the everyday cruelties of anti-immigrant prejudice in Australian society. We seemed even less aware of our country's grotesquely racist bedrock, from the beginning, as a settler colony responsible for the near-genocide of its indigenous people. Like almost everybody else, we were comprehensively blind to one of the greatest cruelties of those times, the abysmal state racism behind the practice of removing aboriginal children from their birth families and placing these 'stolen' children with white foster families: this was the fate of those now known as the Lost Generation. With Bakunin, Reich and the aptly named Max Nomad as our primary guides, not Marx, Lenin or Franz Fanon, we also had a limited class analysis informing our political outlook of 'permanent protest'. The point of our politics was not to proselytise, and certainly never to moralise, which meant that engagements with the outside world were sporadic. While deriding all conventional social hierarchies and cultural exclusions, this enclave of hedonistic radicals was hardly geared to challenging them publicly, let alone to working to overturn them strategically.

However, I remain more sympathetic to some of our other nocturnal assaults with posters and glue, such as that mocking the heavy hand of the police, hunting down one lone convict on Emu Plains, using 800 men, bloodhounds, guns, pistols and tear-gas. With more lasting credibility, and this time in alliance with a broader Sydney Left consisting of the Communist Party, a few (characteristically) diversely aligned Trotskyists, and Left Labour supporters, we marched against the apartheid regime in South Africa, entered into battles with obscenity laws and, from the late 1960s, took to the streets to oppose the war in Vietnam. Wendy Bacon, who joined the small band of more assertive Libertarian women in the late Sixties (just as I was retreating), helped change those obscenity laws, after deliberately provoking charges against the student magazine she edited, *Thorunka*. Arriving in court dressed in a nun's habit, bearing the slogan 'I have been fucked by God's steel prick', she was sent to prison (despite a priest who appeared as a defence witness declaring it a reasonable, if novel, depiction of communion between nun and God).[30]

While Libertarians were well-disposed towards the poorest and most rebellious, always keen to expose corruption, whether of those in government, the police force or justice system (with its powerful links to the gambling fraternity and organised crime), they had little interest in fighting for reform, or capturing any positions of power. For us, all ruling groups, even those resulting from revolutionary change, would soon enough become the basis for self-serving and corrupt elites. They inevitably generated authoritarian practices, according to the Libertarian line – underwritten, for those of a more scholarly bent, by the Italian philosopher Vilfredo Pareto and the sociologist Robert Michels. The many Libertarian meetings I attended in my student years were intellectually challenging, more often than not, whether debating the significance of Freud or Marx, the dynamics of sexuality, the nature of ethics, or the need for permanent revolution. Issuing frequent broadsheets, admiring dissidence, rejecting deference, Libertarian views could never be installed, we all agreed, but only *lived* by those who espoused them: 'If you are interested in anarchism, atheism and free love, then come and listen to us; if you are interested in security, certainty and authority, then Libertarianism is not your cup of tea.' It was a gentle dogmatism, which did not recognize its own orthodoxies. Its principles and practices had been summed up by one true believer in a broadsheet produced in 1960: 'Libertarians believe that pluralism is an account of what is the case … it is utopian to believe that there will ever be an end to the conflict of social interests … whether the millennium be the Kingdom of God, the classless society, the national interest or any other common good.'[31]

Indeed, decades before its time, Sydney Libertarianism prefigured much of the political disdain and pessimism that would launch itself as *Nouveau Philosophe*'s sceptical 'postmodernity', or Richard Rorty's ironic neo-pragmatism, after the iconic failure of the French student uprising of May '68. François Lyotard's rejection of all 'grand narratives' of progress (postmodernism's own founding grand narrative), was robustly embraced in my first political home, although we were, unlike our postmodern successors, keen believers in truth and rationality. Proud of our lack of illusions, we thrived then upon just that sceptical pluralism that would be, this time to my partial dismay, reborn decades later. In the meantime, a new surge of utopian hopes emerged, engulfing many, and certainly me, in the more affluent parts of the world from the late 1960s – at least for a while, sweeping our Libertarian pessimism far behind. Other movements were rolling in, some women this time expertly riding their breakers, not merely sucked into them, for a while eagerly visualizing the shores on which we hoped to alight.

It is not uncommon nowadays for feminists to dismiss the libertarian moment of sexual liberation as wholly exploita-tive of women. Yet, for all its limitations I still believe I found a relatively benign, if rather slow, pathway towards adulthood. Certainly, it was a space that encouraged a woman to speak and act just 'like a man', and hence for us more freely than anywhere else in those days. It was already the 1960s when I appeared on the scene, yet it remained a time when any reference to a single woman's sexuality continued to be taboo. Australia still enforced one of the most rigid censorship regimes in the western world, with quite mainstream and solemn books, such as Mary McCarthy's *The Group* (1963), banned for much of the decade for mentioning women's pre-marital sexuality.[32] Even its grimmest critics would later admit that the Push had created 'an island of excitement in a sea of dullness', at a time when the surrounding levels of conformity meant that 'for some, it was almost impossible to breathe'.[33]

In defiance of this sexual climate, the first significant adult relationships I had were all with those men of the Push, who not only had a type of integrity I had never experienced before, but were usually genuinely affectionate, valued their friendships and, more surprisingly to me at the time, were often touchingly concerned for my welfare. I had not really understood that people could care about each other for reasons other than self-enhancement, remaining for very many years quite unsure that I was capable of experiencing sincere love for others. Although I had earlier come across sexual coercion in more respectable settings (attending parties, while still at school), I never felt used or exploited in sexual encounters on that scene. I still see it this way, despite the overlooked misogyny expressed in the routine jokes about women's sexuality; despite (or, perhaps then, because of) our mutual moving on from one liaison or relationship to the next; despite women remaining marginal in that male-centred group of permanent dissenters, acquiring our status, in large part – though not wholly – from our association with its leading male icons. These key men, living in their unlocked apartments where anyone could 'crash', were the romantic few who never 'compromised' with the mainstream, living off their winnings on race day, at bridge games, driving taxis or taking casual jobs on the dockside, working as 'wharfies'. Other men watched their pleasure-seeking, free-wheeling adventurous lives from the side-lines:

> ... they loomed as Homeric giants, whose lives were one long bland adventure, night after night, party after party, race meeting after poker session and tragic love after tragic love, following only the minute's need or desire, following for its own sake, with no ulterior goal in view, following their own soul's odyssey through all its incarnations with granite amusement ... arguing and drinking far into the night, taking around the hat for incidental abortions, offering no rebuff to anyone who showed up at midnight wanting to sleep on the floor ... conducting their ritual contests, inventing their savage games, and having their parties, parties, parties, all the parties I missed.[34]

I didn't. I went to all the parties, for five years or so. Of course, like almost everyone in that sexually freewheeling world of the Push (men as well as women), I did often feel agonizingly jealous and rejected, emotions we were expected to grapple with and transcend. The one and only talk I gave to a Libertarian meeting, in the mid-1960s, endorsed Freud's pessimistic belief in the inevitability of everyday sexual sorrows, against Reich's utopian notion of the 'genital character' – free from psychic misery. It was during a period of personal anguish at the termination of one of my charac-teristic quests for love, this time from Ross Poole, the finest-looking budding philosopher then in our midst (before he headed off to Oxford, already in the arms of another). But I showed few signs of any premature feminist consciousness: there was considerable sexual competitiveness between the women in our midst, as indeed between the men. Although, in my objection to double standards, as well as in my personal distaste for some of the (often banned) literature the men liked – especially Henry Miller and Norman Mailer – intimations of what was to come were faintly stirring.

I was lucky in my timing also, coming to this lifestyle when I did and facing only a year or two of the ordeal of obtaining effective contraception before the marketing of the pill (provided for me early on by my mother, who had undertaken further training to specialize in gynaecology, with her supplies often passed on through me to other women). However, that moment before the pill lasted long enough for me to shudder at the fearful stories of some of the women around me, in those years when abortion was still illegal. I heard of the death of one who accidentally poisoned herself attempting to induce a miscarriage: 'Lament for her; Time used her poorly,' a Push poet, Lex Banning, mourned, adding (with characteristic gritty but maudlin pessimism): 'Be glad for her; she died young.'[35] But most of us survived. The women in particular moved on, as the more charismatic men hooked up with ever-younger women. I never joined the men in their gambling, although I usually matched them in spending every evening out, forever talking and arguing in our favourite pubs, our drinking interrupted by a cheap meal together at 'the Greeks', before heading off to a Libertarian meeting or back to the pub. A party would usually round off the evening (after collecting bottles at a 'sly-grog' shop), or sometimes a trip to a more salubrious late-night coffee shop at Kings Cross, such as the Russian restaurant, Vadim's. It was there that I first tasted beef stroganoff, learning that there were flavours beyond the totally bland, usually burnt, Australian cuisine of my childhood, or the equally unadorned Greek or Italian fare we usually consumed in large, austere eating rooms. My days were spent reading, or doing necessary college work, finding topics and books critical of the behaviouristic constraints that impoverished the discipline I had chosen to study, psychology.

Regrets, when Push women later spoke of them, rarely if

ever concerned their sexual coming-out in that setting. A few were later sorry that they had been in relationships where they felt unable to choose to have children (though their former partners often opted to do so on reaching middle age). Some felt that they had been forced out of the scene if and when they did decide to have a child. Many women came to question the Libertarian ethos that sexual freedom was not only good for its own sake, but the route to social emancipation. Several of the men would also later question their earlier outlook, admitting (post feminism) that their lifestyle, sexual beliefs and uncompromising political cynicism created problems for women. 'The idea that women were free agents was a self-serving fiction on the men's part,' an early boyfriend of mine, the anthropologist and writer Ian Bedford, later reflected; another of my lovers from much the same period, Roelof Smilde (an internationally successful bridge-player, who at the time managed to live well and exceedingly generously off his gambling), muses over it all to this day: 'We felt there was no other way [but to treat women the same as men] ... I can see no other way we could have acted.'[36]

One other leading figure from that time, who died a few years ago, George Molnar, summed it all up rather neatly:

We had slogans about theory and practice that were precursors of "the personal is political" ... In some respects [however] we were quite blindly the creatures of our time. In the Fifties there was an overwhelming consensus in Australia, to which we were totally opposed. But that put us in such a pathetic minority that there was not the slightest prospect of us influencing the course of events. [We made] a virtue of that. We wove a fantasy ... to justify an impotent little group indulging their particular eccentricities ... [talking] about permanent protest, about the impossibility of change, and although we weren't much good at translating theory into practice we did all insist on the *importance* of translating it. *That* we were into.[37]

I found George one of the most off-putting of translators, with his loud manic harangues, delivered in a gratingly nasal, hybrid accent all his own. As a Jewish boy living in Hungary, he was ten years old when the Nazis invaded his homeland. He and his mother had been abandoned in Budapest and left to face the full horror of Nazi occupation and Eichmann's efficient round-up of the Jewish population. His father had caught one of the last boats out, to Australia, using his wife's papers and the tickets she had secured, substituting his secretary in her place. George only just survived, destitute and starving, hiding out in cellars. Later, having been shunted between refugee camps for the next six years, he and his mother finally made it to Australia in 1951. George was seventeen. This tireless talker on every known political topic never once alluded to his decade of terror, starvation and destitution in Europe. He never forgave his father; he never mentioned the forsaken mother who apparently doted upon her one and only child, this egocentric, wilfully self-sabotaging son. (It was after his death that I learned the details of George's childhood trauma, especially through the writing of his long-time friend, Susan Varga, who finally managed to talk to him about their shared background, as Jews in Nazi-occupied Hungary, in the very last years of his life.)[38]

Ironically, despite a fleeting physical intimacy and my lasting loathing of his irritating dogmatism on every possible topic, George was determined to remain my steadfast friend to the end. Indeed, he was probably the only figure from that time whose life I would influence once I left Sydney to settle in London. To my dismay, he briefly followed in my footsteps in the 1970s, even joining the far-left organization, Big Flame, to which I then belonged. Ours was 'a love-hate relationship', as a mutual friend once quipped, his fondness, my flight: though nothing is ever quite so neat. My son has 'George' as one of his middle names. I don't recall why I chose that name, but George was confident he did. Neither of us seemed to notice then that we were both from Jewish backgrounds, as were, I only now reflect, one or two of the other figures from that time. We never discussed it.

Sydney Libertarianism, thriving on its contempt for postwar conservatism, was already declining by the mid-1960s. After a few years, I simply tired of their favoured hobbies, haunts and habitat. It was not intellectual or political disagreements that disappointed me so much as the aesthetic blankness. I could no longer bear the visual bleakness, virile toughness, brutal directness of its ambience. That the romance of its free-living, insouciant bravado was quintessentially a 'masculine' affair, was something I didn't consciously register, even though my next move was, at least superficially, onto gentler, certainly more colourful, territory.

I stepped sideways into the brand new counter-culture that emerged in Sydney in the mid-Sixties. Determined in their different way to combat Australian cultural conservatism, here was a tribe inspired by the controversial Canadian luminary, Marshall McLuhan (*The Medium is the Message*), the dynamic American inventor and educationist Buckminster Fuller (with his geodesic dome), the pop world of the Beatles, the Stones and slightly more infamous British bands, such as the Kinks (mobbed by young women whenever they visited Australia), as well as assorted North American artists from Andy Warhol, Bob Dylan and Leonard Cohen to Tiny Tim and other weird and wonderful figures arising from the American Underground. During his fleeting moment of fame, the wickedly foul-mouthed Jewish comedian, Lennie Bruce, fighting his losing battles against

US libel laws and heroin addiction, oddly found the time to visit Sydney in 1965, though not the strength to perform there, despite being attended to by our own Push doctor, Rocky Meyers. He was dead within the year, mourned by my old mates from the Push and by the counter-culture, in a rare moment of political accord.

Sydney's counter-culture spawned the resolutely outrageous satirical magazine, *Oz*, which hit the streets on April Fool's Day, 1963, where it sold out within three hours. Future issues were quickly seized, shredded, even burned by the authorities, and its editors charged with obscenity for their brilliantly mocking exposures of police brutality, capital punishment, Church hypocrisy, the 'white' Australia policy. With the medium came the message: it was always packaged provocatively, its words barely legible amid the vivid splash of pornographic imagery and ceremonial salutation to the joys of marijuana. It offered a passionate defence of Joern Utzon's magnificent design for the Sydney Opera House, then fiercely under attack from the mainstream media and the New South Wales state government, culminating in the sacking of this architect of one of the world's most famous buildings. In 1967, its editors, Richard Neville and Martin Sharpe, boarded the boat out, to re-launch the magazine in the heart of 'swinging' London.

It was in this vibrantly pulsing unconventional space, where art was as much the staging of defiant 'happenings', ephemeral publications and throbbing sound, as the production of fine objects, that I crossed paths with young Australian artists such as Gary Shead, Johnny Peart and my long-term friend, the witty, whimsical creator of wonderful art works, Peter Kingston. It was there too that I first met the beautiful Marsha Rowe (then working on *Oz*), who would later become and remain a close friend in London, as well as a host of other elegantly adorned young women. Committed to peace, love and beauty, they preferred dope to alcohol, festive art and music to undiluted politics and gambling, Eastern mysticism to Western rationality. Every home I visited was now lighter and brighter, with incense and marijuana wafting through continuous sound, often the gentle, doleful dirges of Leonard Cohen, or perhaps the deep and meaningless subterranean rambles of Bob Dylan or his clones, no longer merely outraged but now lost somewhere out on Highway '69.

It was on that scene also that I got myself into worse scrapes, finding and falling in love with another type of untamed rebel in 1968: a brilliant artist, James Clifford, temperamentally rather than politically incapable of earning a living or keeping himself out of trouble for long. Self-conscious to the point of paranoia, tall, conspicuous and flamboyantly at odds with the drab codes of masculinity of the day, he was always surveyed with hostility by every passing policeman. Walking with my new lover after midnight, James holding a 'stolen' bunch of flowers from a nearby garden as I clutched a flag picked up from the golf course we'd just traversed, we were both arrested. Charged with the theft of flowers and flag, this time we were not released with a caution. I watched as the police, who quickly identified James – correctly – as homosexual, treated him with aggressive contempt. Soon afterwards, I escaped imprisonment only through the intervention of his rich patrons from the art world, who hired a top barrister to defend us in court. Vicious homophobia, a term yet to be coined, was the ubiquitous treatment of 'poofters' in Australia at the time. It was an injustice which, while not exactly beyond the ken of Sydney Libertarians, with their inclusive tolerance of outcasts, was nevertheless an iniquity barely addressed.

Meanwhile, whether in the alternative spaces of politics

or of culture, women still needed to identify with the boys (though I had found for myself one barely recognized as such). There were no female guides, other than those like Odetta or Janis Joplin belting out their woes. I had by this time embarked on a PhD at Sydney University, still living off the student grants I had received since leaving school, now assisted by a little tutoring work, and topped up by the financial assistance my mother was always more than willing to provide. But my studies rarely seemed to interfere with my switch from near-daily visits to rough pubs, meetings and boozy parties to my new haunts in avant-garde galleries, light-shows, concerts, colourful communes, picnics and marijuana parties. In between, I read all the writers most popular with radicals at the time, a number of them, as I have mentioned, officially banned in Australia – Henry Miller, D. H. Lawrence, Jack Kerouac, Norman Mailer, J. D. Salinger, J. P. Donleavy, Philip Roth, Kingsley Amis. I was regularly distressed by, but barely able to articulate, my feelings about the fear and hostility towards women expressed in all of them. I just knew I couldn't enjoy them as much as the boys. I preferred the classics, Dostoevsky, Tolstoy, Stendhal, Henry James, Chekhov: it is true, they offered little more than heroic feminine victimhood, but they did it without the blatant hostility of the new male rebels, fantasists and tricksters. Where were the women? We did not ask.

It seemed that we had yet to meet any women who did not feel in some buried and resentful way, if not quite explicitly, that it was intrinsically pitiable to exist simply as a woman; we had yet to find those women who could face the world and speak up proudly, let alone joyfully, in the name of women. To say we needed role models is a cliché that barely scrapes the surface of our difficulties. The anguished suffering of heroines in the few contemporary women novelists we read, from Simone de Beauvoir and Doris Lessing to Margaret Drabble or Shelagh Delaney, were just as discouraging for women seeking inspiration on how to lead freer lives. Ironically, it was the black, 'gay' writer, James Baldwin, who supplied the characters I could most easily identify with – not women, of course. Whether in *Giovanni's Room* or *Another Country*, his writing spoke to me most openly about the enchantment and the despair of searching for love. His lugubrious face was pinned to my bedroom wall (where he joined a few more of my favourite sexual icons, Montgomery Clift and Dirk Bogarde, though certainly not Rock Hudson). Today, among my female friends, I find that I was far from alone in feeling stirred and turned on by Baldwin's writing and his sad, deep dark eyes, whether reading his fiction or his essays. The subject position of a gay man does provide certain openings for straight women's fantasies. No wonder some of us in the Sixties were growing very confused.

In 1968 I began living with James Clifford; or rather, he began living with me, along with my sister Barbara and her boyfriend Bill, in a house owned by our mother. (It was one of her planned escape routes from my father, which she never took.) James painted each wall of the rooms we occupied in differing shades of dark cobalt blue, put myriads of tiny flickering lights on the ceilings under pale swirls of clouds, covered every inch of wall with paintings, piling exotic clutter on every surface. Amid this glorious chaos, he stayed on his feet covering large canvases; I sat in the same room, writing up my PhD.

Sojourning in perverse normality

'It seems to have two heads,' the young trainee gynaecologist informed me, completing his examination, in March

1969, when I was already over eight months pregnant. This did not surprise me. My pregnancy was confirmed only after the first three months had elapsed. It frightened me from the beginning. Its consummation approached like some looming tragic farce. I had conceived some nine months after my mother had become anxious about the effects on potential fertility of that early high-dosage pill she had been supplying to me. Following her advice, I stopped taking it and agreed to wait until I began menstruating again before she decided which new form of lower dosage oral contraceptive might be most suitable. My periods never returned until after the birth of my son, the only grandchild she would ever have. The night after the puzzled doctor thought he felt a head at each end of my bloated belly, I went into labour. Unlike my mother's patients, I had attended no antenatal classes; I had not the faintest clue what to expect.

I found myself entirely alone in a hospital bed, hearing on every side of me only the howling screams of other women as a solitary nurse moved from door to door, commanding: 'Be quiet, you're upsetting the other patients.' Indeed we were, but nobody was doing a single thing to comfort us, back then in Sydney's leading obstetric unit, at the Royal Prince Alfred Hospital. My sole consolation was to keep silently murmuring one mantra: 'At least I know, *I don't want a baby; I don't want a baby...*' That much, I did know. (It was the same weird strategy I had used to console myself when in spaces which frightened me as a child, *'You're going to die, you're going to die'*, I would repeat, silently; somehow facing the worst seeming to help propel me onwards.) The next thing I remember was waking up in another ward, no sign of a baby, who was being bottle-fed elsewhere throughout the week I remained in hospital. He had arrived slightly prematurely, jaundiced, and under six pounds, which in those days meant being nursed separately from the mother (who was ignored). When they handed the tiny, wrinkled creature to me to hold for the very first time, as I was leaving the hospital the following week, he had one head – an exquisitely beautiful one. I was still terrified and, bizarrely, homeless. My sister (with a lifelong determination to stay child-free) did not want me returning to the house we had shared, refusing to live with a baby in the home. I have no idea why I agreed to my younger sister's stipulations, nor why my mother would have permitted it, except to suppose that I felt terribly guilty about the consciously unplanned and confusing position I was in. For a few months I squatted in an old shell of a house belonging to another of my by then husband's patrons, before getting a home of my own, as usual, with financial help from my mother.

I now had a baby, and also a husband. A second piece of knowledge was soon clear to me. It was going to be impossible to live with this increasingly paranoid young artist. I could not stay with such a husband. We had married when I was five months pregnant, facing such determined exhortations on the part of my parents that I felt too weak to resist them. They could not abide the thought that their first (and as it turned out last) grandchild might be illegitimate, still a very significant social stigma in 1969. My mother, as well as my father, had dramatic near-terminal health threats that year, which they each blamed on the distress I was causing them. But I knew the marriage was a massive mistake. So too did the official who married us in a register office in the heart of Sydney. Twice during the short ceremony he refused to continue: once because my husband-to-be muttered that he had no idea what the registrar was talking about (following his use of the word 'consanguineous'), subsequently because he turned his back on this official to stare at a painting behind us. The registrar was persuaded to continue only by the forcefulness of Margo

Lewers, one of Australia's best-known abstract expressionist artists (and yet another of my husband's patrons), who was chief witness at the ceremony. Yet, for all my apprehension, I had gone into labour while we were making love, tenderly, although for the very last time. I had been reading the arousing tales of adultery in John Updike's *Couples*, which had just been published.

As soon as he collected his wife and son from hospital, James Clifford saw, with unmistakable clarity, how unsustainable our situation was. He decided there and then that we would have no more sexual contact, acknowledging implicitly (never in words) that he was – even though he believed it a curse – homosexual. 'If my son is homosexual, I'll kill myself,' he later, poignantly, confided to my unsympathetic mother. I would remain the single exception to his same-sex encounters; more tragically, the sole acknowledged sexual relationship of his life, right up to the day he died of Aids, Christmas Day, 1986. He did not ever, even as he lay dying, 'come out' to anyone in his own family.

Back in 1969, he found the thought of my leaving him intolerable, becoming hysterical with jealousy if ever I left the house, or any young man came to visit us. I was living with someone, it seemed, on the point of breakdown, headed that way myself, trying to care for a little creature who, during his first few months of life, had chronic feeding problems and rarely slept for long. For the first time in my adult life, words – even daydreams – failed me. I howled out loud, not just at the moon, but in the daytime too. It almost felt easier to contemplate murdering my son's father, than to find a way out of the situation. Yet, as always before, I had made a few new acquaintances – some friends from the bohemian counter-culture, who offered their warmth and affection. Gradually, together with my new friend Jan Allen, we plotted our very different means of escape from our rather similar predicaments. She too, at the time, had both an infant child and a brilliant, creative young husband causing her anguish, through the drugs, women and itinerant wanderers he brought to their door.

My situation had become unliveable. James was refusing to paint, or to sell the paintings he had completed, feeling that those who could afford to buy them did not deserve them. But I was hardly without resources. Almost by accident, it seemed, I handed in my PhD just weeks before giving birth to my handsome baby boy. I had never abandoned my university studies – in photos I can be seen at parties, on the beach, picnicking, always with a book in my hand, or later resting upon a very pregnant belly. My PhD was a philosophical critique of experimental psychology, with its impoverished conceptual and research agenda, disavowing the distinctiveness of human existence, its social and psychic dimensions. Although quite in line with contemporary philosophical arguments, however, my maverick scholarship served only to exclude me from jobs in either of the two psychology departments in Sydney (despite otherwise near-impeccable academic credentials). Behaviourism was still hegemonic in the discipline – which meant studying either the training of rats, the learning of nonsense syllables, or the measurement of the finer physical movements accompanying perceptual recognition. I was now qualified to work in a university job, but had no access to any such position in Sydney, the place I wanted to live; nor, it must be admitted, could I see myself as what passed for an academic psychologist. Each of the external examiners of my doctoral thesis, one an eminent psychologist in Alberta, Canada, William Rozeboom, the other an even more prestigious psychologist in Texas, USA, Sigmund Koch, offered me jobs in their respective departments. I had not the slightest interest in taking up either of them.

I was lost, confused, unsure and bewildered about what to do with my life, how to live, how to raise my son – although I recall bringing him in a basket at twelve months to his first demonstration, a large Moratorium march against the Vietnam war. In the end, I just took flight, accompanied by my fourteen-month-old son, to the place where folly seemed more fashionable, the land where Ronnie Laing had spent the previous decade writing books to prove, as my life seemed to personify, the madness of the family, the sanity of escape from normality. More conventionally, it had long been customary for students to travel to England on completing their studies – as all of my old lovers who had stayed in higher education had left me to do. Oddly, I was finally conforming to tradition in heading for the 'mother' country, although, as ever, I had still managed to do it a little awry – not single and fancy free, but running away from my husband, with a tiny infant in tow.

My Sixties were over. The Seventies would be another world, or so it seemed. It is that new world that eventually anchored and gave meaning to my life. This is not because Sydney, that most beautiful of cities, had too little to offer, not at all. As many others have found before me, it is merely that it is often useful to flee – at least when still young. We may then manage to re-invent ourselves and find new identities, while perhaps gaining new perspectives on, rather than simply forgetting, our past.

3

Hearing voices

I made it to London in September 1970, just. 'Get onto the plane, get onto the plane,' a concerned official kept whispering in my ear, after my fourteen-month-old son had crashed an empty trolley into the all-glass duty-free shop at the Sri Lankan airport, smashing parts of it to the ground. Surrounded by a hubbub of less friendly officials and stall minders, clutching bags and several paintings in each hand, I headed slowly towards the plane, my sweet and obedient baby boy toddling close behind me. All my other luggage disappeared somewhere in transit, never to be seen again. In London, through contacts of my old Australian friend Mick Taussig, by then an anthropologist working in the USA, I ended up living for a year in a roomy, attractive flat vacated by Doris Lessing on the canal in Maida Vale. Her upstairs neighbour, the English actor Arthur Lowe, true to his pompous, irascible stage character in *Dad's Army*, tried hard to have me evicted. My major misdemeanour, I later learned from the estate agent, was my toilet training practice: my son did not wear nappies in the house, while I encouraged him gently to use a potty. Accidents happened. But how the bilious 'Captain' knew this, I have no idea; we exchanged neither word nor nod, ever.

My adolescence had been one in which Esther Williams'

lavish swimming musicals had provided ideal watching for girls in mid-century Australia; even our vigilant censors could leave them alone. We viewed wondrously energetic young women getting out of bed 'on the right side', performing their unified synchro-swimming, sweetly declaring themselves 'dangerous when wet'.[39] Remove the sweetness, the regulation, the innocence, direct a whirlwind at the waves, and you may start to hear the muffled noises of Women's Liberation, rising anew to speak, dance and sing (perhaps occasionally even to swim) in unison, with the dawn of the 1970s, two decades later. It took me a year or so to hear them. Guiding me, they would very slowly begin to turn around my own quixotic inclinations for evading the mainstream and, despite their unruly, defiant origins, eventually lead me all the way – almost – to its centre.

Following the expansion of higher education in Britain in the 1960s, I slid easily into the first available job, covering classes for a lecturer in psychology on maternity leave from Enfield Technical College, within a few weeks of arriving in London. Again, I was pointed to it through friends of friends, this time the US draft dodger George Segal (no relation), whom I met only once, in my first few weeks in London, accompanied by Ronnie Laing's wildest disciple, a stoned and inebriated David Cooper. I had of course read much of Laing's existential assault on the psychiatric profession, which he accused of officially authorizing the exclusion of those society deemed 'mad' for their failure to play by its rules. Such denunciations of psychiatry accompanied, fist in glove, Laing and Cooper's crusade against the nuclear family, seen as the crucible of invalidation for those who would not, or could not, conform to its furtive codes of practice. I knew, and largely believed, much of their extravagant rhetoric at the time. However, I was much too bewildered to appreciate the exotic company I was in (which was a pity, they were both dead within a few years of this encounter: George Segal from suicide, David Cooper from drugs and alcohol).

With a professional career still for decades the last thing on my mind, I stayed put for twenty-nine years, from September 1970, as my technical college mutated into a polytechnic and was then transformed into Middlesex University. Officially, I was teaching 'Social Psychology'. It was a course that was always popular with students, since it morphed into whatever issues most engaged me, and usually them, at the moment. This included mental illness, viewed anew by anti-psychiatry and some of the shifting frameworks of psychoanalysis; racism, traditionally dealt with in the discipline as an issue of individual differences ('prejudice' almost always emerged as something confined to people who were poorly educated and working class, when measured by psychologists using their favourite, transparent, individual 'attitude' scales); delinquency, now repositioned and extended to 'white collar' crime by the 'new criminologists' (embracing ideas from Gramsci and inching towards what would become critical media theory with the flowering of cultural studies from the close of the 1970s). Alongside R. D. Laing and Wilhelm Reich (the passionately anti-authoritarian, early Freudian dissenter, committed to sexual liberation for the masses), the work of the French-Caribbean psychiatrist and anti-colonial revolutionary writer, Franz Fanon, appeared with the texts of Stuart Hall on my reading lists. Each topic was framed, at every turn, by the new reflection on gender, still ludicrously reduced in mainstream psychology to those putative individual attributes known as 'sex differences', which were in turn perpetually fought over, as they still are, by 'nature' versus 'nurture' brigades. When one external examiner complained that the course was not 'Social Psychology' but

'Social Issues', I obligingly re-packaged it as 'Psychology and Social Issues'.

The 1970s was the heyday of political sociology which, combined with ideas coming from radical philosophy, then inflected by Marxism, enabled me to find a niche and, even within that most hidebound of disciplines, to be quite as iconoclastic as I wished. At the polytechnics, as distinct from the universities, there was little to rein in creativity during that decade, and into the next, should we wish to unleash it. Ironically, some of the radical thinkers who were busy exploring the theoretical oversights, partialities and conceptual or methodological rigidities of our particular disciplines thirty years ago, though viewed askance by most of our senior colleagues, have since been recruited by the old universities. But the places that sustained our pedagogic renovations are now starved of cash and declared failing institutions.

Although I have for the most part enjoyed it, teaching nevertheless seemed to remain a sideline in my life. It would be well over a decade before I even thought of attempting any scholarly writing. My closest colleague at the college soon moved into my flat, introducing her acquaintances, some with peripheral ties to the small militant anarchist formation, the Angry Brigade, who were mainly ex-students from Cambridge and Essex. I had not the slightest sympathy for their maverick actions (nor did she), although as I have already said, I befriended one of the first people arrested for the conspiracy, the winsome Jake Prescott, whom I occasionally still hear from. Like many others, I visited him as he served his ten-year prison sentence for addressing the envelope of an early Angry Brigade communiqué. This was, as I mentioned earlier, my peculiar entrance into Women's Liberation. I moved from Maida Vale into a large house in Islington, bought with my sister in late 1971. The first women I met in my new neighbourhood were those entangled in one way or another with the trial of eight alleged members of the Angry Brigade (begun at the Old Bailey in 1972), who were also eagerly involved in the Women's Liberation movement, on its most radical fringe.[40] Many of them lived a few streets away from me in the large collective household in Grosvenor Avenue, in Islington.

The women from that collective amazed me with their bristling confidence, apparent wildness and determination to enjoy themselves as independent women; they frightened me with their tough stance towards any and all authority, their apparent disdain for the routine practices of life, from the trappings of peaceful domesticity, to career ambitions or home ownership, which I had hitherto encountered only in men, or women in some way attached to them. Motherhood, however, was something they did not disdain, though of course, along with every other facet of life, from the profoundly personal to the far-flung global, they had a clear-cut political analysis of it. It was these Grosvenor Avenue women who had played a key part in, and been arrested at, the Miss World Contest in 1970. They were also the women who had chalked up slogans on the walls of Ruskin College at the first ever Women's Liberation conference in 1970: WOMEN IN LABOUR KEEP CAPITALISM IN POWER, DOWN WITH PENILE SERVITUDE, much to the annoyance of other women, such as Sally Alexander, who had worked hard to organize the event and felt responsible for repairing the damage.

Each one of the half dozen or so women I met in that first, most principled of communes eventually ended up with children and homes of their own. Unsurprisingly, they were a diverse group, each vulnerable and needy in very distinct ways, but to the world they presented a united front. Within a few years these women had all moved on, but for the decade of the 1970s they lived in one form or another of communal household, many of them consisting mainly of women. Meanwhile, as my circle of acquaintances widened, I found and bonded more closely with other slightly less militant women.

To what extent is it possible, I wonder, to offer a portrait of a political moment, placing oneself within it, however cautiously, knowing the limits of retrospection? The Seventies was indeed the decade of Women's Liberation, but we live through the same historical moments, even in the very same places, with such differing proclivities, such contrasting affiliations and encounters, that our stories might seem to emerge from parallel universes. Yet, for all that, there are moments in our lives when we may share with others such a strong sense that we should, and perhaps could, make a difference to the ways of the world that they mark us forever, especially when collective hopes meet with some success. Even so, many witnesses are needed to hold on to a sense of the past and our own presence within it, or else it shrinks to fit the platitudes of the present. Pondering 'identity', Milan Kundera reflects: 'Friendship is indispensable to man for the proper function of his memory [women, one might presume, serve other functions for Kundera] ... memories have to be watered like potted flowers, and the watering calls for regular contact with the witnesses of the past, that is to say, with friends.'[41] Such continuing friendships, surviving comrades, even old rivals and adversaries, 'witnesses in spite of themselves', keep memories alive, pointing out paths even as they diverge, or disappear beneath the fresh tracks laid in contemporary skirmishes.[42]

Fragile beginnings

Planning this book, I asked my friends and other women

from the Women's Liberation Movement (WLM) to send me their thoughts on the personal journeys they had travelled, seeking to register differing accounts of our immersion in shared political dreams. A few dozen replied, most by then in their late fifties. I read all the autobiographical material I could find, talked for hours with my last remaining women's group (tellingly, a small support network of friends who both write and teach as feminist scholars). All of my respondents, like those I talked with directly, had learned to be wary of generalization, stressing their class-bound, ethnic locations (most often white and middle class, though sometimes with parents who had a precarious hold on that economic status). Their words echoed each other's, and my own, when looking back to the close of the Sixties. 'I didn't know who I was then,' Catherine Hall begins; 'I was on the run,' Barbara Taylor echoes; 'It was lonely as an American Jew, trying to be an academic, a New Leftie and a mother,' Cora Kaplan recalls; 'I was very confused,' Sally Alexander explains, 'I think now there was no way to be a woman and to be intelligent and articulate in the Sixties.'[43]

The same words recur in memoirs now assembled in anthologies covering those early years here: 'I was living … with three children, and quietly going crazy,' writes Audrey Battersby, a member of the first UK Women's Liberation group, started in north London in 1969. One after another, voices repeat the same confusion, often triggered by the arrival of children, however much desired. It was motherhood, as Michelene Wandor notes, that created the crisis of identity which set them adrift from the life of the 'active, thinking and working adult' they had expected to lead at the close of the Sixties. 'It was a bleak and frightening time. I was very unhappy,' Janet Rée reflects, on becoming pregnant just before hearing about feminism at the start of 1970. 'I was isolated … I thought I was going insane,' Val Charlton says similarly, recalling having become a mother in 1970, 'just weeks before I heard about the Women's Liberation movement.' 'I went into a lengthy period of subdued shock … I sat with my big, quiet, wide-eyed baby and stared at him wondering who I was, who he was,' Sue O'Sullivan pictures herself that same year, having moved to London from the USA.[44] 'I blame myself for not being "strong" enough to make it in the world, I blame myself for not being consumed with interest for the child and the man, I blame myself for not being sexually glowing and happy. The conflict I feel between the various ideas of what I should be, and the real trap I'm living in, makes me constantly depressed and guilty,' Alison Fell wrote in the socialist feminist magazine *Red Rag* in 1973, of her life four years earlier.[45] These women were all soon at the centre of Women's Liberation, bringing other women along with them as they helped to build their local groups and threw themselves into feminist activism.

Today, new feminist voices writing on maternal subjectivity suggest that the sense of disorientation and loss of self after giving birth for the first time is hardly surprising, the outcome of a type of narcissistic shock as the mother mourns her former self-sufficiency and youthful independence, swallowed up (with metonymic accuracy) in meeting the needs of her baby.[46] True enough. However, careful attention to cultural contexts and contrasts, in addition to the sudden psychic challenges of motherhood, would always be necessary to encompass the diversities of maternal experience. Furthermore, it was facing the turmoil and seeming falsehood of femininity itself, whether or not accompanied by the claims of motherhood, which was alarming so many young women at the close of the Sixties. Recalling those years in one of the first British autobiographies to analyse the impact of the Women's Liberation Movement on her life, Elizabeth Wilson depicts the blankness, passivity and confusion she felt then: 'I was still searching for what I could do and be in life, held back by a sense of imprisonment within my class and within some stifling, artificial prison of gender'; 'All was disintegrating, panic, fear, anxiety, greed ... But in a few months everything would change.'[47]

That sense of being lost, lonely and bewildered, the condition I thought I had brought upon myself in fleeing respectability, turned out to be far from unusual. A similar sense of personal turbulence provided the fragile impetus that propelled many women towards the initial gatherings of Women's Liberation in 1970. Privileged and attention-seeking some of those ripe for women's revolution may later appear, yet having faced the disparagements of womanhood, many felt themselves already rotting:

> I want a women's revolution like a lover.
> I lust for it, I want so much this freedom ...
> To even glimpse what I might have been and never never
> will become, had I not had to "waste my life" fighting
> for what my lack of freedom keeps me from glimpsing ...
> may we go mad together, my sisters.[48]

Robin Morgan's raging verse flew across the Atlantic to land as pamphlets in the makeshift Women's Centres opening around Britain. Just before she would begin to flourish as a feminist writer in the 1970s, Sara Maitland crawled into the decade straight out of an NHS mental hospital, her release date: December 1969. She had already attended her first women's group in Oxford that year; 'may we grow sane together', seems to capture better her hopes for the future:

> My world was transformed. The sky was bright with colour ...
> my ears unblocked and I could actually hear what was going on
> around me ... Too much happened too fast ... but I want to
> make clear my total conviction that it was not my abrupt
> absorption into this new world that drove me into a genuine

nervous collapse, but a complete clash of values. It was the
miseries and repressions of the preceding ten years. I collapsed
from a sudden surfeit of joy. Even then I knew it. I emerged
from the hospital into the Seventies with no doubts at all about
where I now belonged. Things change, of course. But I have
never looked back.[49]

Why were so many of us quite so confused? Raised in the
decade of domesticity ('Happy Families' our first and
favourite card game), we read the flourishing women's
magazines, we saw the fêting of Fifties femininity, the
radiant smiles of women with their hour-glass figures,
adorned in soft pastels, their full flowing skirts swirling in
the sunshine. These were women who would always, in the
end, get their man, the 'right' man. They would be wearing
his band of gold, before having sex, before (the full nine
months before) having babies, before embarking on their
true career – consuming the inexhaustible supply of
household innovations they were everywhere enticed to buy
to keep them serene, purposeful and secure in their domestic
tasks. Housewives were the major target of post-war
advertising, it was their duty to absorb the new forms of
commodity surplus in expanding capitalist markets.[50] More
often than not I felt sick, quite literally, perusing these
magazines in my mother's waiting room (of course, she had
no time to read them herself).

I had yet to learn how very far from alone I was in sensing
so physically the dishonesty of the image, had yet to read
Betty Friedan's excoriating exposure, *The Feminine Mystique*
(1963), of what she saw as this trick being played upon mid-
century western housewives, who would be left 'unnamed,
unsatisfied, drained by the sexual sell into the buying of
things.'[51] Many other young women could not shake off the
hint of harm, the contagion of contempt, the murmurs of
maternal resentment, which shadowed Fifties femininity,

despite all the cultural messages working to conceal them, despite our inability – as yet – to comprehend the nature of our disquiet. We were educated to be happy, healthy, thinking people, and more was invested in and expected of us than ever before. But many sensed the cloud behind that silver lining, suspecting that our growth and fulfilment was not compatible with the image of femininity thrust before us: whether gazing at the Dior-clad models in the bright and breezy background, or surrounded by shiny domestic appliances mirroring conjugal conflicts in the frequently cheerless foreground.

'I was very much the daughter of a 1950s housewife, who lived a life of low-key depression and little personal satisfaction,' Susan Ardill responds to my questions, describing her childhood in Australia, in the now-familiar words I hear time and again from others. Even more harshly at odds with the promises of Fifties femininity, Carolyn Steedman, in her outstanding biography *Landscape for a Good Woman*, sketches the life of her bitter working-class mother, struggling for respectability as well as resources, raising her two 'unwanted' daughters, for the most part alone, in south London: 'The home was full of her terrible tiredness and her terrible resentment; and I knew it was all my fault.'[52] What she did not know, until well into adulthood, was that she and her sister were illegitimate, although she did already intuit, in ways she would so graphically come to depict, that class as much as gender mortifications fuelled the habitual irritation and anger of her mother, who felt herself in every way cheated by life. More women came to Women's Liberation from middle-class backgrounds, yet, as Sarah Benton writes to me: 'As young girls, we had already had a lifetime of feeling snubbed, disparaged and frightened, and by the late 1960s there was no consolation for this in the existing culture (one couldn't say "it pleases God, or my

Father, or even this is my fate") … we just wanted not to be any longer humiliated and shamed.'[53] Without having any words to ponder its paradoxes, many women later recalled, just as I would, that we had more often than not automatically crossed over to identify ourselves with male characters – in books, on screen, in life generally – so uninspiring and dismal were the feminine ones on offer.

The narratives that would address our needs and confusions, if and when we found them, seemed to operate like a spiritual renewal: 'Women's Liberation suddenly lifted the curtain concealing the big world from us, and oh it was exciting,' Sarah Benton continues. I too experienced exactly those moments of sudden awakening. 'Yes!' I thought to myself, reading the short pamphlet, *'Why Miss World? We're Not Ugly, We're Not Beautiful, We're Angry'*, in the bath, after coming home from the makeshift nursery I was helping to run in Islington. Produced by other women from the crèche, including Jo Robinson and Jenny Fortune, it explained why they had been arrested, sneaking into the Miss World contest in 1970, blowing whistles, throwing smoke bombs, flour and leaflets, halting Bob Hope's flippant prattle dead in its tracks. Miss World was never the same again, its innocence gone forever. My own bursts of recognition reading these early pamphlets bounce back to me in the recollections of the other women I knew then, summoning up their own memories. Again the very same words ricochet around between them. They all convey the surge of strength and purpose that animated women when, for the very first time, they linked their own discontents to those of other women, turning to them rather than to men (as all our cultural training had hitherto instilled) when searching for answers, in those early passionate years of Women's Liberation. The women's voices I quoted above, joining others I soon came across, continue their reminiscences as if reading from the same song sheet:

I was bowled over by an extraordinary sense of discovery ...
I was no longer alone.

[It] changed my whole life ... I learned who I was through
the Women's Liberation movement.

[It] was absolutely formative for me, and wonderful ... We
all relied on it for our entry into the public world ... We were
terribly pleased with ourselves.

We began as fragments, guilt-ridden, inadequate as people
(because mere women – no, not women, mere girls then,
whatever our ages) and by bringing our depression to each
other like a gift, an offering of pain, we gradually drew each
other out of our isolation ... It taught me new ways to love
myself, by loving all of us.

Women's Liberation is what enabled me to make sense of
the world ... to live with incomplete but contradictory answers,
[it] gave me an intellectual and emotional curiosity, sustained
me and led me to develop faltering courage in myself. [It]
ushered me so firmly into a politics which encompassed the
public and the personal, with all the attendant pleasures and
pains which that implies.

You had this feeling of being high, and somehow corporate,
part of something, large, public and significant ... It was such a
turbulent change.[54]

Turbulent, indeed. Since it was a politics, as I elaborate in the
next chapter, touching upon every aspect of life, you were
never outside your feminism, at home or abroad – or so it
felt, for some time. Crystallized at the core of feminist re-
awakening was anger at the narrow, recurrently mocking
depiction of women, our bodies and our being, as existing
primarily for men's titillation or maintenance. This accompanied a sense of injustice over women's economic exploitation
and enforced dependency on men, solidified into rage by
growing awareness of the social tolerance for routine
violence against women, within a landscape where we

remained largely invisible or marginalized in political, scholarly and cultural domains. Eyes focused upon women's position in the nuclear family, our still separate, often isolated, and far from equal sphere, as the font of female subordination. It set in motion all manner of confrontations, whether in the all-too-familiar personal and interpersonal arena, or challenging practices within each and every institutional site.

However, in the beginning, one thing every person I heard from could recall was simply their pleasure in suddenly seeing the daring of women around them, captured here in the words of the feminist poet and scholar Denise Riley:

> The compelling first moment for me was when I heard other young women speaking in public at political meetings, around 1969 to 1970. I was amazed at their daring and articulacy. I could only begin to do the same myself, I mean to speak, when I was 26, and went in deep terror to give my first public talk in a course I'd invented (an adult education class, on Women and Socialism) muttering to myself under my breath as I walked there a line from Sheila Rowbotham's writing as a mantra, something about how the Women's Liberation Movement had given to each woman the possibility of courage.[55]

It was a while before we began to unearth our own feminist history, and the differing trajectories behind us. However, if at first with little consciousness of it, we were in actuality merely a continuation of feminism's long and many-sided struggle. Two centuries after Mary Wollstonecraft published her *Vindication of the Rights of Woman*, insisting that women should be fully part of modernity, part of culture, our voices no longer demeaned and marginalised, we were still fighting for full inclusion. Inclusion, however, so most of us thought then, also required radical social transformation.

Revolutionary household rotas

Social transformation was our goal, but tackling the connections between the personal and the political was our method. Women's marginal place in the public sphere was one issue, men's absence from the key responsibilities of domesticity another: flip sides of the same slogan, 'the personal is political'. Courage – at times little more than bravado – would often be needed, whenever the newly celebrated sense of warmth and unity as part of a wider collective of women hoping to change the world collapsed back into the actualities of daily lives. Idealistic, committed and energetic activists many Women's Liberationists became. I did too. 'I am woman, hear me roar', we might sing along with Helen Reddy (when freed momentarily from our daily regime of meetings, poster making, visiting schools, protesting about, when not celebrating, women's lives), yet the newly born feminist, of course, still mumbled, frequently unsure and insecure, jealous and competitive, often embattled in new ways with men we loved or desired over issues of autonomy and dependence.

Men were entangled with feminism from the start, whether they were hostile, wary or, not so unusually, supportive. Especially if isolated at home with young babies, several early recruits first heard about feminist gatherings through the men in their lives, later launching themselves into activism with the support of their husbands or lovers. Sue O'Sullivan, then known as Sue Cowley, was just one such woman, who has recorded her husband John Cowley's initial prompting and continued support for her early feminist adventures.[56] As it happens, when I was still largely friendless in London, I ventured out on my first ever Women's Liberation event, on 6 March, 1971, accompanied by a visiting friend from Sydney, George Molnar. I only later discovered it was the first Women's Liberation march in London, 4,000 strong. It would be several more years before men were banned from our marches, and on that first march we came across another figure from my Libertarian past, Germaine Greer: 'Christ, I hope I don't keep bumping into people I know,' I heard her mutter, as she turned away, or at least that's how I recall her welcome on that day. Supportive, to a fault, were the men I soon hung out with, ready to chastise us should we falter (though I only ever heard of one man who objected to my slinky, low-necked tops).

Nevertheless, few of us realized quite what personal battles feminism would lead us into, when shared housework, equal childcare, sexual autonomy, personal growth, even sexual pleasure, became the *sine qua non* of Women's Liberation. As many of my friends reminded me, it was the lack of ecstasy, or even real intimacy, in sexual engagement with men in the Sixties that first inspired them to talk of their own 'liberation' – not that sexual ecstasy was something I ever expected or managed to find, craving only the attention and hopefully love of a man I admired. Some women had experienced both the orgasms and the intimacy so publicly celebrated in the 'Summer of Love' of 1967. Nevertheless, few felt free from sexual doubts and conflict in their relationships with men. With feminists suddenly discussing, reading and writing about their sexual feelings, many soon decided that it was male-defined notions of sexuality, in particular the 'myth of the vaginal orgasm' (usually angrily attributed to Freud), that left us so often self-conscious and dissatisfied, barely able to speak of our bodies and their potential pleasures.[57]

Personally, I never relinquished the psychic investments of penetrative sex, however 'culturally conditioned' (to use the unsatisfactory terminology of the day). Nor did any of my friends, even though some felt freer to mention the variations they enjoyed to their male partners. I was shyer than some in talking about the details of my own sexual encounters, even when with close female friends, let alone male lovers, having no desire to share the 'submissive' fantasies I dreamed up to heighten desire. Beyond sex, feminists now sought both commitment and responsibility from men, while inevitably often competing with other women for just those men (and, increasingly, just those women) who excited us with their traditionally alluring qualities of strength, authority, charm and glamour, even though exercised in less traditional arenas. Like Don Juans of old, men's sexual magnetism usually sprang from a certain phallic confidence (and the dangers this threatened), which we were criticizing. So too did women's sexual allure, just to confuse matters more. Celebrated as it soon was by a significant minority in this feminist milieu, lesbianism had never before been quite so visible, nor proved quite such a popular choice for women, as it became at the height of Women's Liberation.[58] Yet, for the most part, desire still refused to obey principled rules; least of all, our rules.

Some Seventies feminists, myself included (transporting me back to my critical reading of Reich in the 1960s), had always puzzled over the refractory life of desire, conscious that orgasm, and how to 'make it happen', was not the beginning and far from the end of the story. But most, as I later tried to elaborate, had yet to understand the awkward complicities of desire's entanglement with power. Attempts to detach sexual passion from deference or conquest, cravings for approval or demonstrations of dependency, laid down landmines for the future.

By the close of the Seventies, splits in Women's Liberation over 'the problem of men', and how we should, or shouldn't, relate to them, saw the emergence of a small vanguard of political lesbians. Pushing aside other lesbian feminists (those I was always closest to, and remain firmly bonded with today), these self-selected few chipped away at straight women's dreams of sexual liberation. Feminists who slept with men were criticized for their heterosexual privileges, our sexual desires dismissed as ineluctably hostile to feminism. 'Coming together' sexually, in the literal prescriptiveness dictated by self-styled 'revolutionary feminists', was to be no word play or pun, but the only feminist ideal, a rigorously lesbian affair. Here, any hint of heterosexual roles or routines (butch or femme), along with the dildo, let alone a 'strap-on', were strictly taboo. The many possible pleasures of 'penetration', any excitement attaching to thoughts of power or powerlessness, and the place of passivity and thoughts of submission in sexual encounter remained firmly unacknowledged.[59]

Slightly younger feminists, in particular those who came to the movement at the close of the 1970s, have recalled the tensions this induced: 'I felt like an undercover heterosexual (though a pretty inactive one for a long while, thanks to feminist pressure and guilt),' the journalist and film producer Jill Nicholls writes to me.[60] This particular version of radical feminist scrutiny led to the barnstorming against pornography in the 1980s, which, in the apocalyptic idiom and imagery of Andrea Dworkin and Catharine Mackinnon, seemed itself to double as a form of vicarious, if disturbing, titillation. My long-held sense of this duplicitous manipulation of desire was entertainingly illustrated recently when a new, now very close, friend explained to me how she discovered an unexpected, keen sexual yearning for women. In the 1980s she was a happily married radical feminist, active in the anti-pornography campaign in Norway; attending one of their screenings of 'harmful and degrading' images of women, she was so aroused that she returned home sexually voracious, frightening her husband with her sudden leap in desire. She very soon turned to women, beginning with her pursuit of the feminist campaigner conducting the screening. She has remained a contented lesbian feminist ever since, though eschewing the anti-pornography campaign.

For my part in this fraught arena of sexual politics, the very first reflective article I ever published (apart from calls for militant action, or reporting on such events) was one illustrating the partial disjuncture between the psychic and the social in the sexual domain. As humorously as I could, I illustrated the folly of prescribing a necessary harmony, let alone homology, between the nature of sexual desire, fantasy and fulfilment in the psychic domain and feminist struggles for equality, justice and autonomy in the public sphere. Indulging the pleasures of sensual passivity, escaping the self-reliance we usually seek to assert, lies close to the heart of erotic yearning for many women. For many men too.[61] I thought then, as I think now, that such contradictions at the heart of desire, far from undermining calls for a more helpful feminist sexual politics, make the need for trying to understand some of the complexities of intimacy and its responsibilities all the more pressing. Influenced by the women in their lives, most of the men I knew had joined anti-sexist men's groups by the end of the 1970s, where they puzzled over how to be less sexist, patriarchal and predatory in their relations with women. Since some of them were on the dole, most were involved in low-paid community or caring jobs, all shared the housework and the cooking and none of them were property owners, it might be thought that their patriarchal privileges were somewhat meagre. However, we women had convinced them that they could never completely escape the cultural ascendancy of their birthright. Unlike men a decade earlier, most accepted our analysis, although in their self-criticism, they usually preferred self-parody to self-flagellation: 'I'm in a men's

group, and I'm OK. I don't compete but I win anyway,' as
two men sang at our Islington Socialist Centre Christmas
party in 1979, to a full audience in our regular venue upstairs
at the Hemingford Arms pub. In those years I did not meet,
though I would later, men in relationships with fervent
radical feminists (usually living in Leeds or Bradford) who
had been disciplined into going without penetrative sex
altogether, as intrinsically 'anti-feminist'.

The majority of the hundreds of women I encountered
politically in the 1970s, who were mostly in their twenties
and early thirties, lived in some form of shared housing.
With or without men, collective living was viewed by many
feminists as not just a more economical arrangement than
settling down either alone or within the traditional family
unit, but one which could encourage more open, supportive
and creatively shared forms of companionship, domesticity,
childcare, political work and community engagement. Those
choosing communal households usually attempted to
embody the libertarian catchphrase 'live your politics', pre-
figuring a vision of the social relations they hoped to see in
the more egalitarian future. The poet and writer Michelene
Wandor depicted this domestic dream early on:

> let us reject some of the old means
> and grope towards a new accuracy
> …
> Make all houses big and make them homes
> Make all people lovers and parents, make one word mean that
> …
> "how"? is another poem.[62]

I don't think she ever wrote it.

Absorbing these ideas from the feminists and community
activists I came across in Islington in the 1970s, I was soon
living in a household organized along collective lines, after

my sister moved out to live with her partner as a couple in 1973. It was a large, draughty, un-renovated Victorian house in Highbury, where property was still cheap and mortgages easy to come by if you were, as I was, in secure employment. By 1973 a group of feminists lived in the house, with our boyfriends of the moment passing through, or sometimes, as in my own case, taking up residence. Three single mothers, all connected to the Women's Centre we had set up in Islington, were at its heart. One of them was the then budding poet and writer, Alison (Ali) Fell, who moved in, although I was not at all sure we would get along, because she had been evicted from her squat, and her son was already a close friend of my son. At the time she was fiction editor on the collective of the successful feminist magazine, *Spare Rib*, eager to launch her own literary career. Her first novel, *Every Move You Make*, would provide an accurate, if unflattering, sketch of the house, written within its walls:

> And now this house, a tall, crooked house which sucked in draughts. It stood on the corner of a street lined thickly with sycamores which in summer hid the tower blocks to the east ... a dense wild undergrowth of lime trees and privet overhung the steps which led up to the front door. It would have taken money, care, commitment, to put it all to rights. Permanence. None of us had ever been too sure of that. People passed through. Few of them stayed longer than a year. They left to buy houses or have babies, or to live alone.[63]

She drew an even less flattering sketch of me at the time, living with my son and my partner, as she saw us all inside the collective household. We are easily recognizable, my name changed, incongruously, to Marie:

> There was Marie, who darted around the borough on political errands, Tom, her taciturn lover of many years, and Zac, her nine-year-old son ... Marie, up to her neck in local politics,

exuded urgency. She worked on the same community paper
[that I had worked on] founded back at the beginning of the
seventies. [So I] understood the pressures all too well. There
was always this or that council meeting one had to keep an eye
on, or a new split in the Labour Party to investigate, or such
and such a shop-steward to interview. I couldn't bring myself to
carp at her just because she let the domestic side of things slide
a bit.[64]

Yes, I remember it well. I seem to recall that we all let the
domestic side of things slide a bit, but perhaps I was more
challenged than some. I've yet to learn to bake a cake, but I
do now know how to create what I see as an elegant and
welcoming home. The other single mother then living in my
house with her daughter was Noreen O'Connor (later to
return to her maiden name, Noreen O'Faolain), who had
married young to escape her own wretchedly unhappy
Dublin family. She identified strongly, back then, with her
sad, crushed, alcoholic mother, abandoned much of the
time by her cavalier, philandering husband (a popular
journalist), who left his wife largely on her own and unable
to cope with raising their nine children, in growing poverty
and increasingly serious neglect as the years went by.[65]
Living collectively, Noreen began to catch up with the
education she had missed out on, in the end achieving her
goal of becoming a solicitor and working for Islington
Council in child protection.

The one thing that was sacred in the 1970s, while our
three children were still young, was compliance with the
domestic rota, on which names circulated daily: one for the
evening meal; one for getting up, making breakfast, taking
the children to school and collecting them afterwards; one
for putting the children to bed, reading to them, child-
minding for the evening; one for allocating differing
housework jobs; one for the weekly shop, using money from

the few pounds we all put into the kitty. No one paid rent. Essential repairs, although not the mortgage, were to be paid from a house account, but since we had no fixed system for putting money into the account, there were disagreements at our monthly house-meetings over how to organize and pay for household maintenance. My position, as both house owner and highest earner, when some of the others lived off social security, meant that I was not supposed to display my 'privilege' by paying for repairs out of my own pocket. (Not surprisingly, largely unspoken tensions over disparities of income could be a source of bitterness in collective households, especially towards those with more income.) Also, our styles of dealing with the children differed. I was scolded for not being strict enough with them. This was probably true. But I was offended at the time, as it was generally agreed that my son, despite my permissiveness, was always the most cheerfully obedient and the least troublesome. He really was!

Dreadful conflict only arrived when two of the women – the two other mothers who had been very good friends (Noreen and Ali) – fell out with each other. Predictably enough, in this then exclusively heterosexual household caught up in a lively social scene promoting personal autonomy above 'dependency' or 'exclusiveness', it was over a man. He lived elsewhere. But shortly after his relationship with Ali ended, he and Noreen began what would prove to be a permanent relationship. So destructive was the fallout from this rift that we called in the recently established feminist Women's Therapy Centre, attempting – unsuccessfully – to handle the crisis. I think, as 'sisters' then, we all suffered from certain levels of guilt over jealousy and competitiveness with each other, even knowing that the few on that scene (who might be either women or men) who suggested that you could abolish jealousy through shedding individual 'possessiveness' were to be avoided for their dogmatism, dishonesty or self-deception. Trying to live differently, in looser forms of intimacy, is not in itself impossible, especially when you are young, and sustained at least partially by sincere commitments to mutuality and shared political goals. But there are no political solutions to individual heartaches and frustration, even among women who tried, and all too often failed, to avoid causing them. This left shared households of female friends, not unlike siblings, especially vulnerable to rivalry and sexual tensions.

I was never without a sexual partner during these years and, for a while, was so fearful of rejection (or causing pain myself) that I sometimes rather surreptitiously had two. I was also so busy anchoring myself in this new political milieu, trying to feel secure in my occasionally fraught household, that I returned to Sydney only once during the 1970s, though my parents visited their three children, now all living in England, more often. Apart from the painful ending of one relationship, my memories of life in that decade are mostly of the friends I made, and the fun we had, particularly talking and plotting, dancing and singing, in the feminist or other alternative Left cabals we had formed. I shall return to the varied political activities we embarked on in the next chapter, but mixed in with them, on a near daily basis, was an intensely social and surprisingly diverse cultural life, as radical artists, musicians, theatre groups, alternative cabaret, and other creative endeavours gained our interest and support. The regular rendezvous in pubs, cafés or wine bars tied in with the schedules of meetings; the dancing kicked off at the fund-raising benefits staged at least every other week in support of some campaign, resource centre or other cause. Life was always quite as rich and as full as we could manage to sustain.

Yet some who were new to feminist gatherings no doubt

found it harder to join in, perhaps sensing unspoken rules and rituals of engagement that they must traverse to be accepted, their spirit evident in the dress code of the day – loose, practical, relatively unadorned and economical. Liz Heron has described her version of this feminist sartorial stylishness in those years: 'In 1976 I bought some denim dungarees, a red-necked cowboy-style shirt and some brown "desert boots"; and for the next year or so this was the outfit I felt most comfortable in, with variations.'[66] However, as I see from photos of myself with friends, whether at home or on demonstrations, some of us preferred the round, plunging necklines of the Biba T-shirt, or floppy, floral tops, even the broad flowing skirt and occasional mini dress. Nor was I ever without some subtle form of high heels, lipstick and eyeliner: the dress code was never as rigid as subsequent caricature would suggest. Hippie divas, as a friend reminds me, could feel at home in feminist circles then.[67] But twin-set and pearls, the smart matching suit (skirt or trousers) with briefcase, would be unthinkable, underlining the limits of our flexibility. Most women wore bras, though I never did, either before or long after Women's Liberation. Nor would I go to a commercial hairdresser, home cuts allowing us to expand our range of skills. One good friend later told me he thought I looked as though I'd been dragged through a hedge backwards, but I liked my now loose, shoulder-length hair.

Some of my friends from those years remain my closest friends today, but the vibrant community activism of the 1970s faded rather fast as the political climate changed at the close of the decade. By 1980, the original women in my household had all departed; the two single mothers were re-housed by the council in houses of their own. The decade of living primarily with women was over; so too was the grass-roots feminist activism we had jointly helped to initiate. The

Islington Women's Centre had closed, and feminist campaigns were moving into the political and media mainstream, no longer primarily networks of local groups. The women who departed had lived in my house for several years – not quite the fast turnover suggested in Alison's fictional version. The nature of the collective household changed – together with my son and myself, three activist, comprehensively pro-feminist men remained in the house. The four adults lived collectively, sharing the house for well over ten years, while working together politically, attempting to build resistance to the rolling back of welfare and workers' rights during the Thatcher years. We were soon at the centre of a north London group of activists affiliated to the then small but dynamic far-Left libertarian socialist organization, Big Flame, and later, shifting gears just a little, we joined the North Islington Labour Party, then at its radical best. Big Flame's political leaders had included Pete Ayrton (now my publisher) and Paul Thompson (who subsequently mellowed sufficiently to chair the centre-Left Labour Co-ordinating Committee). Domestically, the Eighties were very peaceful. The three men, two musicians and one artist (a member of the editorial collective on the anti-sexist men's magazine *Achilles Heel*), had all, like me, worked for many years at Left print-shops and on alternative community newspapers. They also played a significant part in the upbringing of my son. He was now the only child in the house, although his mates were ever present, something I encouraged and he, always a popular and gregarious young person, wanted. Discipline was never our forte.

'How come you've kidnapped the sexiest men in London and got them holed up here servicing you?' my charming American visitor, the feminist writer, Barbara Ehrenreich, would tease me, with characteristic exaggeration. To this day, I am sent e-mails, like this one (arriving only last week, as I write) from an old Australian contact, Roseanne Bonney: 'I heard a wonderful story about you in Paris. I fear, unfortunately that it is not based on fact … an Australian writer said to me: "Lynne Segal? Isn't she the woman who lives in a four-story house with a different lover on each floor?" Is this true Lynne??' Ah, such tales! Such sweet times, when rumour like this might circulate! (The problem for me today is how to keep it alive, since desire feeds on – imagined – desire, like boredom on boredom, even sleep on sleep.)

Until the mid-1980s there was a grain of half-truth in the teasing, but only in the sense that the man in the basement, Chris Whitbread, was an ex-lover, and the one at the top of the house, James Swinson, was my then lover, and perfect housemate. As I could have said in those years, 'I'm pretty monogamous when I'm monogamous', in line with the serial coupling that was the pattern of our particular culture, before our middle age ended all this – although only for the women.[68] These two ex-lovers, plus Steve Skaith, the captivating singer-songwriter from the band Latin Quarter, were still living in the house when I met the great love of my life in 1986, the radical philosopher, Peter Osborne, the one I knew I'd love till 'the salmon sing in the street'.[69] Although I'd typically managed to get conventions the wrong way around again, looking up to a man fifteen years my junior, by the close of the 1980s we had begun living as a traditional (only slightly unusual) couple. My son, now twenty, had left home, the collective household ended and we relied upon each other for what, to my continuing surprise, proved incalculable intellectual and emotional support. I shared fourteen years of astonishing happiness with Peter, before time took it away, and he – by then the same age as me when we had met – fell in love with someone else. It was the year 2000. I was into my fifties.

Feminism and motherhood

Despite its demographic shifts and Spartan comforts, the decades of communal living had suited me. An accidental, apprehensive mother, I came for many years to feel sure about only a few things in life. The first was that it was best for my son, as well as for me, to live with other people who had bonds of friendship and commitment to both of us, ties that were more relaxed than any I had known in nuclear families or couples. We both seemed to like it this way. It certainly worked well for me, enabling me to do all the things I wanted to do, hold down a job and be politically active and socially gregarious, live with children around, while ensuring my son was cared for and loved. He will say to anyone that he had a 'wonderful' childhood (although he has yet to enter therapy, and learn what mothers do!). Some children raised in collective households have since been quoted in media coverage expressing more ambivalence, although I have detected no consistent pattern in their comments: some felt neglected, some that they received too much attention, and were expected to join in and account for everything they did.[70] I now question aspects of my own mothering, worried that I was neither sufficiently mature, nor sufficiently selfless, to get the balances right, feeling that I could do better today.

Yet the main problem, as my son often reminds me, is that I raised him for a different world, for the gentle world of our dreams – uncompetitive, compassionate, and tolerant. He emerged as an adult into a culture and workforce that was its uncompromising antithesis. Only in hindsight can I even begin to think how I might have done things differently, preparing him better for the world he entered. It would have involved more focused parental attention than the laid-back, carefree domestic haven of his young life, where children confronted few challenges, and nearly everything was permitted. It matched only too well the near complete failure of the inner-London comprehensive schools in the 1980s to expend energy pushing pupils to reach their potential. How we parent, I now know, has many ingredients: the imprint of the parenting we experienced (which I thought, in genuine self-deception, I had inverted), our age and readiness for parenting, as well as all the intricacies of the intimate and wider world we are inhabiting. Few are accessible for conscious evaluation, while staying afloat, holding a child, in the murky waters of deepest intimacy.

The dilemmas surrounding feminism and motherhood have proved enduringly challenging, clearly encompassing far more than my own personal afterthoughts. It is unyielding dogma today that Women's Liberation ignored the needs of mothers. Dozens of books support the charge. Stubborn accusations of our betrayal come as much from other women, including feminists, as from men. This tells me two central things about women and mothering: how appallingly easy it remains, even now, to make women feel guilty about the issue, whether or not they have children; and, how compelling are the forces tipping all manner of problems onto mother's lap, a creature we know, definitively, to be female. As I write this, one leading daily newspaper in Australia, *The Age*, has for years been hosting a series of articles with such titles as 'The sins of our feminist mothers'. Middle-aged women are held responsible for the fact that, supposedly, their daughters are now 'childless and angry': 'Why did feminism forget motherhood?'[71] They show no interest in exploring the formidable social obstacles contributing to young women's reproductive decisions, such as the ever more competitive workforce, in the contemporary cultural context obsessed with celebrity, money, individual success and failure. The berating continues elsewhere, with some of those feminist mothers themselves, such as Anne Roiphe or Elizabeth Fox-Genovese in the USA, joining the populist rants, scolding their feminist peers (while exonerating themselves) for disrespecting mother-hood.[72]

It is as though, back in the naughty 1970s, Adrienne Rich had never written *Of Women Born* (1976), acclaimed by feminists the world over for its account of the wisdom and wonderment of motherhood (along with its anxieties), while carefully distinguishing the mothering experience from its coercive regulation by patriarchal institutions. From that time onwards, there was widespread celebration of maternity in much feminist writing, with two other highly influential texts, Jane Lazarre's *The Mother Knot*, and Hélène Cixous' essay 'The Laugh of the Medusa', also appearing in 1976, followed quickly by a host of other books exploring the experiences and significance of maternity, from Sara Ruddick's shrewd *Maternal Thinking* to Phyllis Chesler's far more contentious *Sacred Bond*.[73] When the feminist publisher, Stephanie Dowrick, searched for women to articulate the diverse experiences of motherhood for her anthology, *Why Children?*, at the close of the 1970s, she could not find one feminist prepared to write *anything* negative about their mothering experiences.[74] However, I am glad to see that over the last decade a few more of those early Women's Liberationists (some of them now psychotherapists), alongside younger women in their wake, now do feel confident enough, finally, to address the intense but typically ambivalent experiences of mothering. It is not an ambiva-lence stemming from their feminism, quite the opposite. Rosie Parker, Wendy Hollway, Brid Featherstone, among others, have elegantly conveyed both the guilt so easily generated in mothers from sources both within and without, as well as the potentially productive nature of accepting and working with just such ambivalence.[75] Indeed, as Ann Snitow suggests, facing up to her own infertility, while Women's Liberation once hoped to support women's choices, whether to have children of their own or not to, it is in practice maternal experience that we have primarily marked and honoured.[76] She is right.

However, as in my own case, back in the beginning many of the key instigators of Women's Liberation were already mothers. We fought tirelessly and in the end extremely successfully for changes in maternity care and more respectful gynaecological attitudes and practices. We placed the subject of nurseries, shared parenting, 'working' time, children's health requirements, play space, schooling, mothers' housing needs, anything else we could think of in relation to women and children, on political agendas. Above all, we undermined the stigma of single motherhood and illegitimacy. Single mothers became the stars of Women's Liberation. Our babies, at least in my experience, could not have been more welcomed and loved within our circle; we created a sense that men were privileged to be able to relate to children and put time and energy into them (their own or those of friends and comrades), to run crèches or to find jobs working with children. That was a rather glorious ideological shift.

Have we really forgotten the panics of the days of my adolescence, without available contraception and no possibility of a legal abortion? How easily we cast from our minds the limbo so recently threatening western woman facing 'an illegitimate spawning', fearful as much for her child as for herself, as Seamus Heaney captures exquisitely in his poem of a girl drowning her illegitimate baby: 'He was a minnow with hooks/Tearing her open'.[77] In her wonderful memoir written just before her tragic early death, Lorna Sage vividly evoked the terrifying drama of her accidental pregnancy at sixteen, somehow occurring prior to her knowingly even engaging in penetrative sex. She found the humiliations endured by women in public maternity wards in 1959 so devastating that a week after giving birth to her daughter, still running a temperature, she plotted to jump out of the window leaving her baby behind. She screamed at the punitive day sister that she would rather die than remain in the hospital a moment longer:

> Anything that might make you feel less wrecked and dirty was disallowed on principle ... mothers were dirt and fathers barely came into it at all ... visiting hours were brief. There were no public phones ... Confinement was the right word, but it wasn't solitary. The curtains round the beds were only drawn for intimate examinations or bedpans – except for one bed where the curtain was always drawn, because the large, sulky girl in there was an unmarried mother. Her privacy was a badge of shame.[78]

How can we explain the resolute censure Seventies feminism receives? In the USA, the self-styled feminist economist Sylvia Ann Hewlett has spent two decades attacking feminism for ignoring mothers. Here too, apparently more sympathetic voices, such as that of journalist and writer Maureen Freely, accuse feminism of 'betraying' mothers: 'the women's movement was dominated by women ... who were desperate to escape from motherhood.'[79] Is it merely that past hopes are never safe in the hands of history? This was the decade in which Women's Liberationists set up refuges for battered women, almost all of them mothers; won legislation to enable women to obtain a court order against a violent husband or father; and campaigned successfully for child benefits to be paid to the person caring for a child, not the husband in the family.[80] Times change, and the stories we tell change with them. Feminists who thirty years ago fought for better conditions and resources for mothers and

mothering are for the most part horrified today at what is re-
packaged, often meretriciously in 'our' name, in the current
neo-liberal consensus: mothers on benefit are coerced into
employment; women's role in an ever more competitive,
market-driven culture of the workplace is ambivalently
applauded, pitting women with children against women
without. In regimes where public rank and fiscal reward rule
supreme, a high-flying working mother can sometimes be
found once again, weeping in the women's loo, nowadays
not because she is frightened to speak, but because she
misses her baby.[81]

There are, however, further nuances in play here. Mothers
who joined the WLM tended to be women who had children
when still quite young. Women overall embark upon
motherhood when older and less needy today, especially
middle-class women. Age makes a difference; money as
well. The loss of selfhood accompanying motherhood can be
greater for those who have as yet only a shaky grip on their
adult identities, who have still to find secure sources of
recognition and support that might create and sustain them.
As younger mothers, we needed to create our own alterna-
tives, and so we did. I had no family to help with childcare
('granny' was a busy professional woman on the other side
of the world). I never once in my life paid for a babysitter, let
alone dreamed of a world with 'nanny' back in the nursery.
'The great gain,' as feminist philosopher Kate Soper
commented, recalling those early domestic tussles, 'was co-
parenting, a new gender division of labour ... I shall always
be a passionate defender of it for both the parents and the
children themselves.'[82]

The society we fought for – the battle we lost – was to
shorten the working day to enable those with the commitment, ability and desire to do so, to look after those in need
of domestic care. We were not defeated for lack of trying: if

that is 'betrayal', it comes only from the minds of those who project it as such. Off-loading all the demands of caring for children, or other needy dependents, onto a single paid worker was complete anathema to this outlook (the idea of employing another woman as a cleaner was quite simply unthinkable). I recall a terrible row breaking out over dinner in the mid-Seventies when someone mentioned the possibility of a 'service' wash at the local launderette, the informant taken to task by Noreen, who had once worked as a home help, for expecting some low-paid woman to service us in this way.

How fast things change; some things, at least. We did not envisage how easily women would slide into using other women as nannies and cleaners. Today's older professional woman pays out daily for childcare and faces rather different problems: not so much an ontological challenge (the sense of no longer knowing who she is, or once was struggling to become, before baby appeared on the scene), but rather the anxious juggling of the demands of her career and the responsibilities of her home. It is true that we were guilty, we second-wave feminists, of not addressing the needs of this immanent post-feminist life form. But her day had yet to dawn. Ambitious professional women, wherever they were in the Seventies, did not for the most part embrace Women's Liberation in the days of its high radicalism. It was seen then, probably correctly, more as an impediment than an advantage for career success. Many would later declare themselves to have always been feminist, while – because they came to it later – remaining, in the spirit of Polly Toynbee, disdainful of its earlier forms of collective activism: 'the "women's movement" of the '60s and '70s never really existed.'[83]

Today's career woman resides in a world apart from those alternative dreams of mutuality back then, when troubling dilemmas around self-reliance and personal authenticity meshed with the desire to create a fairer world in ways that were dedicatedly 'anti-careerist': 'I never had a notion of a career, in the typical Sixties complacent way, I just thought you lived for politics and earned enough money to survive,' my friend Sheila Rowbotham confided to Michelene Wandor about her life in the days of Women's Liberation.[84] 'We lived then, all of us, inside the loose embrace of feminism,' her counterpart in New York, the writer Vivian Gornick, echoes; 'I thought I would spend the rest of my life there.'[85] Strange, surely mythical, are the creatures that lived behind our always accessible, collective doors, when surveyed through today's neo-Darwinian lens, focused sharply on individual, competitive survival.

4

Escape into action

'Can't you find another word for "struggle"? You keep repeating it,' the woman from a London radio station cautioned us in the mid-1970s. She was interviewing me and my comrade and lover at the time, Ralph Edney, trying to pin down the goals of the alternative local paper we both worked on throughout much of that decade, called, oddly, *The Islington Gutter Press*. We found it hard to oblige her. In these more politically alienated times, it is daunting trying to convey to readers the personal inspiration that propelled us optimistically into the concatenation of meetings, street theatre, demonstrations, leafleting, lobbying, union work, community liaising, staffing of resource centres, reporting, publishing, poster making and more, that absorbed the committed feminist activist of the 1970s. Yet, for many years, taking me from my twenties into my thirties, I felt increasingly more confident about the significance of the political work we did in that decade. It was not that I thought we would achieve all our goals, I was never blasé or unrealistic about that, but I felt secure about their intrinsic worth. 1968 had proved the high point for many male student radicals, but not for me. That was the year when, accidentally pregnant and completing my PhD in Sydney, I grew ever more insecure and confused, blinking blankly over the Situationist slogans occasionally reaching me from Europe: 'Be Realistic, Demand the Impossible'; 'Live without Dead Time'; 'Form Dream Committees' ... hmm.

Dream committees, of a sort, became routine in the 1970s. Settling in Islington in 1971, well before it had become the expensive location it is today, put me in touch with the loosely associated radical community then within it – feminists, socialists, gay liberationists, anarchists, radical philosophers and philosophical radicals. At that time around half the borough lived in council housing, bringing tenants' activists, squatters, social workers, teachers, community lawyers, co-operative business entrepreneurs, students and the unemployed together in jumbled militant alliances. We shared a desire to express solidarity with anyone who joined 'the struggle' – that ubiquitous word again – against embedded inequality, 'from Hackney to Haiphong', as our paper spelled it out: parochial internationalists, we might have been called. (Interestingly, 'Glocalization' is the clunky linguistic innovation used by sociologists to describe today's reverse process: local forces attempting to attenuate the unsettling impact of global processes). Our battles for parity might be against grievances entrenched primarily through economic disadvantage, or the cultural diminishments of ruling-class elitism, racism, sexism, homophobia. We embraced the lot.

Life as politics

Class and cultural forces were seen as always entangled, in line with New Left analysis of culture as a key site in the production of social hierarchy. These ideas filtered down from Raymond Williams, E. P. Thompson, André Gorz and, soon enough, from each other, with Sheila Rowbotham and Barbara Ehrenreich just two of my own early mentors and friends. Joined together, all these voices inspired our goal of building an open, heterogeneous socialist movement: 'Women you have nothing to loose [sic] but your chains', one poster on my bedroom wall declared, depicting a woman, hands aloft, breaking through chains. We also had to learn to spell, I scrawled alongside it.

The emphasis on organizing from your 'own oppression' combined (at times uneasily) with support for working-class struggles, especially at their most militant, organizing directly from the shop-floor. In Islington in the 1970s, manufacturing firms were selling up fast and moving out of an area where the price of property was spiralling upwards, leading to a series of unsuccessful occupations against closures. STRIKE A BODY BLOW TO CAPITALISM, however, which some of my local gang of libertarian men and feminists spray-painted onto the blackened walls of empty property in Kings Cross at the time (1972), was not exactly the cry of our more strictly organized 'brothers' – or sisters – in the labour movement. The structure of feeling here, to sound another Raymond Williams note, resonated with our identification as outsiders in the straight world. Women, like those who were racially oppressed, unemployed, imprisoned, or in other ways disrespected and excluded, had long been largely ignored by the orthodox left of the labour movement and (what was then still seen as) its Party. Women's traditionally distinctive concerns were, for the most part, similarly marginalized within the organized far Left groups or parties.

Most days of the week throughout the 1970s, I emerged from my collective household to spend some time at the large, squatted, shabby building, less than a mile away, which provided shelter for the various machines and dark room constituting the alternative Islington Community Press. The building also housed various other radical projects, including the Under-Fives Campaign, the Rights of Women (ROW), Islington People's Rights and the Squatters Advice Centre. I must have been the only person who occasionally managed to sunbathe amongst the matted brambles out the back. When not producing the paper, there would be some other urgent work to be done, perhaps assisting the other community groups using the resources available at the press. It might be the Black Parents' Movement, campaigning against police harassment, headed up by the impressive Caribbean leader, the late John Le Rose, from New Beacon Books. We also helped out the local Greek Cypriot and other immigrants' rights groups. The lists grew longer year by year, supporting anti-racist, anti-apartheid campaigns, working with Troops Out (of Northern Ireland), or any of a multitude of diverse liberation struggles around the globe, from Eritrea to East Timor. Even the mother of the controversial chess player, Bobby Fischer, arrived on our doorstep one day before going on hunger strike outside Downing Street – I've forgotten exactly why. Locally, we would be lobbying for prison reform, supporting mental patients' unions, or radical social workers producing their *Case Con* magazine. Today, my mind reels at the very thought of it all.

Responding to calls for direct action and building networks of solidarity, not party building, was always the strategy favoured by most of these grass-root activists. This sustained our belief that radical community organizing was as crucial a site of struggle as organizing in the workplace. Most of the women I knew were networking locally, then meeting nationally for a few years as socialist feminists (from 1973 to 1975), later gathering regionally to exchange ideas. However, some women might prioritize working on specific national campaigns, perhaps as legal workers (in ROW) campaigning for changes in the law to get money directly into the pockets of women most in need, or for women's increased reproductive control with the National Abortion Campaign (NAC). Meanwhile, many of the men, for a while at least, formed men's groups to discuss ways of promoting anti-sexist practices. Another long-term friend, Barbara Taylor, captures the spirit and lifestyle characteristic of this swathe of left-wing feminists in a recent essay on her own political journey:

> [My] leanings were towards the libertarian left – a natural home for many feminists – and my social world was fervently experimentalist. I lived always in communes, spent most of my evenings in political meetings, and had nothing but contempt for conventional middle-class ambitions and lifestyles … Women's liberation was not just a political ambition but my life's agenda.[86]

Our life's agenda. The first crop of women's newsletters and manifestos, merging this desire for women to take charge of and change their lives ('Organizing Ourselves'; 'Manifesto on Motherhood'), combined with diverse legacies derived from the New Left's democratic Marxism, aligning women's liberation with the libertarian left ('Women on the Buses, 'Television and Women').[87] 'We come together as groups and individuals to further our part in the struggle for social change and transformation of society', the founding document of the Women's Liberation Workshop in London concluded, in 1970.[88] Those words were echoed in the opening editorial of the alternative local paper I helped produce in Islington: 'This paper aims to be a forum where all those groups in the borough who want to control change, instead of being controlled by the forces which badly affect us, can get to know each other.' (Elegant prose was not, as yet, our strong suit.) Despite a certain disdain in the women's movement and libertarian left for the 'soft-cops' of welfare, therapeutic or religious bodies, feminist activism often looked rather like full-time, unpaid missionary work, at least in hindsight: 'we wanted to do good in the world,' as Sally Alexander recalls.[89]

That fervour reverberates in her description of the first effort of the London Women's Movement to support working-class women, in this case, night cleaners fighting for better wages and conditions. In a piece she wrote soon after the partially successful completion of the campaign, in 1971, Sally describes how feminists responded to a call for assistance from the cleaners' spokeswoman, May Hobbes. Young women, who were neither cleaners nor members of the Transport and General Workers' Union, could be found nipping through the night into offices to persuade women to join the union, returning later to collect their dues, negotiating in the daytime with reluctant trade union officials to make them take their new recruits seriously.[90] This was the beginning of many campaigns to support women fighting for union rights. For many socialist feminists, union work would become the 'key site of struggle', as Sarah Benton reminded me. Then a young journalist in her twenties, Sarah was active in the Association of Cinematograph, Television and Allied Technicians (ACTT), where in 1973 a group of women pushed through the groundbreaking resolution demanding union investigation into the media's general stereotyping of women and discrimination against them. They fought on afterwards to win the even harder battle to give her (rather than a man) the job which resulted: 'The report I wrote was the first ever published by a union on the topic,' she writes to me. 'This has since become commonplace and incorporated into all union traditions; one forgets how revolutionary it was at the time.'[91] One certainly does. Equally radical battles from the NAC would eventually force the general Trade Union Council (TUC) to support abortion rights, while on a broader canvas feminist economists and allied intellectuals began meeting together to devise an ambitious feminist Alternative Economic Strategy.

Although speaking at nurseries to encourage unionization and supporting local workers' struggles in their places of work, I was not especially active in my own union for Teachers in Further and Higher Education (NATFHE). Shunning exhausting battles within the labour movement, other Women's Liberationists, to whom I was closer, were more likely to be found in campaigns such as the Claimants Unions, defending those surviving on the meagre welfare available to single mothers. Supporters accompanied single mothers to their Social Security offices (*NEVER MEET THE SS ALONE*, leaflets cautioned women), sometimes going en masse to 'occupy' these offices, demanding an end to the snooping and harassment experienced by women on benefits. Occupation in those days was a popular tactic in this politics of 'direct action': its sudden, dramatic effect, if rarely successful, gave maximum publicity to the relevant issues. Papers on Fleet Street were occupied to protest against their sexist portrayal of women, or the pathologizing of lesbian mothers. Homeless people from the London Squatters Organization occupied the skyscraper, Centre Point, in the heart of London – deliberately kept empty since its completion in 1967. Squatters also occupied the London Electricity Board, this time demanding the reconnection of supply to their homes (for which feat Ralph Edney, mentioned earlier, would receive and serve a six-month jail sentence). The post office at Trafalgar Square was briefly occupied by hundreds of feminists in 1972 – and this time I was there – demanding that the family allowance be paid directly to mothers (rather than appearing as a tax deduction on their husbands' wage packets). Again there were arrests, but no jail sentences.

You needed to have supportive domestic arrangements, to think carefully about how best to live, if you were going to keep pace with this level of constant political activism. Alternative lifestyles were all the more significant if, as a woman, you were also responsible, as I was, for children's welfare. This is why communal living was the usual choice of those I was closest to. Conversely, of course, you could escape some of the insecurities and personal anxieties involved in forging alternative lifestyles, embarking upon unconventional and less secure sexual relationships – or perhaps alleviate the tedium of unfulfilling jobs – by immersion in political activism. Seventies feminists were busy organizing on all fronts, often alongside men, to support themselves and others in the workplace and, especially, to improve what still then felt like our own local 'communities'. We had friends and supporters in the council, as well as in the main tenants' and housing associations and at all the local resource centres. I not infrequently sat through the monthly monotony of long Council meetings in Islington Town Hall, spending my birthday, at thirty-three, at just such a meeting, its dullness lightened by the birthday cartoons Ralph drew to keep me amused – which I still have.

Throughout this time, my job as a lecturer remained secondary to my life as a community organizer and activist, whether working at the community press, spending time at the women's centre, or more loosely supporting a shifting array of radical campaigns, from the Working Women's Charter group to the National Abortion Campaign. Most people I came across in political associations would have no idea of my professional status. I remained an undercover academic, but an 'out' revolutionary of the officially leader-less brigade, at times mocked in my political life (sometimes with affection, sometimes with envy) by those who knew my professional position and home-owning status. In that sense, apart from my weekly childcare night, I had not moved so far from my Sixties' student persona, especially as I usually ended up in the pub with friends following whatever meeting or social event I had attended – whether it was a campaigning, educational, or more pleasurable, usually fund-raising, occasion. The difference was that I was now working more hopefully for some form of immediate progressive change, rather than remaining primarily suspicious of it, as in my Sydney Libertarian days. If I had drifted into a form of lifestyle politics in the 1960s to find a moral compass, I had an altogether firmer sense of belonging throughout this high tide of socialist feminism.

Nevertheless, a certain ambivalence over political goals was never fully resolved, nor did I really expect it to be, then or since. On the one hand, there was always uncertainty over issues of 'reformism' in my libertarian and feminist milieu, with fears of people being 'co-opted' or diverted from their fully egalitarian goals by the compromises made with those in local government, or other structures of power and funding. On the other hand, doubts were expressed about radical 'interventionism', where militants parachuted themselves into others' struggles to impose their own 'revolutionary' agenda. We did fight for policy changes at both local and national level, joining with organized Left groups, in particular the International Marxist Group (IMG), to oppose clawbacks in welfare, launching 'anti-cuts' campaigns against the tightening of public spending that began after Harold Wilson replaced Edward Heath as prime minister in 1974, his government almost immediately issuing circulars demanding savings in council spending. Our campaigns intensified a few years later, in 1977, when James Callaghan, with his chancellor, Denis Healey, tightened monetary controls, making significant cuts in education and health spending. But the vernacular, expressed in a half-joking way, was always a rhetoric of 'revolution': 'And I suppose we'll see even less of you after the revolution,' one youth worker, Dave Robins, amused us, recounting a recent visit to the 'class enemy' – his mother! 'Has anyone seen the parliamentary road to socialism?'; 'a few small reforms quite soon please', Ralph Edney would quip, deriding the Communist Party's cautious moderation in all things, diligently following their famous programme, *The British Road to Socialism*, issued in 1951. The CP had a stranglehold on the Islington Trades Council, as well as the local Federation of Tenants' Associations and NALGO (then the largest public-sector union in the area), regularly frustrating the more militant actions favoured by us. For instance, they boycotted the main anti-cuts campaign as much too radical.

Ralph was the charismatic cartoonist and chief writer on the *The Islington Gutter Press*, as well as the dominant presence in our particular political arena. In his creased baggy trousers and open-necked denim shirts, his shaggy, unkempt locks framed fine features that moved constantly from laughter to derision in his indefatigably entertaining repartee. As I mentioned, he was also my lover for three years in the mid-1970s, between his restless moves from one woman to another during that decade. All the women flirted with him, even as he lingered for a year or so with one or other of the local 'sisterhood'. I never lived with him, although for six years or more he dutifully looked after the two boys from my household, my son and Alison Fell's (an earlier ex-lover of his), on our key night for socializing – every Friday. I was always grateful, and the boys enjoyed their time with him just as much, and perhaps more securely, than his latest girlfriend of the moment, snuggled up beside each other, whispering and laughing, in his big double bed in another communal household – always in some sparsely furnished, previously empty, squatted house, usually owned by the council. Many of those communal squats – the ones that didn't accidentally burn down – would eventually mutate into a local housing co-operative. This was the result of campaigns to obtain tenancy rights in the empty property the new occupants had 'liberated' from its fallow state.

Ideas in the void?

What did it all amount to? Elizabeth Wilson, a friend of mine who was a teacher in another London polytechnic, as well as an acerbic feminist writer, was sharply critical of the libertarian left. Along with a small group of other socialist feminists, she had joined the Communist Party in 1973, presumably looking for ways to keep class at the centre of feminist concerns, while reining in the permissiveness of the new social movements with more disciplined Party formations. In her view, lack of formal structures of authority produced disguised leaderships, cliques and exclusiveness. It created 'tiny ghettoes' of alternative lifestyles, exhausting its advocates in activism and perpetual confrontations that tended towards nihilism, the romanticizing of outcasts and, above all, failing to address the central question of 'how you take power'.[92] The Trotskyist Left voiced this last criticism interminably; indeed, it was the central mantra of their revolutionary liturgy. One might have thought these factions were always on the point of taking power, rather than the marginal ghettoes they actually were. This is presumably why the far left, as the Trotskyist groups were known, imagined that they needed to expend the greater part of their energies not so much on fighting the injustices of capitalism, as on 'the rather more urgent war against other left-wing organizations', as the literary critic Terry Eagleton noted caustically, recalling his days in the Workers Socialist League.[93]

In my view, then and now, all the Leninist groups tended to undermine attempts at left unity through their own self-appointed vanguardism. Nevertheless, I took Elizabeth's criticism very seriously at the time, although I failed to persuade my comrades at the Islington Community Press to discuss her particular critique, published in the Marxist feminist journal, *Red Rag* (when I was briefly on its editorial collective). Was she right? Was there anything useful, or enduring, which came from our sense of belonging to that amorphous collective, to that 'we' of non-aligned (largely libertarian) left feminism, the admittedly small rock on which we tried to stand? Well, yes, I would still argue. This 'we' did open up and transform some of the working practices of the council, whether widening the language net for addressing topics previously suppressed, forcing long-standing grievances higher up council agendas, providing a firmer voice for existing organizations of all sorts, or facilitating the growth of a plethora of local resource centres and cultural events. Nevertheless, the criticism made of our diverse and disorganized ways of working has a compelling ring, its notion of 'the tyranny of structurelessness' almost a truism today.

All radical activism, unpaid and unrewarded by conventional canons, relies upon the personal and shared confirmation of 'doing the right thing' in displays of solidarity with others. On the left, it springs from commitment to some compelling vision (forever fought over, fluctuating, ideally open-ended) of individual autonomy, equality and people's right to live free from basic physical peril and psychological intimidation or disparagement. Inevitably, collective affiliation courts dangers of moralism, elitism, in-group references and exclusions, whether revolving around shared behaviour and dress codes or distinctive jokes and curses. However, with closeness, familiarity and mimicry the common forms of all human bonding, their manifestations here were no more (and no less) inevitable or reprehensible than anywhere else – though politically they could prove counter-productive. The potential of oppositional groups fighting to shift old ways of thinking to facilitate new movements for change surely turns on their capacity to highlight the already familiar, but with a partial twist. It is this partial twist, the finding of just the right words to alter ways of seeing and talking, which can suddenly open up new spaces for acting, despite all the established presumptions necessary for sustaining old collective loyalties. The process is much too context-bound to be predictable.

Purism could certainly be heard on the libertarian Left, some of the most regular rants coming from those who opposed any form of organizing as inevitably a type of domination. A minority of feminists, if often a noisy one and, exasperatingly, a voice the media provocatively delights in highlighting, developed a special sort of intransigent moralism in their attacks on men, and even boy children.[94] It left anti-sexist men confounded and many feminists confused or, like me and my friends, in outraged dispute with their stance. It took some years for women to discuss and begin to theorize the dangers that stalked political affiliations based upon shared injuries: resentments could harden into a self-righteousness that threatened to undermine the broad-based solidarities needed to effect change. The occupation of such moral high ground usually served primarily to paralyse, shame or silence precisely those with any sway in progressive arenas, those already most attentive to particular claims of victimhood.[95] Nevertheless, at the best of times, those most active in Women's Liberation and community politics put enormous effort into reaching out to others. This was frequently accompanied by an undercurrent of self-mockery, and awareness that the world at large viewed us askance, if and when they saw us – stern but still smiling – sprinting from meeting to march, leafleting to law court, public gathering to picket line.

There was always mild ridicule of political correctness (PC) in both the feminist and mixed political worlds I inhabited, applied by us then to those seen as over-zealous in policing the views of others. This was long before the Right stole the notion from us – like much else – twisting it to their own ends, which had nothing to do with self-criticism, but was merely a cheap way of mocking anyone seeking ways of achieving greater social equality. Nothing was more constant in my memory than the lighthearted put-down with which we greeted our own actions: 'Just think, we can do this all day, every day, after the revolution,' one person would joke, as we circled tables, collecting up and stapling leaflets, before racing off to shed them in the chilly streets of Islington. 'Lacking the strength of character to bear much joy, nevertheless he refused to deny all his higher tendencies simply because they came under the modern suspicion of being rackets,' Ralph Edney began his cartoon book of the adventures of *Lazarus Lamb*: his eponymous hero a perfect parody of himself as a depressive, scrawny 'minge-bag', 'prattling on about the world like an escapee librarian'. Few on that scene were so blinded by doctrinal purity that they did not indulge in some form of self-examination: 'A stranger to certainties himself, Lazarus knew the pain of doubting, but counted stilling doubts in others a sharper pain.'[96]

Chronicling this still largely unrecorded community activism and workers' militancy of the 1970s, the Islington Community Press published a pamphlet, *Beyond the Fragments*, in 1979. It was reissued successfully as a book the following year, leading its three authors, Sheila Rowbotham (the major voice), Hilary Wainwright and myself, to organize a conference in Leeds in 1980, searching for more effective ways of organizing to confront the ominous prospect of a new ideological and economic conservative offensive, which arose after Margaret Thatcher's election in May 1979.[97] Three thousand people came to the conference, but divisive sectarianism destroyed any hopes of coherent outcomes, though a few follow-up meetings ensued. Criticism rarely came from the grass-roots activists around Britain, but was most abrasive from almost every organized Left and some feminist groups that attended, as well as one or two sceptics claiming to be anarchists. Addressing the opening plenary, Sheila Rowbotham could only whisper due to a throat infection. It was perhaps the only time some in the huge audience, those who had arrived with their own pre-set agendas, strained to listen to our calls for unity on the Left: a unity we had hoped to see forged both despite, and through, the recognition of differences and diversity of outlook. Like many before us in the UK and elsewhere, we found ourselves uncomfortably caught between the vanguards and the differing agendas of the fragments: the 'fraggies' as Edward Thompson, a supportive participant, called us affectionately, 'NANAs' (the National Association of the Non-Aligned), as Paul Foot, who stayed well away, dubbed us with Trotskyist disdain, despising our lack of party 'discipline'.

It was true enough that the shifting universe of non-aligned activists did not have any means, or even plans, for 'taking power', either at the national or the local level. However, given that there was no political formation even remotely resembling a mass revolutionary movement in Britain, we suffered rather less from the hubris of proclaiming its possibility. Arrogant, impatient, naive we may have seemed; nevertheless, it was our working away to support rather than commandeer a diverse array of particular struggles that now seems the less absurdly grandiose strategy. However, those working hard to create unity and pursue change through flexible consensus and networking were (and still are today) beset on all sides by vanguards that already believe – despite dissension all around – that they have the answers.

Notwithstanding these snares, from the early 1970s until well into the 1980s, forms of grass-roots activism, incorporating much of Women's Liberation and Left libertarianism, did begin to transform the content and style of politics. Links were made between activists and the Left of the Labour Party, with ideas flowing across from the array of new social movements and more traditional community politics, promoting forums for more participatory democratic practices. Although often mutually mistrustful, such interaction left a clear stamp on mainstream politics, broadening political agendas to include problems hitherto barely discernible, including the intricate nuances and discrete issues raised by those involved in race, ethnic, sexual orientation, disability, mental health or prisoners' rights politics. It also made it possible for many more activists, myself included, to make their way into the Labour Party, in what were for us its glory days of radicalism in the 1980s; for others, its wilder years of inelectability. In fact, we did get a few radical MPs elected, as in my borough of North Islington, campaigning successfully for Jeremy Corbyn as our MP. He is one politician whose feet till this day remain solidly set in the ideals of those times. It was the success rather than the failure of militancy at municipal levels in the inner cities of England, Wales and Scotland, which led to Thatcher's offensive against any sources of public funding for more participatory democratic practices, curtailing the power of local councils in the process. New Labour has done little to reverse this.[98]

However, it was without doubt feminist activism that had

the most lasting impact, interacting as it did with shifting economic and labour requirements as service industries and the financial sector expanded to replace traditional industrial investment in Britain. It placed a host of women's issues irrevocably on mainstream political agendas. On the home front these included childcare and domestic responsibilities, women's health and sexual agency, issues of violence against women and sexual abuse; in the workplace, it had highlighted sexism in employment practices and the delivery of services, sexual harassment and the existence of household sweatshops; more generally, the complex interface of race and ethnicity with gender issues was being analysed. In the wake of feminism, women's lives were scrutinized in all their diversity, inside and out, from birth to old age, in their pleasures and in their pains, across class and region. Tensions between women with children and child-free women, reflection on heterosexual privilege and the perils of lesbian lives, numerous hierarchies between women, all were now relentlessly aired when women spoke out in public forums. The differing requirements, resources and skills of specific groups of women were mulled over, whether in relation to the state, education and training, or oral histories and cultural expression. Hidden sources of women's power, reservoirs of rage, triggers for female embarrassment and unease, nothing at all seemed too grand, or too trivial, to escape some form of feminist attention or debate. Over time, addressing these issues also helped smooth the way upwards for particular groups of women, especially professional women.

That the concerns feminists raised can today sometimes be seen to affect the lives of men as well as women testifies not to the tunnel vision of those who addressed them – however dismissive of the dilemmas of men and masculinity some may have been – but to the significance of these freshly identified, now named and recordable human tribulations. With or without feminism, male culture is still loath even to admit that men can be raped, let alone to make it easy for male victims to declare themselves rape survivors. Men also remain reticent to report spousal violence or experiences of sexual abuse as children. The decade of militant feminism permanently altered ways of seeing women in all places touched by the global media, even though the world's way of seeing feminism would often become more than a little distorted. It might be twisted into altogether new manifestations, when women's interests were invoked in the mainstream to service very different agendas from those of feminists who battled for change in the 1970s. In 1969, the coming decade was ushered in with the long-haired, miniskirted, youngest-ever female MP, Bernadette Devlin, entering Westminster at twenty-one, as a socialist and a feminist, supporting the Republican cause in Ireland. She was immediately ticked off for whistling in its corridors, before proceeding to scandalize every authority by becoming a single mother during her time in Parliament. The decade was ushered out, ten years later, with the election of the regally coiffured, first ever female prime minister, Margaret Thatcher, leading one of the most conservative Parliaments in British history. Women were on the move, that much was certain, though far from headed in the same direction.

Women's cultural renaissance

More than anywhere else, it was in the cultural arena that feminism had its greatest impact in the 1970s. If it is hard to cover the diverse political tracks laid during that decade, following women's cultural interventions is even more daunting. The two entwined, obviously, with cultural productions seen as both a political weapon and the passionate unshackling of women's hitherto stifled or disparaged creativity. Liberation rhetoric fired the explosion of creative work from women, in theatre, music, fiction, film, fashion, publishing, poster- making, dance, art works, crafts; indeed, every conceivable imaginative and scholarly arena, as the vicissitudes of women's lives – loves, hopes, fears, responsibilities, skills and interests – spiralled outwards from the early fiercely critical, yet soon surprisingly confident, militant platforms of Women's Liberation into the more popular arenas seemingly ready to receive them. A polyphony of women writers and artists were suddenly determined to portray female futures with lives that would offer fuller, richer possibilities than any of their creators had ever hitherto imagined for themselves. Feminist rock bands such as Jam Today (at their peak in the mid-Seventies) would seem to transport these joyful promises right into our midst. For a while, there was certainly dancing at this revolution.

As Marsha Rowe writes to me today, of the period just before she and Rosie Boycott launched by far the most successful magazine of Women's Liberation, *Spare Rib*, in 1972:

> How can women now understand what it was like then, for a
> woman to be viewed by the world as less than a man?
> Releasing ourselves from that restrictive hold came with a big
> punch in the air, partly, it must be said, of resentful anger and,
> following that, joy, exhilaration. Suddenly, words were
> possible. Words that were at one with your own thoughts,
> rather than twisted into what would fit with some extraordi-
> nary notion of being the inferior section of the human race. Not
> only words, but pictures, music, poetry, engineering, science, all
> resources, love with no holds barred; daily life took on a new
> sublimity, as our potential was released on all fronts. One was
> flying. Eventually we had to land. That came with a bump, as,

of course, conflicts and responsibilities were grappled with. But reality itself had changed. We had changed the world, we were changed ourselves, and that dialectic is still going on, to my great fascination, giving me optimism and courage.[99]

Those same thoughts are reiterated by Michèle Roberts, who was poetry editor for *Spare Rib* in 1974:

We knew the male-dominated establishment would not be interested in our work. We felt we were revolutionaries with everything to fight for. Women's theatre expressed the excitement of it all, as some of us had just experienced in our Women's Street Theatre group. We never dreamed of being victims. Just felt passionate and passionately creative.[100]

Back in 1978, Michèle said, when interviewed for *Spare Rib*, 'I'm very conscious of having written from my sense of gender identity in quite a pain-filled and angry way ... The writing enabled me to reclaim something I thought was lost forever with childhood – which was a sense of creativity, of play, the sheer enjoyment of making something.'[101] This passion and creativity would lead Michèle, a few years later, to publish her first, semi-autobiographical novel, *A Piece of the Night* (1978), in a writing career that took her, two decades later, to the shortlist for the Booker Prize for Fiction and to winning the WHSmith Literary Award for her novel, *Daughters of the House* (1992). Her friend from those days, Sara Maitland, who also published her first novel, *Daughters of Jerusalem*, in 1978, was interviewed that same year, along with Michèle. She too spoke of writing as 'an act of power'. Because you have complete control over your fictional characters, she said gleefully, you can bring out more of the confusions, contradictions and even the unsisterly things in feminists' experience and behaviour, 'without being heretical': 'You can deal with [your characters] in exactly the way society deals with you – *as it chooses*. I like having that control.' [102]

A 'feminist literacy' spread quickly into the mainstream from the early 'consciousness-raising' novels of the 1970s, many of them published by the new feminist presses soon sustaining women's emancipatory zeal. In Britain, Virago began the process, publishing its first book in 1973 and becoming independent and self-financing in 1976 (with Ursula Owen, Carmen Callil and Harriet Spicer at its helm). In the UK alone, several other imprints swiftly followed, while similar ventures arose in most of the more affluent cities around the world, those in the USA reaching the broadest audiences internationally. Feminist writers' groups were formed to foster women's talents, support and criticize each other's work, their ventures sometimes first appearing as collaborative productions of short stories or poems. One such writing collective in London, including Zoe Fairbairns, Sara Maitland, Valerie Miner, Michèle Roberts and Michelene Wandor (all of whom would become recognized feminist authors), produced a number of publications together, beginning with the collection *Tales I Tell My Mother* (1978).[103] The fifteen short stories it contained aimed, characteristically, to explore the experiences of contemporary women in general, and the authors' aspirations as writers, feminists and socialists in particular, while enmeshed in their everyday lives of families, friendships and other relationships. Another compilation, again distinctive of its day, carried the graphics and poetry of five feminist poets. Celebrating this style of joint effort, it included a poem written by a white South African feminist then living in London, Ann Oosthuizen, 'Bulletins from the front line'. The setting, as it happens, was Alison Fell's bedroom, in the middle of my house:

Regimental HQ, Ali's room;

Three windows, two desks, one bed
Papers everywhere,
Five women meet; a council of war
Our strategy still unspoken.
We are not in uniform, there are no medals.[104]

Comparable collaborative ventures were set up in every other cultural arena, from film and theatre to poster making or mural projects, all of them regularly reported in *Spare Rib* and the various other feminist newsletters and outlets that came and went over the years. Their combined efforts often prevailed, even over protracted stubborn rebuffs in the more prestigious public domain. In 1974, for example, no major gallery in London would allow the New York curator, Lucy Lippard, to stage her exhibition of women conceptual artists. By 1980 the Institute of Contemporary Art (ICA) in London hosted not one but three major feminist exhibitions, Lippard's show prominent among them.[105] Why was there such a shift? It was partly because, like all the women I knew, so many of us had been so eagerly consuming feminist cultural work that we had created not just an audience, but a market. Some aesthetic efforts might stay within a smaller, determinedly feminist audience, including much of the most thought-provoking work. However, it too would sometimes permeate well beyond initial dedicated enthusiasts. For instance, from our bookshelves in the mid-Seventies, many of my friends were reading and discussing *The Three Marias*, a text that had been immediately banned when first published in Portugal in 1972, with its three female authors arrested on charges of public indecency.[106] These writers were for us instantly emblematic of women's struggle for freedom in a country that was still largely in thrall to the patriarchal shadow of its old authoritarian ruler, António de Oliveira Salazar, just before its popular revolution in 1974. The book is today a classic of European literature. Another charismatic feminist heroine from later in the decade, who would also soon face banning and imprisonment in her own country, Egypt, was Nawaal El Saadawi. In 1977 she published *The Hidden Face of Eve* in which, drawing upon her work as a psychiatrist and public health administrator in Cairo, she wrote with compelling energy on the abuses of women's minds and bodies in Arab culture. However, El Saadawi never failed to mention what she saw as the oppressive effects of attitudes to beauty and the cosmetic industries on western women.[107] I read her writing, both fiction and non-fiction, alongside many fascinating interviews with this progressive Islamic feminist, just a few years before hearing her speak to an enthralled audience in Sydney in the early 1980s. This was on one of my visits back to my homeland, which became a little more frequent after my father died in 1980, and my mother was for many years living on her own.

During these years, some of the most accessible feminist material had immediate mass-market success, especially books arriving from the USA. Lisa Alther's *Kinflicks* (1976) and Marilyn French's *The Women's Room* (1978), to name two, both sold in their millions worldwide. For years I too enjoyed these semi-autobiographical feminist bestsellers, if sometimes irritated by the staunch self-regard rarely far from the surface. Unlike the tales of angry young men many of us had imbibed in the 1960s, portraying its male heroes (or anti-heroes) on the move, enraged at the subservience or conformity of their class roots (for which they blamed women), we now had a type of feminist *Pilgrim's Progress* all our own. It created a new genre of utopian fiction mapping women's journeys from the world as it was, to a deliverance yet to come. Protagonists emerged out of the humiliations, harms and constraints of girlhood, navigating past the frustrations and impediments of marriage, surviving isolated, disregarded motherhood (in the company of arrogant, selfish and difficult men), to arrive at redemptive liberation through personal honesty, growing autonomy and confidence, helped by the understanding and support of other women – not infrequently, at least if still heterosexual, ending their voyage standing alone, but always wiser, and just a little more hopeful.[108] Some of these new heroines, at times, might shed their heterosexual shackles to experience the women-centred secrets of sexual fulfilment in the knowing caresses of a female lover, like Ginny in *Kinflicks*, or as the Dutch writer, Anya Meulenbelt, more ambiguously portrays herself in *The Shame is Over* (1976).[109] These questing females, always depicted as both intrepid and vulnerable, mostly remain unsure of their futures at the end of their journeys but they have, like Ginny, always gained in autonomy: 'She left the cabin, to go where she had no idea.'[110] It was only in the lesbian fiction that the heroines often alighted, enduringly confident, in the arms of another, as in Rita Mae Brown's ribald celebration of the joy of women's lovemaking, *Ruby Fruit Jungle* (1977).[111] More often, however, the commercial bestsellers maintained heterosexual protocol, but substituted dashingly rash, daringly unrepentant, picaresque heroines, such as Isadora Wing in Erica Jong's runaway success, *Fear of Flying* (1974), selling more than ten million copies worldwide.

One of the first off the block to commercial fame in Britain, Fay Weldon's *Down Among the Women* (1971) portrays its female friends with wickedly acerbic humour. They are all disappointed and dissatisfied in their different ways: 'I sit on my park bench and cry for all the women in the world,' its anchoring voice observes.[112] Each of these young women struggles to survive their passions for selfish, narcissistic, domineering or dismal men. Few succeed. As a result, there is a seemingly hopeless paradox at the heart of the novel. Weldon wants to spell out her version of feminist wisdom: 'In the end men are irrelevant. Women are happy or unhappy, fulfilled or unfulfilled, and it has nothing to do with men.'[113] Men are irrelevant? Weldon seems at odds with herself! Her own characters are rescued by nothing other than the love of a good man, although these fictional creatures, like their author, dream of an evolutionary shift. Their daughters, she predicts confidently, with feminist battles behind them, will turn into something 'strange and marvellous', 'free and happy'. They will, finally, no longer resemble their mothers. Rather, they will look pityingly at them. We learn of future possibilities through the words of the iconic granddaughter, Byzantia, whose coming into existence opens the novel and whose wry dismissal of her mother's world closes it: 'Fancy seeing success in terms of men ... [it was] a fearful disease from which you all suffered ... It is enough to tear the old order down.'[114]

It is still pleasurable rereading this book today. But I no longer experience the frisson I recall, turning its pages in 1974 (on a trip to Portugal, being driven speedily through fascist Spain, to celebrate the fleeting hopes for a brave new socialist democracy to succeed the military dictatorship established by Salazar). I scribbled confident but self-critical words in its margins, urged my sister Barbara (who never shared my feminist affiliations) and my friends to read it, seemingly unaware of its thoroughly unconvincing denouement. In my defence, I could say that I was particularly moved by Weldon's account of the failings of the women who felt powerless in the face of their own difficulties in life and love: 'I cry for my own malice, cruelty, self-deception and stupidity,' its authorial voice murmurs.[115] So did I – although I would, rightly or wrongly, delete the cruelty. Nevertheless, turning to other women for inspiration as well as guidance (some of them, anyway) seemed a particularly wise move. Weldon has always been most persuasive in her depiction of human folly. Just like Doris Lessing a generation earlier, she gleefully attributed near seamless flaws to men, before, with feminism no longer fashionable, she turned on feminists in the 1990s for following in her footsteps. She now claims that men are the new underclass, socially and emotionally, blaming feminism for being unfair to men: 'Women are elbowing the men out. The boys get anxious, the girls swagger.'[116]

Neither activist politics nor lesbianism make an appearance in her fiction, but Weldon was nevertheless a significant feminist presence in mainstream British culture in the Seventies. Apart from Margaret Drabble, who established herself as a successful writer before second-wave feminism, no other feminist novelist in Britain was as successful. Weldon was also, early on, a contributor to the feminist magazine *Spare Rib*. Drabble herself was among the very few famous women novelists who gave *Spare Rib* one of her stories to support the brand new Women's Liberation magazine in the first year of its existence. When Marsha Rowe, one of the two founding editors of the magazine, met her again in 2005, she took the opportunity to thank her once more. Marsha tells me that Drabble responded by saying: 'what we were doing then seemed confined to such a small group of women, with Women's Liberation seen as so extreme that she knew it just had to be supported, unlike nowadays, when it's all accepted as part of normal life.'[117]

Apart from the Nigerian writer, Buchi Emecheta, the British feminist voices we read in the 1970s were still predominantly white, though this was about to change.[118] However, black writers from the USA were already crossing the Atlantic, and ever more successfully, even more cogently, conveying the significance of black women's struggle against both racism and sexism. I first came across these powerful new feminist voices in compilations, such as Toni

Cade Bambara's *The Black Woman*, and Mary Washington's *Black-Eyed Susans*. They sit, heavily underlined, in my bookcases still. And soon afterwards, the powerful novels of these black women writers began arriving in the UK.[119] In my household, I recall us all reading and discussing Toni Morrison's books, *The Bluest Eye*, *Sula*, *Song of Solomon*, each of them conveying the visceral sense of being black women, forced daily to absorb the crushing economic and social reality, the noxious poison, of race hatred from surrounding white society.[120] Paule Marshall's semi-autobiographical *Brown Girl, Brownstones*, which I also read in the mid-1970s, is another text whose impact I can still feel, its heroine (with whom I somehow managed to identify) caught between sympathy for the predicament of her irresponsible, romantic father, recalling his Caribbean life, and conflict with her dour, hard-working, ambitious mother, rising upwards as an immigrant Barbadian in New York. For Christmas in 1976, I was given the passionate, theatrical verse of Ntozake Shange's *For Colored Girls Who Have Considered Suicide*, a few years before seeing it performed. Its lyrical tales of young impoverished black American women, were soon supplemented by the writing of another forceful feminist voice, Alice Walker, in her essays recalling her days as a civil rights activist, and not yet quite the celebrity she would soon become.[121]

Back in Britain, Virago published an influential book on Asian women in 1979, *Finding a Voice*, by Amrit Wilson, ushering in a decade when black feminist texts became ever more significant.[122] Black and Asian women had begun organizing and writing regularly in feminist outlets in Britain, although, with some exceptions, such as the writing of Joan Riley, the black literature we read was still primarily from the USA.[123] In retrospect, the popularity of this writing can be seen as a sign of intensifying struggles over difference and diversity that would overturn the idea of any unitary feminist identity by the end of the decade. In 1984, Virago Press began distributing the exuberant writing and poetry of Maya Angelou, publishing the first of her four autobiographical narratives, *I Know Why the Caged Bird Sings*.[124] These books would sell over a million copies in their Virago editions alone. Women's Press, the second largest feminist publishing outlet here, obtained the rights to Alice Walker's novels, including the spectacularly successful *The Color Purple*, published in 1983.[125] Another feminist publisher, Sheba, was set up in 1980, with the specific aim of prioritizing the work of women of colour and lesbians. Their first publication, *Feminist Fables* (1981) by Suniti Namjoshi, retold myths and legends from a lesbian-feminist viewpoint. It was Audre Lorde, however, who many feminists would name as their favourite writer of the 1980s. Her prose and poetry on the significance of recognizing differences between women, written from her strategic position as black, female and lesbian in the USA, could hardly have been more powerful, or more thrilling, than when we read it in what she called her 'biomythography', *Zami: A New Spelling of My Name*. In that book she recalls her experiences in the bars and streets of Greenwich Village, in the 1950s, when 'so far as I could see, gay-girls were the only black and white women who were even talking to each other in this country':

> Each of us had our own needs and pursuits, and many different alliances. Self-preservation warned some of us that we could not afford to settle for one easy definition, one narrow individuation of self ... It was a while before we came to realize that our place was the very house of difference rather than the security of any one particular difference. (And often, we were cowards in our learning.) It was years before we learned to use the strength that daily surviving can bring, years before we learned fear does not have to incapacitate, and that we could appreciate each other on terms not necessarily our own.[126]

Black writers from earlier times were also rediscovered and published anew, immeasurably enriching cultural horizons around the world. 'I do not weep at the world – I am busy sharpening my oyster knife': the assertive words of Harlem Renaissance writer, Zora Neale Hurston, were unearthed from her young adulthood in the 1920s.[127] Such flamboyant defiance was offered in the face of her knowledge that 'De nigger woman is de mule uh de world so fur as Ah can see,' as we heard again when her long buried words floated back to us from her now classic novel, *Their Eyes were Watching God* (1937), reissued, along with another of her novels, by Virago in 1986.[128] It took skilful searching by Alice Walker, forty years her junior, to discover Hurston's unmarked pauper's grave in 1973. By then, however, it was impossible to dispute the enduring impact of this new generation of black feminist writers and poets, so many from the USA. They could hardly have made a bigger splash in the classic canon of western literature, supported by, critically appraising and incalculably enhancing, the evolving cultures and political agendas of feminism.

From the 1980s some of these black writers were also contributing to, or routinely being written about, in *Spare Rib*, which had become increasingly more radical since its opening instalments in 1972. In testimony to the practical skills and experience some women acquired, at least partly through the feminist milieu they moved through, one of its founding editors, Rosie Boycott, would end up, briefly, editor of the *Daily Express* newspaper; my friend and fellow Australian, Marsha Rowe, on the other hand, stayed within the creatively alternative, non-commercial world she had always inhabited from her days in the underground magazine, *Oz*. Women's Liberation would prove a portal for extremely diverse journeys through life. Some women, who would later make their living through writing, started with the encouragement they received to contribute to movement magazines, such as *Spare Rib*. A few, in turn, honed their new skills, setting up literacy and writing groups with working-class women in adult education classes or community centres.[129] I was one of a host of unknown women who first reached a wider audience through doing occasional book reviews, or reporting on some new women's initiative in *Spare Rib*. That magazine had an impressive lifespan – over two decades (1972–1993) – and with no major financial backers was remarkably successful for an alternative monthly. With a distribution of over 20,000, *Spare Rib* was read by women of all ages, reaching well beyond the core of the movement. For a while, especially from the later 1970s into the early 1980s, the appearance of a few of the increasingly celebrated feminist voices helped sustain the magazine's more popular appeal: the successful singer-songwriter, Joan Armatrading, did a benefit to support it, while other regular fund-raising evenings kept the magazine afloat and our feet tapping. Amrit Wilson regularly covered the specific tensions Muslim women in Britain confronted daily, while Republican women kept feminists aware of struggles across the Irish Sea. The registering of significant differences between women was, of course, at the same time undermining notions of shared womanhood, or any simple binary conception of sexed difference.

Contesting injuries

With some of its members emerging from alternative journalism, but most arriving straight from higher education, *Spare Rib*'s editorial collective toiled tirelessly (on meagre wages) to challenge and reframe fixed images of women. They straddled the growing divide between Left-leaning socialist-feminism and the tightly woman-centred focus of radical feminism, while becoming heatedly entangled with the explosion of differing feminist voices from the close of the 1970s. This most flourishing movement magazine soon became a crucible for discord, receiving and reflecting back the creativity and the quarrels within the wider movement. Only towards the end of the first decade, however, did the rapid growth of feminism come to display the signs of its own downfall as a coherent, if complex, movement. Feminists coming into Women's Liberation from the mid-1970s have pointed out to me that their women's movement was not quite the same as mine or those other voices I have mostly drawn on from its opening years. Slightly younger women had sometimes encountered feminism's precepts at school, as already established opinion, or in their higher education, in places where the very first women's studies courses were starting up. The journalist and film producer, Jill Nicholls, was one of these somewhat younger women, encountering feminism as a student at Cambridge. She started writing for and helping out at *Spare Rib* immediately after she left university, in 1974, but continued to feel 'like an outsider' there until joining the collective a year later:

> ... the fragility and fearfulness of the first women's libera-
> tionists, I don't think I felt like that, coming a bit later. We were
> not so tentative. But then there was always the sense of not
> having invented it, not being so authentic ... For me, it did
> become a noose, more than for you I think ... I did feel the
> heavy hand of political correctness, especially towards the end
> of my time on *Spare Rib*.[130]

Jill hastens to add that Women's Liberation would also provide for her 'the most inspiring, joyful and formative period of my life', giving her the skills, the direction and the framework for the rest of it.

Nevertheless, working on *Spare Rib*, as it grappled publicly with contention breaking out in the movement, was taxing. Often attacked by a variety of women on the outside, the magazine (along with the movement) was tearing itself apart from within: accusations of anti-lesbianism, heterosexual privilege, racism, anti-Semitism, class privilege, divided women. Sue O'Sullivan, another member of its editorial collective from 1979 to 1984, later wrote of her confused feelings: 'Joy was still swirling on the dance floors of feminism in the early 1980s, but joy's partner was often anger.' Trying to grapple collectively with everything that needed to change to create a fairer world for women everywhere, feminists not only confronted the sexism of the world at large and their own feelings of inferiority, but needed to acknowledge the deep inequalities between women themselves, which meant, as she concludes: 'The anger women once directed so confidently at the perpetrators of sexism was now ricocheting within the movement, and *Spare Rib*, the most widely read feminist publication, became the forum or repository for many of these struggles.'[131]

Though Sue does not say so, one woman on the collective, whose enraged voice remains with me from so many of the public meetings in those years, was Linda Bellos, vociferously occupying each and every injured position as it arose. As well as being female, black and lesbian, the last 'injured' identity I heard Bellos speak from was as a victim of anti-Semitism. Indeed, it was as a Jew that Bellos finally resigned from *Spare Rib* in 1982, departing to help produce the short-lived magazine *Shifra* soon after. I could trace the distressing encounters around any number of contesting identities, but simply because it is one that has returned to haunt me today, I will focus, in a highly selective way, on this particular quarrel over anti-Semitism.

The crisis emerged after Palestinian and Lebanese feminists in London had used *Spare Rib* to denounce Israel's siege of Beirut and South Lebanon in the summer of 1982, which culminated in appalling massacres occurring in the Palestinian Sabra and Shatila refugee camps.[132] For me at the time, the 'Jewish' identification conspicuous here merely underlined what seemed most troublesome about identity politics, offending both my Jewish, anti-Zionist heritage and, more importantly, my desire for justice for Palestinians. The refusal to allow criticism of Israel's invasion of Lebanon was not representative of the stance of all self-identified Jewish feminists, but it was typical of the bitterness often expressed in the clashes then circulating in feminist circles. That same year, the influential American feminist Letty Pogrebin declared anti-Semitism 'the hidden disease of the Movement', in the flourishing magazine, *Ms.*[133] Seizing upon the hyperbolic rhetoric of victimhood that had crept into some feminist writing, a phantasmagoric spectre of anti-semitism was unleashed: 'Our children are tortured every time they set foot inside English schools,' one feminist wrote to the *Women's Liberation Newsletter* at this time. Eager to join the indignant chorus, her non-Jewish girlfriend added her voice: 'My family accuse me of putting them in danger by associating with Jews; they are convinced there will be a knock at the door one day, and they will be taken [away] for collaborating with Jews.' Bizarrely, these two daft contributions (along with equally contentious claims from quite different sources) were reproduced as 'key writings' in the last anthology ever to appear from the British Women's Movement, *Sweeping Statements: Writings from the Women's Liberation Movement 1981–3.*[134] It was the beginning of the end of any coherent women's movement, I thought sadly, reviewing the collection for a socialist magazine at the time.

As Sue O'Sullivan again spells out, the problem was

certainly not that the issues addressed were unimportant, rather that strategies for dealing with them could get lost in a politics of anger and resentment. Nonetheless, like the majority of feminists I knew, she herself never lost sight of the movement's broader goals, calling always for that 'lightness of generosity' which enabled women to work together across their differences: 'Women's Liberation transfixed and transfigured me and millions of other women. Through it, I became who I am today.' [135] She is today deeply involved in the International Community of Women Living with HIV/Aids around the world. In a variety of ways, most second-wave feminists managed to move on into broader arenas where they would continue to raise gender issues, despite the tensions and splits that threatened former feminist projects and coalitions.

The rise of what would at times prove a divisive identity politics was as much due to the success as the failure of Women's Liberation, as women explored both the potential strengths and the particular suffering of their multiple identifications. Moreover, the effects could prove enduringly creative. One of the most successful radical women's organizations in the UK, for example, arose among Asian women in Southall, asserting their own situation in relation to the multiple prejudices and injustices experienced by their ethnic communities from the world outside or, as women, from patriarchal practices within them. For over twenty years Southall Black Sisters have campaigned for resources for Asian women experiencing domestic violence, often in the face of opposition from their own male community leaders. They have found ways of confronting the successive political challenges to their notions of freedom and justice as black, Islamic or ethnically oppressed women, whether tackling violence against women in their native communities, confronting the global rise of religious fundamentalism and ethnic violence or, as I write, explaining the costs of US-led military assaults in Afghanistan and Iraq.

Despite the clashes that could develop between competing feminist voices, working together with other women and negotiating more generally with those whose politics were very different from your own could also, in my experience, at times increase open-mindedness, at least when there was clarity in joint objectives. Looking back, Kate Soper suggests that 'second-wave feminism became quickly sensitized to the "cultural imperialism" of its model … [and] in its criticism of the goals of its own original feminist project (white, western, middle-class, urban, and so on) it began opening up new views on the nature and limits of emancipation itself'.[136] An optimistic assessment.

Personal retrenchment

Decades are never simply chronological, serving instead as powerful metaphors for their most salient moments, usually constructed retrospectively. The era of trade union mobilization and expanding social movements in the 1970s subsided into increasingly sporadic and fragmented political struggles after Thatcher's defeat of the miners' resistance to pit closures in 1984–85, followed the next year by her ruthless closure of the highly popular, progressive Greater London Council (GLC), under Ken Livingstone. The final collapse of the USSR, in 1991, was seen as emblematic of the pacification of class struggle and the ideological defeat of Keynesian legacies of public planning. Little, it seemed, could flourish for long that was not geared to the profit-seeking whirl of global capitalism. The 1990s was thus seen by many of my group of leftists and feminists as the dreariest decade they had faced. The view was widespread. John Major was almost ubiquitously ridiculed as one of the most dispiriting prime ministers to preside at Westminster – 'I'm still here', comedian, Rory Bremner, mocked him – triggering neither admiration nor aggression, as his opponents waited patiently for a Labour government, finally, to overturn the long years of Tory rule. In the USA, as well, Bill Clinton quickly became a bitter disappointment for many Democrats who had eagerly celebrated his election to the White House in 1993. Indeed, with only the most meagre resistance, the Clinton years proved a mere interregnum between the Bush presidencies heading up the militaristic, neo-liberal, predominantly Christian fundamentalist far Right in control of the USA, stewarding ever-deepening social inequalities within its own population, and enforcing global trade agreements intensifying the North-South divide worldwide.[137]

In place of political ideals and collective action, mourning and nostalgia have never been more popular than in the 1990s, extending well beyond the old Left and former movement activists. 'The only New Worlds still to be discovered in the 1990s,' the historian Mark Mazower suggested, 'lay in the past.'[138] He was registering a form of cultural and political resignation the émigré Russian scholar, Svetlana Boym, later analysed in her book, *The Future of Nostalgia*.[139] Yet, for me, then in my forties, resignation was not at all what I had in mind. It was, it is true, the decade in which I too first looked back, although not to mourn but rather to take stock of the recent past. I began to write and speak about the many victories that we had worked so hard to secure, noting too the struggles still in full flow, while knowing how far we remained, in some ways, further than ever, from our dreams of a more equal, compassionate world. Living happily with my partner, Peter Osborne, it was the period in which I settled down, finally, more fully and confidently, into teaching and writing, both of which I had begun doing more seriously in the 1980s. Ironically, a bad political moment overall provided a good transitional space for a certain personal retrenchment, thinking back, as I saw it, not to generate individual nostalgia, but rather to encourage possible critical retrievals. The idea that rudiments of the creative optimism of the past can be nurtured in the present as prompts for imaginable futures was what my friend Sheila Rowbotham had always argued, as captured in her title *The Past is Before Us*.[140]

In 1984, Ursula Owen, then the joint head of Virago Press, had invited me to write an assessment of contemporary feminism and its future, and also to join the Virago Advisory Board to suggest ideas for commissioning similar books in future. It was very much her support, combined with that of Ruthie Petrie, then Virago's Senior Editor, which led to my first book, *Is the Future Female? Troubled Thoughts on Contemporary Feminism*. I not only needed encouragement to write in those days, but to feel that it would meet a receptive political audience. The book, appearing in 1987, did receive the type of engagement I was hoping for, both positive and negative, in the discussion of its two central themes: scepticism over recent moves to highlight sexual difference as the grounding principle for feminist struggle; arguments for keeping feminism aligned, however critically, with the more general politics of the Left. It questioned the expedient cultural mythologies of women's intrinsic virtues, associated at the time with popular feminist writers such as Dale Spender, Andrea Dworkin or Robin Morgan, emphasising instead feminism's potential to offer a more subtle analysis of the complexities and ambiguities in both women's and men's mentalities and access to power. While always needing to confront the ubiquitous negation of the 'feminine', women's struggles could neither be reduced simply to gender, nor solved purely by revaluing the 'feminine'.

My next book, *Slow Motion: Changing Masculinities, Changing Men* (1990) was a type of sequel to the previous one, this time focusing on masculinity. Again it challenged the conservative mood of the moment, echoed by those feminists suggesting that we could neither see, nor expect to see, signs of significant change in men's use and abuse of power and privilege. A literal battle of the sexes had returned in one perversely popular version of feminism, equating 'male sexuality' with 'male violence', and declaring it the root of all troubles, near and far. In contrast, I highlighted the writing and research revealing that both resistance to and acceptance of change was actually a constant feature in men's lives, reflecting the complexity of forces generating very differing patterns of masculinity across time and place. The same theoretical agenda inspired my next book, *Straight Sex: The Politics of Pleasure* (1994). It surveyed the notions of male activity and female passivity that both construct normative understandings of heterosexuality and underpin the language of male dominance, but without the accompanying disparagement of straight sex appearing in much feminist writing from the late 1970s. As ever, I was striving to capture the volatile fluidity of sexual experience, despite our limited phallocentric language for depicting it.

For better or for worse, all my writing has a political inflection, attempting to address both an academic and a popular audience. However, it is only the first book that reached well beyond an academic audience; by the 1990s it was less clear what broader intellectual Left movement existed. Nevertheless, at that time, significant political battles were certainly still being waged within higher education, encouraging productive, and not so productive, engagements within it. In the wake of the activist movements of previous decades, the 1980s and 1990s were the years when feminists, postcolonial theorists and other cultural dissenters, hitherto either marginalised or merely the object of interrogation in the construction of knowledge, themselves joined the interrogators. Our whole raison d'etre in the academic world was to challenge traditional canons, insisting upon our distinctive cultural and research agendas, beyond the contours of existing disciplines. Again, we were surprisingly successful. The courses young people can study today, especially in the humanities, are rarely untouched by the issues radical newcomers brought into pedagogy. As a gender theorist, my own work and teaching kept me searching across disciplinary domains, whether exploring the intricate, shifting social contexts in which identities are enmeshed, or the most disruptive particularities of psychic life, with their often tortured relation to social expectations and familiar discourse. At its best, it is psychoanalytic litera- ture that has tried hardest to understand the central, always fraught, place of sexual difference in the grammar of the unconscious: the married man who feels compelled to risk cruising in public spaces; the transsexual negotiating myriad hazards in search of gender re-assignment. At its worst, psychoanalysis has been used to attack feminist and gay insights, pathologising those who failed to conform to traditional gender and sexual norms.

This shake-up in higher education did not, of course, go unchallenged. In particular, the immense success of cultural studies, with its awareness of the ties between language, knowledge and power, generated frequent conflicts, from within as much as from without. From without, in the upmarket media and educational or political forums, cultural studies (usually seen as loosely incorporating gender and other forms of identity or ethnic studies) often became the butt of derision. Primarily because of rather than despite its success in recruiting students, cultural studies was attacked by the defenders of traditional disciplinary scholarship as intellectually frivolous and abstruse. From within, however, some of the most fashionable cultural theorists were themselves penning grandiloquent attacks on each other, rather than using their critical insights to reinvigorate richer cultural and political agendas. Symptomatically, though with his own unique brand of humour and provocation, the influential Slovenian critic, Slavoj Zizek, combined a worship of Hitchcock and Hollywood, Hegel and Lacan, with fierce theoretical assaults on cultural studies for providing a home for feminism, postcolonial and queer studies, rather than promoting 'proper political struggle' in the service of his enigmatic notion of 'absolute negativity'.[141] Intervening in some of these academic skirmishes in recent years, I argued that such metaphysical excess is hardly the soil for renewing either cultural or political agendas, serving more as a form of high entertainment and rhetorical posturing confined to academia.[142] Trivializing the forms of scholarship that cultural studies helped foster encourages a type of 'contemporary amnesia', as my friend Bill Schwarz comments. It negates the significance of enabling issues of gender, race and other forms of systemic oppression to be fully incorporated within the knowledges and cultures of modernity, for the very first time.[143]

Some of the new conflict within the academic realm thus merely reflected the old deadlocked polarities of the Left, disputes between those wanting to prioritize economic or class issues and others committed to promoting the recognition of 'differences' and 'diversities'. Nevertheless, it seems to me no bad thing that there should be some 'return to economics' in cultural studies in the late 1990s. Less rhetorically, and hence for me more compellingly than Zizek, the writing of the Indian Marxist theorist, Aijaz Ahmad, has for some time been pointing out that the promotion of multiple identities in the 'community of difference' has been incorporated as a key strategy of the global capitalist order: eager to service people's avid need for signs of authenticity, on the one hand; working to dilute any trace of politics, on the other.[144] The most interesting work today is that transcending the 'culture' versus 'politics' clashes, revealing how the cultural industries service global economic exchange at every level, deploying an emphasis on 'difference' and 'diversity' in the process. But it is only certain differences and diversities that are recognized, others remain suppressed.[145] Such thoughts can be usefully applied to the diverging legacies of feminism. One face of global woman today is that of those few women who have clambered up the corporate ladder or, like Condoleezza Rice or Hillary Clinton, attached themselves to the pinnacle of world power. The other face of global woman is that of those on the move at the base of the world, leaving their own families behind to arrive in richer countries to perform the labour of caring work, domestic chores and sexual servicing in new forms of super-exploitation of third-world women. But this face is only recognized and addressed on agendas where feminism still combines with forms of Left politics.

Twists of time

The troubled afterlife of Women's Liberation saw feminists heading off on a variety of differing journeys, whether working in groups or, increasingly, individually, as the movement imploded in the 1980s. Both despite and because of feminism, women's lives continued to change and diversify, the transformations cultivating their own shifts in words, meanings, contexts and perceptions of contemporary life. It is clear that new ways of thinking, talking and organizing pioneered by Women's Liberation, which at first felt so fragile, eventually succeeded in placing women's interests and outlook on mainstream political and cultural agendas (especially with occupational openings expanding for women). But they could not forestall the appearance of new modes of manipulation. What was beyond words yesterday may become cliché today; the silent scream, once heard, can be isolated to mute out other signs of distress, even those once perceived.

The lucrative trade in individual self-help manuals and 'recovery' programmes, mostly targeting women, has been one appropriation of some of the discourses of feminism, although erasing most of its original political message. Inside strictly feminist domains, battles continued within its 'house of difference'; outside, feminism might be held responsible for disrupting the natural order of things one minute and invoked as a model for promoting equality and wellbeing the next. Feminism has been accused of effacing women's 'difference' in struggles for equality, even as eminent feminist scholars battled to preserve their conception of the 'feminine' as inherently subversive of our still resolutely male-centred language, culture and world. A resulting media ploy is to encourage battles between women: whether in the name of defending feminism, or belittling it, being of little consequence.

I traced some of the residues and renovations, uses and abuses, of feminism in my last book, Why Feminism? Gender, Psychology, Politics (1999). As my own writing exemplifies, feminism was elevated into a form of knowledge in the academy, mutating into gender theory, to include the scrutiny of men and masculinity, alongside accounts of shifts and continuities in relations between the sexes and ever more sophisticated theories of the embodiment of gendered subjectivities. In other public realms, feminist agendas also

diverged, showing signs of multiple revisions and reloca-
tions as certain women advanced in professional life or the
managerial mainstream, even as others endured harsher
times.[146] However, my chief concern at this juncture is with
the backward glances of feminists themselves, reflecting
upon the peculiar intermeshing of life cycles with political
cycles in my generation, knowing it is youth that most easily
attaches itself to utopian politics and cultural experimenta-
tion. As women, we found our voices through politics, but
have we anything left to offer the very different world of
today, as rising inequality, ethnic violence, poverty and new
imperial wars overturn so many of the progressive hopes of
yesterday?

'I feel like a survivor of a lost world, a pre-Jurassic relic,'
Denise Riley writes; 'at the same time I have the impression
that, for some younger women, there is a strong eagerness to
know how we experienced things.' Times were affluent, the
number of jobs increasing in the developed/overdeveloped
world we entered as adults, and horizons could and did
expand for many women across differing social groups.
Seeing so much change so rapidly in our lifetime, high
expectations came easily to many of us. Generations are of
course hybrid and fluctuating entities. Yet, there seems to
have been a certain closing of the generation gap between
my generation and that of women born after the 1960s, with
nothing like the same psychological gulf that we felt divided
us from our own mothers. As Kate Soper comments: 'I
suspect that intergenerational friendship is not uncommon
today … some of my best friends are less than half my age.'[147]
She hastens to add that this may perhaps be more
pronounced in her academic milieu, and that the affinities
she feels with the young might be less than fully reciprocated. Interestingly, her view is strongly supported by wide-
ranging empirical surveys comparing the closeness of adults

from different generations to their parents. The 'cultural gulf' that those born in Britain in 1946 reported had greatly declined in the group born twelve years later (with both women and men more likely to say they felt 'close' to their parents as adults), a trend still evident amongst those born in the 1970s.[148] Nevertheless, whatever the nature of generational affiliations or conflicts, the political climate my own post-war legion of female 'bulge' babies discovered on entering 'the golden age of capitalism' in adulthood had definitively altered by the close of the twentieth century.[149]

'I miss the optimism we had that now things are starting, they will go forward, these changes are irreversible,' Cynthia Cockburn writes.[150] It is the loss of this shared confidence, when it seemed, as the social researcher Ursula Huws has written, that 'the boundary between understanding the world and changing it was dissolved,' that so many old radicals mourn today, whether within or without feminist trajectories.[151] In fact, Cynthia, in her sixties, seems quite as militant as ever, organizing with the global networks of Women in Black working for justice, peace and multi-ethnic democracies by opposing what they see as the 'continuum of violence': their silent vigils illustrating 'a way of doing things that ridicules and counteracts all the sexist, masculinist posturing that goes with militarism on every side.' But the mood is different now, 'sorry, gloom gloom', she writes to me. For those of us born into times of relative affluence and apparent peace, the gloom is hardly surprising: fear rather than expectation dominates the political landscape; displaced populations, militarism, revamped colonialism, ethnic strife and religious fundamentalism are ominously in ascendance, and now a new threat in our midst, the suicide bomber in western heartlands, placing bombs that harm only civilians on tubes and in buses, as in London in July 2005. Immediate access to the worldwide web and instant knowledge banks also mean that we are more aware of the depth and complexity of these problems, if we want to be, than ever before. This knowledge can also be paralysing.

However, many women's liberationists look back a little more ambivalently on their heyday of activism, while perhaps minding grandchildren, tending gardens, or working harder than ever in today's restless work cultures. Sally Alexander reflects:

> I found strength in having a collective identity. I find it hard without one, which doesn't mean that it was better then. I also found it very painful being part of a movement, always trying to put it first. I think now I negated personal relationships a little, spent less time with my children, because I was so bound up with the ethical dimension of our politics.[152]

As I suggested in my last chapter, I too worry that I did not devote more time exclusively to my son. The extraordinary energy devoted by women to both our inner psychic states and calls to collective action was, as Catherine Hall agrees, a very difficult thing to carry off: 'It was a strength, but a burden too.'[153] Yet one and all, every feminist I have spoken to felt proud of what their struggles had achieved, though usually regretful that it had benefited some women more than others – 'those already poised to benefit,' as psychologist Wendy Hollway puts it.[154] 'My confidence grew and my fears receded as I lived through more and more years of involvement in politics ... as I negotiated my way through personal misery and happiness ... [Today] I am prepared to admit differences, question dogma and fight for my ideas,' Sue O'Sullivan sums up her three decades of feminist involvement.[155]

Certainly, many older feminists are now critical of the way in which apparent respect for women's rights can be

deployed meretriciously to sideline or attack other significant struggles against class or ethnic injustice. We are even
more enraged on hearing moral conservatives, such as
George Bush, daring to raise 'women's rights' (while
routinely attacking them both at home and abroad) as part of
their current imperialist rhetoric for advancing 'the
American way of life'. Within the profession of higher
education, where I still work, feminists were particularly
proud of the gender issues they had brought to the opening
out of scholarship and scrutiny in almost every discipline,
where feminism has had a somewhat less ambiguous, if still
contested heritage. A minority of my informants, such as the
economist and still tireless activist Irene Bruegel, nevertheless blamed 'academic feminism for ... distancing itself
intellectually from the lived experience of many women and
hence impeding the success of women's struggles.' Although
a familiar criticism, this is not a sentiment I can agree with. It
is, first of all, far too reductive to expect knowledge to be
always politically expedient. Secondly, women's activism
declined along with that of the rest of the Left. The rise of
academic feminism as one of the most successful outposts of
Women's Liberation for some professional women, and the
nature of the issues it addressed, was as much symptom as
cause of that decline. The area of greatest agreement that
almost every woman I spoke with or heard from mentioned,
the most cherished gain from the past, was the enduring
network of friends they had acquired through Women's
Liberation: whether celebrating, along with Cynthia
Cockburn, 'the strong and reliable universe of feminist
women that resides in every country on earth ... wherever I
go I feel at home with them, learn something new from them
... it's wonderful,' or simply valuing that old network of
feminist fighters, who had become enduring friends.[156]

Yet, there is a further twist to the interconnecting generational and political lineage of the feminists I have known, where personal life can seem to shrink in gloomy counterpart with political hopes. It is hard to unpick general patterns of ageing here from the more particular trajectories in play. Some feminists now live alone, many who never expected to, having devoted much of their younger lives to building up support and friendship networks, sometimes pioneering alternative family forms. They had often used the freedom and independence they so valued to move on from relationships when love died or, increasingly as they aged, struggled for the strength to allow long-term partners to do so without too much bitterness. These are issues I will return to. Let me close this chapter with the words of my friend, Sarah Benton, living alone while battling heroically with the frightening effects of multiple sclerosis, supported inadequately, in my view, by her old friends: 'we had an unforgettable, if unique experience, which is incomparable.'[157] For the most part, the gains were almost always thought to swamp the pains and regrets, no matter what became of Beauvoir's dutiful or defiant daughters, those dreamers of Women's Liberation and transformed worlds.

5

Political timelines

The London I had entered in the 1970s, at least the one I noticed and attached myself to, was one where the ashes of revolutionary fervency smouldered on for at least another decade. The Libertarian politics that seemed so homegrown in Sydney had its resonances, as well as its differences, with the radical politics appearing in other western capitals in the 1960s. Times being increasingly affluent, expectations had grown in labour movements and on university campuses alike. Both reform and revolution re-entered a world where politics had been largely in abeyance as western Europe and its allies recovered from wartime traumas, leaving the USA to consummate its moves towards global economic and cultural hegemony.

I understood little about the roots of the Left, or its shifting contexts, during the time that political activism dominated my life, but I have a strong urge, as well as many more resources, to do so today. I was far from indifferent to the idea of looking for those roots, thirty years ago, attending endless meetings and study groups, my head then often buried in the latest Left or feminist literature addressing our intellectual forebears, when not more comfortably imbibing women's fiction. But it is impossible to grasp the diverse ways in which collective struggles leave their mark till well after their victories or defeats. The complex legacies of historical struggles tend to blur the distinction between success and failure. So it is only now that I realize how little I understood about what sustained the political affinities of the men of the Left, or the women either (usually somewhere backstage), that predated my socialist feminist milieu. Yet they had triggered much of our early resistance, even while, less obviously to us then, inspiring many of our goals. Nowadays, reflecting upon the transmission of generational histories appears to me more important than it ever could have before.

Battling for words

Nobody has captured that raw moment of resistance better than Sheila Rowbotham who, in 2000, published an account of her own enduring radicalization four decades earlier, in *Promise of a Dream*.[158] The legacy of that tumultuous decade, the 1960s, when prosperity and transformation seemed equally pervasive, was by then a battleground. Today, the iconic 'Sixties' perhaps arouses fondness or loathing, but more often dismissal as the last moment of irresponsible, self-absorbed dreamers. 'Retrieval has become an act of rebellion,' Sheila suggests, when radical ideas and fashions once inspired by genuinely egalitarian movements are later repackaged – commodified, sanitized, toothless.[159]

Trained as a historian, she returned to her diaries, interviewed friends and acquaintances, read everything available until, 'drowning in memories', she recaptured her often-fraught embrace of the seditious decade. Her midnight salvage proved a lonely, often disturbing process, sifting through relics for 'evidence' to narrate 'the tangle of coincidences which contribute to the particular fatality of living a life.'[160] Useful as her memoir is for my own retrievals, however, it is hard for me to offer an impartial appraisal, when Sheila was not only one of my first feminist mentors, but has become over the years my longest-lasting English friend. We share other idiosyncratic biographical details, having both been skinny, sickly, bronchial children, banished from home to Methodist boarding schools at a young age, supposedly for fresh country air. We both passionately preferred our mothers, remaining disdainful of overbearing fathers who brought no joy to their wives – although her gruff domineering Yorkshire father's shaky hold on respectability as aspiring lower middle class (giving her the Northern accent for which she would later be mocked) bore little resemblance to my own irascible father's speedy upward mobility from the poverty of Jewish immigrant roots into Australia's professional middle class.

Distilling the promise of a feminism that transgresses the barriers between public and private, Sheila looks back at her hectic route through the Sixties, not to lose herself in politics, nor to disown it, least of all to provide her own life as exemplar, but rather to resurrect her young selfhood the better to understand the apparently sudden emergence of a whole social movement of women, knowing its tide has since ebbed, then receded. Women such as her, caught between vibrant cultural change and militant political action against newly visible inequalities, violence and inhumanities, near and far, were bound to feel a queasy disorientation in relation to the subservience expected of them, of us – and, just sometimes, desired as well – in fulfilment of 'feminine' destiny. Adept penmanship, Methodist missionary zeal, perennial introspectiveness, fanciful flights, all made Sheila a key – if somewhat surprising – catalyst for other women at that moment: surprising, given her unassuming style; unusual, given her heightened sensitivity to her own and others' hesitant mutterings (vacillations suppressed by the single-minded folk she admired, who got things done); invaluable, because she could express the contradictions and doubts of political lives, just when a rising constellation of women was eager to hear them. This was the decade of sexual revolution, with the restraints on women's sexuality beginning to lift, yet Sheila was typical of most of us then in remaining for years ignorant about almost everything to do with sex: 'I was not the only one steering without a compass between the dreaded Scylla of frigidity and the humiliating Charybdis branded "nymphomania".'[161]

Nor had she been the only one, on joining Oxford's elite students in 1961, to discover its cunning ways of putting down anybody who was not male and upper class, with men's sniggers routinely greeting female undergraduates, who were still barred from the Student Union and subject to harsh and petty restrictions in women's colleges. Sheila was rescued from her alienation in this terrain by the kindness of the few older Left historians she managed to encounter, mostly former Communist Party (CP) members, such as Richard Cobb, Bridget and Christopher Hill and, most crucially, Edward and Dorothy Thompson. They were interested in people without power, not the dull diplomatic history she was forced to study in most of her courses. Her new mentors offered a non-dogmatic Marxism, expressing the creative intellectual life of the New Left, although she was equally attracted to the more mystical, introspective counter-culture of the 1960s, with its unstable mix of hedonism, and contempt for greed and competitiveness.

Sheila's socialist leanings were strengthened at nineteen on linking up for a few years with the young Marxist economist Bob Rowthorn, who – from a working-class background and aware of Beauvoir – supported women's emancipation.[162] He introduced her to the then still illicit ways of obtaining birth control, as well as to the new genera-

tion then (as now) in control of *New Left Review*: Perry
Anderson and Robin Blackburn. But she hated the toxic
sectarian combat between rival Trotskyist factions she soon
encountered, especially on briefly joining the Hackney
Young Socialists the year Harold Wilson's Labour government assumed power, in 1964, heightening hopes for social
reforms and cultural change. 'United Front, *Yes*; Popular
Front, *No*,' the member from Militant explained when she
arrived, warning her against his enemies from Gerry Healy's
Socialist Labour League: 'I blinked, trying to concentrate. It
would be easy to get this the wrong way round, and his tone
suggested the consequences could be dire.'[163] Scrutinizing
the battle of dissenting certainties, she was quickly an expert
on the ritual differences between the small Trotskyist sects,
admiring their tenacity (always angry, acerbic, alert for
betrayal); appalled by their arrogance and dogmatism
(usually driving away any working-class youth they
managed to recruit). This was the beginning of Sheila's
permanent aversion to vanguardism, which she came to see
as far from the most effective way of winning people for
progressive ends, while also sowing the seeds of potential
intimidation or abuse – thoughts fully elaborated some
fifteen years later in her influential critique of Leninism in
Beyond the Fragments.[164]

Back then, she was swept up in the extraordinary
activism of the late 1960s, supporting the surge of trade
union struggles, befriending Third World radicals and
immersed in the Trotskyist-led Vietnam Solidarity Committee
(VSC). Yet, as her diary jottings reveal, Sheila was simultane-
ously nursing serial heartaches, and endlessly confronting
the frustrations that seemed so intrinsic to heterosexual
passion: all her goals for autonomous, mutual loving were
stymied by experience and by her own ambivalence.
Meanwhile, the chronically niggling mortifications

connected with being a woman, from sexual denigration to marginalization in men's conversations, remained quite separate from her political activities. Only in hindsight could she see how 'profoundly disjointed and askew' she was feeling by then, without yet having words to explain her sense of 'the tragedy of the sexual divide and the way it had hobbled me.'[165] Sheila's activism resulted in her being invited to join the editorial board of *Black Dwarf*, as one of the very few women around it, a few months after it was launched in 1968.

The year had kicked off with US military morale shattered by the Viet Cong's Tet Offensive, followed by Enoch Powell's 'Rivers of Blood' speech, inciting racism and encouraging the National Front, with Left revolutionary passion reaching a peak in May as French students occupied the Sorbonne, their revolt spreading – for a few amazing months – to over nine million French workers demanding changes in working conditions. Students may have wanted social transformation, but when Sheila tried to address them on a public platform in her hip miniskirt (at the founding of the Revolutionary Socialist Students' Federation), the full force of 'revolutionary' sexism turned her into 'an object of derision':

> It was like a living nightmare. Stubbornness kept me in front of the microphone … Somehow through the whistling and laughter I managed to speak about [the under-funding of] further education.[166]

Some things never change. The class-based under-funding of Further Education colleges in Britain, at least when catering primarily for poorer working-class students, is with us still. Other things do change. Public guffawing at a young woman trying to address a meeting would, within a few short years, be frozen in the throats of men – whatever she was wearing.

Militancy had been forced upon women; a box reopened and the spirit of feminism flew out again. Although, in Sheila's reminiscence, for a while the impromptu meetings between women occurred mainly in the toilets, while she repeatedly wound up feeling once more stifled and 'annihilated' by Left comrades.[167] She remained at the *Dwarf* just long enough to solicit and write articles for an issue heralding *The Year of the Militant Woman*, appearing in 1969. Preparing for that special issue, she read through Lessing and Beauvoir, hunting for ideas on how to bring women's personal issues to politics, while at the same time interviewing sewing machinists on strike at Ford factories and other militant working-class women who, alongside female guerrilla fighters in Vietnam, provided early role models for Women's Liberation. 'I had *become* a woman,' she later wrote: 'As the words splattered out on the pages, it felt as if I had reached a clearing.'[168]

As we know now, many other women quickly found their own way into that clearing. 1969 was the year the brashly sexy Australian Germaine Greer (then working with the radical porn magazine *SUCK*) was busy writing *The Female Eunuch* which, both despite and because of its snipes at women and feminism, became an instant bestseller in mainstream culture, popular with men and women. It was, as we have seen, the year the first Women's Liberation groups appeared in the UK, a year after they became visible in the USA. From the beginning, American feminism was a critical catalyst in the growth of British feminism. The first National Women's Liberation Conference in the UK was set in motion that year, after Sheila announced a meeting (again to guffaws) for those interested in talking about women at one of Raphael Samuel's History Workshops. Just for a change, she later wryly notes, the assertive predictions of a Left paper 'had been vindicated by history'.[169] The year 1969 *was* the turning point in the rebirth of the 'militant woman' in Britain. Summing up her views in an article that year for *Black Dwarf*, 'Cinderella Organizes Buttons', she realized she could not bear to defend her views before what would be a largely hostile, all-male editorial group. Instead, she wrote a letter of resignation, suggesting that to understand why it was so hard to discuss what she had written on women, the men should spend two minutes 'imagining they had cunts'. The silence her speech briefly evoked was one of embarrassed anger, not creative compliance. 'This is outrageous,' they finally agreed. It would take twenty years for her novel challenge to become commonplace – if only on 'queer' platforms in academia, gleefully subverting gender orthodoxies.

1969 was also the year Sheila began writing her first book, *Women, Resistance and Revolution*, exploring how women had managed, historically, to educate themselves and fight for better lives. The times were exactly right for her thoughts to inspire women around the world. She had always stressed her indebtedness to others; now her former lover, Rowthorn, joked that others could take heart from her, since they would realize that anything she could do, they could do too. Not so much vanguard, one might say, as vigilant forager: 'I seemed often to bumble along almost unconsciously into doing a lot of things in my life which have then connected me to some radical mood in the culture.'[170] When that mood began to change, a decade later, the audience for her style of politics began to evaporate, even as her own thoughts shifted, just a little, to embrace new challenges.

The rise and fall of socialist man

Women's Liberation came into being, at first inadvertently, within the Left. But what were the cross-currents that had fed into that Left's own confident resurgence at the time? Today's interest in memoir writing has encouraged some lifelong radical campaigners to venture into the genre. Their reminiscences not only convey a far richer sense of the world of these earlier political travellers, but also enable us to puzzle over what often kept them committed to working for goals long after they became unfashionable, or bore any obvious relation to their immediate self-interest. Their journeys were already largely misconstrued by or mysterious to my immediate post-war generation. It is something I can only belatedly regret, meanwhile observing our own stories trashed or rewritten today, as I ponder the complexities of generational legacies.

As one of those post-war rebels Sheila encountered early on, the poet and broadcaster Michael Rosen would later recall his Communist mother's angry sense of being profoundly misunderstood by her son, the Trotskyist, and most of the radicals of the next generation, *my* generation, in our impatient criticism of older CP members:

> It's all very well for you to sit there in the 1960s and talk about the betrayals of the CP over the years, but for us, as Jews and socialists in the 1930s, there was no choice. The CP were the only organization that had the power and organization to oppose Mosley ... it was the only possible route to take.[171]

She was largely right. Back in the 1930s, with war in the air, unemployment soaring worldwide, and with Oswald Mosley and his fascist supporters on the move in Britain, 50,000 people joined the British Communist Party (CP). They marched against Mosley, supported the Unemployment Movement and Hunger Marches, and above all, opposed the emerging fascist regimes in Europe.

No choice, was the forceful explanation given by Eric Hobsbawm, one of Britain's leading historians, explaining why he joined the British CP in 1936, as a Jewish teenager who had just escaped from Berlin: at that moment, for him, and so many others, 'the October revolution represented the hope of the world.'[172] Hobsbawm's memoir, *Interesting Times*, spanning much of the twentieth century, exemplifies perfectly the ways in which political commitment, in certain times and places, can provide the soil for cultivating lifelong selfhood: 'The Party was what our life was about. We gave it all we had.'[173] Moreover, as Hobsbawm also notes, the cultural conservatism, bureaucracy and obedience found in Party members in the mid-twentieth century mirrored the manner, if not the minutiae, of the psychological conformity so hegemonic in the 1950s. Hobsbawm remained in the Party until its demise in 1991. Yet, for all his political intransigence, distrust of cultural projects and disdain for all he dismisses as 'identity politics', this indomitable campaigner ends up defending the uses of political memoir:

> Historians of my age are guides to that crucial patch of the past, that other country where they did things differently, because we have lived there ... we know what it felt like, and this gives us a natural immunity to the anachronisms of those who were not there.[174]

A partial immunity, perhaps. It is not that memory is reliable, far from it. Nevertheless, simply 'being there,' provides us with associations that may help to challenge the imposition of new orthodoxies onto the past. Indeed, in the face of the failure of the communist dream to put an end to class exploitation or halt western imperial aggression, this ex-Party man, now in his mid-eighties, can still launch a persuasive argument that social injustice can (and must) be fought: 'Let us not disarm, even in unsatisfactory times. Social injustice still needs to be denounced and fought. The world will not get better on its own.'[175] It is a sentiment, of course, a little at odds with his traditional Marxist epistemology, in which change is always immanent in the universal dialectics of the historical process itself.

Twenty years younger than Hobsbawm, another Left historian who became part of my network of friends, the late Raphael Samuel, provides an even more detailed snapshot of the pains and gains of Party members who made politics their lives, penning his vivid reflections in the 'The Lost World of British Communism'. Recalling the intense neighbourhood networks, friendships, discipline and hyperactive optimism of the Communists he knew as a child, he concludes: 'To be a Communist was to have a complete social identity, one which transcended the limits of class, gender, nationality.'[176] Indeed, as he later reflects, mid-century Communism created an exclusive identity and private world all its own, 'a moral vocation as well as a political practice', not unlike a religion or tribe, suspicious of outsiders, protective of members, socializing, drinking, even holidaying abroad with their own kind. The constant political activism also served as a way of practising together-ness: 'our demonstrations, though intended as "mass mobilization", could be seen in hindsight as rituals of reassurance.'[177] Strange as it might seem nowadays, Raphael suggested that for his mother's generation being a Communist, as so many in her extended family were, was 'a way of being English, a bridge by which the children of the ghetto entered the national culture', shedding the hostility or coldness that had greeted them elsewhere. It occurs to me now that it was also, perhaps, distinctive as a way of discarding their Jewishness in still deeply anti-Semitic times (as Raphael's father feared when his son refused to go to synagogue). Of course, it was equally a refusal to affirm *any* exclusive identity, whether gendered, racial or ethnic, in favour of an internationalism, committed to the social and cultural advance of all. Raphael's own life, however, also exemplified what it took to break away from such a background and forge a new identity, working to create a contrasting political world, the one I would enter.

As so many later testified, it was Raphael who was the initial dynamo, inspiration and indispensable catalyst of the New Left, when it arose in 1956 from the combined fallout of Khrushchev's confirmation of the state terror under Stalin and the Soviet invasion of Hungary. In full flight from the purges and horrors of Stalinism, and still critical of the failings of the British Labour Party, the many former Communists and their fellow travellers in this New Left tried to hew a more open, participatory politics, critical of the whole notion of leaders and led. Some departing Communists remained close to the old traditions; others moved ever further away. The Cambridge literary theorist, Raymond Williams, who like Edward Thompson had always been interested in the cultural dimensions of class, was soon lining up with younger radicals, including Stuart Hall, to make an even more definitive break with the Communist past.[178]

This New Left, with its commitment to journals, clubs, even a short-lived coffee bar, began the turn towards placing cultural analysis at the heart of politics, seeking out the contesting forces mediated within popular culture. Its ideas were soon embodied in the first of the post-war 'new social movements', the Campaign for Nuclear Disarmament (CND), launched with a massive meeting in London in 1958, and sustained by its popular, colourful Easter marches to Aldermaston. Attacking the banality and conformism of capitalism at home, supporting anti-colonial movements abroad, this early New Left sought to forge cross-class alliances.[179] But it was history itself that became Raphael's abiding passion – history converted into politics, politics converted into history – his mission becoming that of inspiring everyone he encountered, myself included, to believe that they had an interesting story to tell, whether emerging from a bedsit in Bromley, a suburb of Sydney, or a jungle in Bolivia. He was a unique catalyst in pushing excluded voices to assert their place in the world. Through a determined, if chaotic and wily ruthlessness, Raphael was also someone who could redeploy the skills of his old Party training to make things happen.

Yet, for all his desire to bring others to recognize their roots in history, suggesting that possible futures may lie dormant in the present's past, it was only three decades after leaving the Party that Raphael would burrow back into the 'lost world' of his own young life. His turn to personal memoir was triggered by seeing that community on the verge of permanent extinction in the late 1980s. Again reflecting more general trends, it was the old sense of collectivity that he realized had all but vanished in the final decade of the Party's life in Thatcher's Britain. The rising 'eurocommunist' wing of the Party, represented by the newly fashionable magazine *Marxism Today*, was in fierce conflict with its mostly ageing trade union loyalists, grouped around the *Morning Star* newspaper.[180] The real importance of this battle inside the CP, however, was its resonance with changes on the Left generally, not least its declining fortunes. Earlier Marxist thraldom to the 'working class' as vanguard of revolutionary change tied in with trade unions growing ever stronger throughout most of the twentieth century. In Britain, serious defeat of union power began only in the 1980s, after a decade of exceptional strength and militancy. What had disappeared on both sides of the Communist split was any confidence in the possible success of revolutionary transformation, despite *Marxism Today*'s switch from homage to working-class struggle to embracing the idea of

*Right: Lynne's mother,
Iza Joan Harris, in 1921,
age seven*

*Below: Iza Harris, taking
up very little space when
graduating as a surgeon
in the early 1930s. She
was the second woman in
Australia to graduate
with this qualification*

Left: Lynne's father, Rueben Segal, around 1909

Below: Iza Segal, with her three children, Lynne, Barbara and Graeme, in the 1940s

Left: Lynne (right) with her sister and brother in the early 1950s

Below: Lynne as a teenager in Australia in the late 1950s

Left: Lynne with Ross Poole, mid-1960s

Below: Lynne at home in Sydney, 1968

Above: Lynne (centre) with husband James Clifford and sister, 1969

Below: Lynne with her baby, Zimri, 1969

On the steps of the house in Highbury, called Balfour Lodge, 1976, with (left to right) Ivan Coleman (son of Alison Fell), Janie Prince, with Mischa Prince on her shoulders, Lucy Prince, Marion Conway, Noreen Conway, Lynne, Zim. All live in the house except Janie and her children

Left: Alison Fell cutting young Zim's hair, as Marion watches, inside the collective household, mid-1970s

Below: Islington Community Press, with (left to right) Pete Mullineux, Geoff Holland and Chris Whitbread, 1970s

The protest against Miss Islington organized by the Essex Road Women's Centre, mid-1970s

Hackney and Islington music workshop preparing to play at the Thornhill Community Festival, organized with housing activists from the run down estates in the south of the borough of Islington, late 1970s

Right: The cartoon drawn by Ralph for Lynne, as they both spent her birthday attending an Islington Council meeting, in 1976

Below: Ralph outside the squatted building occupied by the Islington Community Press and other groups, including the Islington Squatters Group, The Islington People's Rights Group (IPR), the Rights of Women (ROW) and the Islington Under Fives group

Right: Lynne and Noreen at the People's Field Day, Highbury Fields, in 1976. This was a large festival organized by practically everybody active in local politics in the mid-1970s, from a host of grassroots groups to representatives from the organized Left. Music came from local bands

Days of protest: on the march against racism and the rise of the National Front, walking alongside Ralph Edney and Rick Johnston with the Islington Campaign against Racism and Fascism at a march to Victoria, spearheaded by the Anti-Nazi League, in 1978

Men supporting women's right to choose at the 50,000-strong, TUC march against the Corrie Bill (the third attempt to restrict abortion rights) in 1979. These three men were members of **Big Flame**, *the libertarian Left group to which Lynne belonged: Max Farrar, Chris Whitbread and John Tuman*

Lynne and Sheila Rowbotham in Whitby in 1980, having fun while planning for the large Beyond the Fragments *conference which took place in Leeds*

Lynne with Zim, photographed for the Guardian *in 1983, to accompany a feature written to promote her first edited collection,* What is to be done about the Family, *published by Penguin Books (in association with The Socialist Society) for the series* Crisis in the Eighties

In the kitchen at Highbury, with old friends Janet, Tony Skillen, James Swinson and Ross Poole, late 1980s

James Swinson with Steve Skaith at the book launch for Lynne's first book, Is the Future Female?, *1987*

Above: friends on the stairs (left to right) John Mepham, Sheila Rowbotham, Lynne, Janet Rée, Paddy Maynes (front) at one of the annual summer garden parties held now for around twenty-five years at Balfour Lodge

Left: Pete Ayrton and Stuart Hall at a Latin Quarter gig in the mid-1980s

Left: Lynne and Peter Osborne at home, Christmas 1990

Right: with Alan Sinfield, 2002

Below: with Irene Bruegel and Bruce Robbins in front of the Al-Aqsa Mosque in East Jerusalem, attending a Faculty for Israeli-Palestinian (FFIPP) Peace Conference in 2004

photo: Sophia Robbins

photo: Éamonn McKeown

Above: with Misha Hadar, about to leave after spending four months at Balfour Lodge, to serve four months as a Refusenik in various Israeli jails, 2005

Right: with Agnes Bolsø in Trondheim, in 2006

the new social movements, such as feminism – although just when these movements were themselves beginning to weaken and fragment. Despite its impact on an equally embattled broader Left, four years before it voted to dissolve itself, Raphael could justly describe the Party's internal squabbles as a 'war of ghosts'.[181]

Following his tragic early death, at only sixty-one, I joined the large gathering at Raphael's funeral in Highgate in 1996, to see him buried not too far from Karl Marx. One mourner after another would later describe that day as the moving enactment of the end of an era, sensing that those attending represented a bygone age, one that would not come again – at least in our lifetime. Certainly, the combination of confident, outspoken self-identity, committed not to personal ambition but to political change, community building or, at the very least, to understanding and voicing opposition to the injustices of the world, is thought anachronistic across the greater sweep of public life today. Yet, on its fringes, Pied Pipers do continue to emerge in the global arena, encouraging young people into battle from Seattle to Genoa and beyond. As one of Raphael's oldest friends, pondering the uniqueness of his political formation, concluded:

> What strikes me most profoundly is the way he managed continually to remake himself, and to confront the irreversible transitions ... through which he passed ... without ever really losing his way, renouncing his political convictions or letting go his attachments to the worlds and values which formed him.[182]

Living with difference

Much the same could be said about the presence and impact of the man who penned those words, Stuart Hall. He is, in my view, the most charismatic of all the New Left figures, and the one I personally know best. Crucially for me, Stuart has spent much of his life locating political matters in their cultural and historical conjuncture, while also exploring private worlds of identification and belonging. Half a century after arriving in Britain from Jamaica, he is still politically engaged, still constantly rousing audiences on public platforms, still offering friendship and encouragement at every turn. Again, it is only late in life that Stuart has felt able to look back and assess the significance of his Jamaican past. His childhood, he now reflects, was a crucible of the destructive permutations of class, 'colour', fantasy and all the longings for status that are implanted as lasting legacies of colonial subordination, 'lived out as part of my personal history'.[183] Recalling the anguish he escaped from as a black West Indian embarking on his own long political journey, he concludes: 'In a sense, it has taken me fifty years to come home … It was a space I couldn't occupy, a space I had to learn to occupy.'[184]

It was not just that skin colour was such a prominent feature in the middle-class family Stuart was born into, in 1932, but his paler-skinned mother, with relatives who could pass as 'local white', identified completely with the island's white settler past. The older he grew, the greater his alienation from his parents' unrelenting aspirations: the school friends he liked were too 'black' to bring home; the sports clubs his father wanted him to join were places in which the son saw his father demeaned by white people; the old colonial world his parents identified with was one others were working confidently to overthrow. Indeed, the very week Stuart first attended secondary school, he recalls that Michael Manley, already a teenage rebel, was expelled from school for throwing a textbook at the English history teacher for his colonial interpretations – proleptically revealing (in ways self-styled postmodernists would quickly forget) the unique impact of a *combined* practical and deconstructive textual assault. But it was only in England, after winning a scholarship to Oxford, that he learnt for the first time that he really was 'black': 'I became Caribbean there, in Oxford.'[185] It was this experience which accentuated Stuart's characteristic stress on the contingency of any identity, its lack of fixed origin, only called into being through the different ways we find ourselves placed, or position ourselves, in narratives of the past. It was this experience too, reflecting back upon the toxic colonial mix he had escaped that he suggests broke down forever the distinction between the public and the private self:

> I could never understand why people thought these structural questions were not connected with the psychic – with emotions and identifications and feelings because, for me, those structures are things you live. I don't just mean they are personal, they are, but they are also institutional, they have real structural properties, they break you, destroy you.[186]

This takes me back to the place where Stuart Hall laid down tracks I and so many others would shortly follow, remaking himself – after Suez, after Hungary, after his Caribbean friends in London had returned home to work, unsuccessfully, for their dream of a united, socialist West Indian federation – to become another prime mover in the New Left in Britain. His was the most inspiring voice now putting culture and personal life, alongside anti-colonialism, at the heart of the Left's political agenda, struggling for a regeneration of ideas and ways of organizing outside any of the old party formations. Stuart became the founding editor of the *New Left Review* in 1960, setting its initial utopian tone, working for a 'society of equals' where people, no longer needing to escape immiseration, had access to the resources necessary for pursuing meaningful, pleasurable lives.[187]

However, like the 'new social movements' hovering on the horizon, this first New Left soon found itself weakened by organizational dilemmas, 'trapped between the "Vanguards" and the "Fragments",' as Stuart later put it.[188] In ways I still find true of the residual Left I align with today, one could say it already found itself trapped between following leaders and leaderless follies. Nevertheless, thirty years on, Stuart tells me he remains as attached as ever to the project of finding a third space for the renewal of democratic and socialist politics, but without knowing quite how, or where, to do so. Indeed, he added wryly on one occasion, 'When I'm talking nowadays I've begun to feel that people listen, but they have no idea what I'm saying or where it's coming from. It's as though it's from outer space'.

Back in the early Sixties, after two years as editor of *New Left Review*, Stuart bowed out to a vanguard led by Perry Anderson, eager to take over the magazine. The new editorial leadership was altogether less libertarian in thought and style, with ties to the centralized Trotskyist Fourth International. Alongside the New Left, competing Trotskyist groups had also begun to flourish from the close of the Fifties, following the final collapse of the decades of dominance of Communist Parties as the only legitimate representatives of Marxism worldwide. They were all largely dismissive of the early New Left style of grass roots resistance. Meanwhile, Stuart had accepted Richard Hoggart's invitation to start up a new Centre for Contemporary Cultural Studies (CCCS) in Birmingham University, in 1964, thereby inaugurating what quickly proved the remarkable rise of cultural studies. It was a transdisciplinary new field, enthusiastically uncovering the political manoeuvres concealed within cultural formations, both dominant (hegemonic) and marginal (subcultural). Stuart's stress on Gramsci's belief in mapping the 'historical conjuncture', with its contesting forces of control and resistance, would provide one of the few abiding principles for those who to this day remain faithful to the Birmingham heritage of cultural studies. Its founding texts addressed histories and ruptures in working-class life and cultures, but its objects of study and investigative tools were soon broadened and honed with each hub of cultural dissidence. Such evolving enthusiasms often made the Centre a dangerous place to dwell, its most contentious moment surfacing as feminism erupted in its midst: 'The personal lives of everyone there were knocked sideways,' Stuart later ruefully recalled.[189]

Like Raphael, he had been among the first to notice and try to repair the New Left's blindness to women's marginality on its platforms and programmes: supporting Women's Liberation from the beginning (alongside his ardently feminist young wife, Catherine Hall), he invited feminist thinkers to work with the Centre. Yet, in a paradoxical but for me now all-too-familiar swerve, it was often those people most open to change who tended to become its first fall guys, hurt and distressed in the process of the upheavals they helped to engender. As the indisputable paternal figurehead and leading light at the Centre, Stuart soon found himself targeted as 'patriarchal enemy', hostile to and bewildered by the demand that women students should meet and work separately from the men: 'Living the politics is different from being abstractly in favour of it. I was checkmated by feminists; I couldn't come to terms with it, in the Centre's work.'[190] In retrospect, with Women's Liberation still in its confident 1970s heyday, we can see already ghastly anticipations of the traumas soon to engulf feminist collectives themselves.

Stuart's battles against the reductionisms of class politics and the Leninism of Marxist practices continued, even as he turned his attention, decisively, to the theorizing of race and ethnicity as hybrid, contingent cultural identities. In the 1980s he became the pivotal intellectual influence on *Marxism Today* as it turned against its own former doctrinal beliefs, if not equally against its former strategic conceits. He launched his groundbreaking analysis of 'Thatcherism' in 1979, stressing the definitive swing to the Right symbolized by Thatcher's victory.[191] Ten years later, years which had seen Thatcher's symbolic defeat of Arthur Scargill and the miner's strike (in 1984), her defeat of Ken Livingstone and the days of creative resistance from municipal councils (the GLC was abolished in 1986), throughout which *Marxism Today* had continued its attack on 'the British Left' for its inability to jettison old habits and face up to the 'new times' of 'popular capitalism', Stuart would declare the death of 'Socialist Man':

> The problem now is to rethink the politics of class as, and through, a politics of difference. I truly did believe for a time that it was not me but 'Socialist Man' who would appear somewhere, homogenize all differences, and "make socialism" ... [but] 'Socialist Man' has gone over the hill and far away, and thank God for his departure. *Finito!* Now any future is a future of difference, any future society a society of diversity.[192]

I was somewhat shocked when I heard Stuart utter this obituary, with his familiar ringing rhetoric. I remain troubled by the sentiments it encourages, despite having myself always opposed the rigidities, moralism and other glaring deficiencies of traditional labourism, even more the 'self-dramatising vanguardism' of putative revolutionary groups with their sectarian squabbles.[193] Those I have worked closest with politically were mostly unhappy with *Marxism Today*'s persistent attacks on the Left and the labour movement. It was as if, catching up with our critique of its earlier trade union orientation, this Left magazine could now speak from some uniquely transcendental position, just when its former allies, whatever their faults, were most in need of and most open to advice and assistance. Retrospectively, I have not changed my mind. Nevertheless, piecing together Stuart's own political journey now, I understand far better how he has remained one of the most persuasive figures on the Left – his fighting egalitarian spirit unbowed and unbroken.

I have been studying these particular journeys, which impacted so directly on my own, not hoping to find exemplary political lives, even less any necessary strategies or structures for progressive transformation. The complexity of gaining political leverage at the level of national government, not to mention in the global arena, encompasses such arts of pressure and compromise that any such notion of correct practices becomes absurd. Committed to universal principles of freedom and equality, Communists and socialists have always believed in an internationalist outlook. However, people are mobilized to support egalitarian causes and oppose inhumanities and injustices in line with the cultural images and political structures most visible and relevant to them at any particular point in time. Although it could, at times, confront capitalism with one of the most powerful of weapons – strike action – in pursuit of its economic goals, the rise and fall of Socialist Man was itself lived out as a type of identity and a significant community belonging quite as much as the political affiliations found in the so-called 'identity' politics of more recent times, whether gendered, ethnic, sexual, anti-colonial or religious. Dissident identities emerge only when the disadvantaged and disparaged consciously and collectively begin to contest visibly unfair constraints. But the possibilities for them uniting in battles against local, national or global exploitation or denigrations will depend on how compellingly they can envisage and work for broadly conceived alternative, open and more egalitarian futures. What I learn from pondering the political reflections of these men of the Left takes me back to one message Stuart Hall is eager to deliver from his own journey, which is that new times, however revolutionary the dream, reconfigure as much as they transform the old – which calls, as I see things, for a softer burial of Socialist Man. We reproduce what we are breaking away from, even heading towards and beyond profound ruptures.

Women's disputed legacies

It is not unusual, still, to hear the disgruntled voice of older men of the Left blaming feminism for the disintegration of the socialist vision, exhausted by what Britain's liveliest Marxist literary scholar, Terry Eagleton, for one, dismisses as those 'dreary old bickerings between feminists and socialists'.[194] Certainly, post second-wave feminism, it was impossible to be as moved as Communists once were by Brecht's passionate elegy to the professional revolutionary back in 1930, eating his meals between battles, forever on the run: 'We, who wanted to prepare for kindness/Could not be kind ourselves.'[195] Even the staunch female Communists or militant socialists prior to my generation of women, although perhaps supporting equal pay for women, believed that the serious business of politics overrode all personal concerns, as though the two were necessarily at odds with each other.[196] For my generation, the apparently spontaneous burst of female collectivity, the sudden desire to bond with each other, did not initially spring from contacts with an older generation of activist women. Those who had remained dissidents in the mid-twentieth century, squeezed between the first and second waves of feminism, rarely gained their inspiration or sense of solidarity from other women. Some had kept faith with the Communist Party from its heyday in the 1930s, as Yvonne Kapp elegantly illustrates in her memoir, *Time Will Tell*; others tried to find a home in the Labour Party.[197] Nevertheless, in pondering the encouragement or resistance younger women might feel for my generation of feminists, I now find it helpful to look more closely at the disputed legacies of a few of the women who, usually in highly contentious ways, did leave their mark upon the feminism that took root in the 1970s. As I said in the preface to this book, yesterday's female agitators seem particularly prone to generational misunderstandings, with older women's envy of youth and younger women's need to affirm their distinctiveness promoting barriers at every turn. Nobody illustrates this paradoxical exchange between generations better than Doris Lessing.

Ironically, although claiming to be passionately antagonistic towards us, the one-time Communist who did capture the interest of second-wave feminists, myself included, was Doris Lessing. Born in Rhodesia in 1919, as a young woman she joined the Communist Party in Southern Rhodesia in the early 1940s, rejoining for a while after arriving in London, the following decade. Lessing's political outlook had been decisively shaped, she says, by reading *The Story of an African Farm* (1883) when young, written over a generation before her by the South African socialist, suffragette and crusader for peace and racial tolerance Olive Schreiner.[198] But she became a Communist, we learn, 'because of the spirit of the times', meeting so many refugees fleeing fascism in Europe, most of them Jews.[199] Whatever the Zeitgeist, however, Lessing's views were also a product of her resolute flight from the fate of women around her, not just her bitter English mother, who always felt isolated and abandoned in rural Rhodesian exile, but from the frustrated housewives she met as a young woman. She 'simply refused', she would later write, to join those 'nagging white housewives'.[200] She was never a typical Party member, however, her persistent concern with the ties between the personal and the political itself the proof of this. Unlike most political memoirs, Lessing's autobiographical writing, *Under My Skin* and *Walking in the Shade*, is steeped in reflections about sex, desire, relationships, loneliness, confusion and sorrow.[201] Despite constantly drawing upon periods of her own active engagement with politics, her chronically inchoate political ideas ensure that her strength as a writer has never come from her assessment of world affairs, or depictions of those fighting for justice.[202] Her special strength – whether in fiction or autobiography – has always been her incisive personal voice.

Added to the beauty of her prose, it was Lessing's concern with the hazards of women's lives, including the failings of male comrades, which made her so popular with second-wave feminists. All her writing dwells upon the dilemmas of the unfolding phases of womanhood: the experience of resentful daughters with harsh, demanding, unhappy mothers; the boredom of wives with uninspiring, uncomprehending husbands, or facing the condescension, cruelty even, of male gynaecologists; the guilt of mothers, struggling to combine childcare with writing and other passions of the heart and mind; and the anguish of older women, facing the fearful pain and isolation of ageing. This was her childhood. These were the men from whom she had fled. Those older women, feeling unwanted and useless after their children leave home, mirror her own mother, whom she can hardly bear to think about: 'She could have lived another ten years … if anyone had needed her'.[203]

It is just these patterns of female misery that Women's Liberation would seek to turn around only two decades later, declaring 'the personal political' and thereby a site of struggle and change. How puzzling it might seem that the woman we admired, so discerning about women's lives and longings, should denounce feminism when it came along, condemning us as 'avaricious', 'vindictive' and guilty of 'crude stupidity.'[204] 'I have nothing in common with feminists', she said again in an interview just a few years ago, 'they never seem to think that one might enjoy men'.[205] The enjoyment of men, it must be said, is hard to find in Lessing's novels, or in her memoirs, another reason for her appeal to the generation of feminists stealing up behind her. Indeed, athough I was reading Lessing from the late 1960s, I often found her near-seamlessly bleak portrait of relations between men and women, of male betrayal and the breakdown of women, more depressing than I could handle. I abandoned *The Golden Notebook* halfway through. It is thus Lessing herself who almost invents man-hating feminism. Yet, in what Freudians would describe as a peculiar form of splitting, she hates her own invention.

Nevertheless, contemplating Lessing's reflections on her long and creative life helps me understand more about generational suspicions. What I realize, only today, is that the mystery of Lessing's scorn resonates with the feelings of many other women who, coming of age between the two waves of organized feminism, still managed, against all odds, to become professionally independent (to a limited degree), successful (in certain respects), despite all the hurdles and the heartaches: the blanket sexism, the sexual harassment, the back-street abortions, the abandonment by lovers, the betrayal by husbands – despite, in short, the many costs and frustrations they faced, more or less alone, with next to no support from other women in those years. My own mother was, of course, one of them. She too had been the target of the full gamut of sexual aggravation, betrayal and painful pregnancy terminations, which at that time only intensified in her, as in most of her contemporaries, a sense of the inferiority of women, rather than igniting thoughts of feminist subversion.

With heroic exceptions, this all too often made younger women, in so many different ways, a source of envy and distress for successful older women. Their earlier, stoical route to individual survival and success could be seen as undervalued by young feminists, now collectively combating all the obstacles in our way. It clearly seemed, at least to Lessing, that the regiment of angry young women in her wake was made of weaker stuff, our complaints too expedient, our success – if we had any – too easily achieved. Younger women all too easily become the targets for women of a certain age, substituting for the impervious men who have discarded or disappointed them. They are responsible for the pain that can devastate an older woman, as Lessing reflects, musing upon a 'pretty girl of twenty', deliberately displaying her beautiful body for inspection: 'Pain was slicing through me for what I had lost. And, too, because I knew that I had been every bit as arrogant and cruel as that girl'.[206] Older women, as Lessing comments (with weary resignation), lose men of their own age to younger women; moreover, it is young women who successfully pursue these older men. It is a 'heartbreaking unfairness' that she sees as genetically encoded.[207]

Adding a pinch of Freudianism to her putative Darwinian mantra, men are doubly exonerated by Lessing for the pain they cause women: '[They] have to fight so hard to free themselves from their mothers, but then circumstances and their natures make their wives into mothers, and they free themselves again ...'[208] With eyes so open to, heart so wounded by, what she sees as women's inevitable lot, Lessing could never accept it. There was no feminist movement in her youth, and she could never become a feminist when older. Her desires, identifications and attachments remain with

men, never with that abjected mother. Such is her fear of
facing life alone as an older woman that, following her
rejection by the American writer Clancy Sigal, at thirty-nine,
she describes herself as for a short while sliding into
alcoholism, 'feeling abandoned, unloved, unwanted'.[209] It is
this sorrow that not only feeds Lessing's fear of younger
women – as the source of her annihilation – but also, it seems
to me, triggers her estrangement from politics more
generally: 'About politics there is nothing to be done finally
but laugh.'[210] Or cry, one feels. As a source of strength,
politics failed her. Finally, she found spiritual consolation
from the disappointments of both sex and politics in the Sufi
teachings of Idries Shah. Lessing's autobiography closes
with her encounter with an 'unlikeable young woman'
(arriving with a baby in a push-chair) who comes knocking
at her door, a single mother, 'demanding' money from her,
and displaying bitterness and 'rancorous envy' towards
her.[211] The rancorous envy she experienced coming from
young women would seem, at the very least, to be mutual.

Lessing did not write the third volume of her autobiography. Instead, she substituted a fiction, *The Sweetest Dream*,
to revivify her reminiscences of the 1960s and beyond. Here,
her contempt for political ideologies, Leftist, feminist or
utopian, is absolute. She ridicules and stereotypes them all.[212]
As chance would have it, I was one of the young women
Doris Lessing encountered briefly in her middle age. I took
over the lease of her flat in Maida Vale in 1970. I was at the
time much too shy, lost and insecure, as a single mother,
newly arrived in London, to make the most of the encounter.
She seemed to me eccentric: moralistic about the threatening
ways of the young, though concerned about the stray cats of
the neighbourhood. We surveyed each other with mutual
incomprehension. I continued to enjoy and admire her books
during the following decade, but I have recently wondered

whether I was the 'unlikeable young woman' she depicts (arriving, with my infant son on her doorstep, as she is leaving her flat). However, I have been told of other feminists of my age who met her at that time, who wonder the very same thing.[213] A composite picture, no doubt.

Phallic mother

Lessing claims to be angry that *The Golden Notebook* became the 'Bible of the Women's Movement'.[214] Her compass is, reliably, awry. It was not so much Lessing, but Simone de Beauvoir who, in the beginning, supplied the text, set the goal and lived the life (or so it seemed) of an independent, politically committed woman, helping to inspire women the world over to think again about their own emancipation. 'Women, you owe her everything,' declared one of those who like to see individuals embodying the spirit of history, the French scholar, Elisabeth Badinter. She was addressing the five thousand who attended Beauvoir's funeral in Paris in 1986, after her death at the age of seventy-eight.[215]

For all the controversy it would engender, nowhere more viciously than in France, only rarely in history have books had the impact, the long slow burn, of *The Second Sex*. Selling 22,000 copies in the week it was published in 1949, it is still selling, still debated, over fifty years later. It is not an easy read, but one maxim crystallized out of the ink that was spilt to fill the hundreds of pages Beauvoir penned on the situation of women, drawing upon a medley of historical, philosophical, psychological, anthropological, biological, biographical and economic research: 'One is not born, but rather becomes a woman'. In that becoming, readers learn, woman is installed in her condition as 'object and prey' for man, never as 'sovereign subject'. Women have yet to be recognized by men as 'free and autonomous' beings, just like them. Beauvoir's goal was to establish that a woman's behaviour is not dictated by her physiology, but rather 'shaped as in a mould by her situation': her grasp upon the world, the world's grasp upon her. Hardly anticipating all the criticism in store, Beauvoir did notice the age-old dilemma confronting 'an emancipated woman', who must refuse 'to confine herself to her role as female, because she will not accept mutilation', while being aware that 'it would also be a mutilation to repudiate her sex'.[216]

Just as she intended, Beauvoir's life itself became a public attempt to transcend that dilemma. She was legendary as she lived it, even to women who had not read a word of her books. Beauvoir's symbolic presence at the time, as self-styled 'liberated' woman, choosing to remain single, steering clear of conventional family ties, to pursue a sexually active, free and independent life, was uniquely significant for many of the post-war generation of women I knew. Her four autobiographical volumes, her various polemical novels (all commentaries on her life and times), above all, the post-war media attention on the King and Queen of existentialism (Jean-Paul Sartre and herself), along with the lasting glamour of Parisian bohemia, all made her an iconic figure.[217]

In almost identical words, one early second-wave feminist after another recorded her impact on their younger selves: 'I was seized by a desire to imitate her,' as a teenager in Canada in the 1960s, Lisa Appignanesi recalls. '[We] were grateful, regaled, awestruck and disturbed … [Her] denunciations opened windows on to a great gale of air. We shouted yes,' Sylvia Lawson relives her delight on discovering *The Second Sex* as a young middle-class mother in my own home town, Sydney, in 1960, immediately sharing her reading with friends. 'For us, the young women in the 1960s who became the Women's Liberationists of the 1970s, her life was truly exemplary, to be pondered and explored for clues [on] how to live differently,' another Australian contemporary of mine, Ann Curthoys, notes; 'she demonstrated an art of living.' Yet another, Margaret Walters, adds: 'It helped me make sense of my confused and isolated depression.' 'It was a siren call,' Kate Millett claims, alighting upon *The Second Sex* in New York in the 1960s. '[She] indicated a new and transformed possibility – the movement from passivity into freedom,' Sheila Rowbotham agrees, writing in one of the founding texts of British feminism, *Women's Consciousness, Man's World*. Judith Okely broadens the picture, years later: 'I was fortunate in receiving the testimony of some women from the Third World,' recording favourable responses to *The Second Sex* in India and the Middle East.[218] My own initial encounter with the book was less enlightened, seeing it in the bedroom of a male lover during a brief relationship in my first year at university. It was there because of its sexy cover in the early, truncated Penguin edition (the back of a naked woman, half turned to expose her breasts) and because of its titillating accounts of lesbian sexuality, which he had underlined and read out to me. A few years later I read the rest of the book, discussing it excitedly with some of my new Libertarian friends in Sydney, both women and men.

'Idealized mother', maybe, as Appignanesi suggests, but – archetypically – never less than difficult: morphing from idol to irritant when feminism reinstated itself as a collective force and analytic framework in the 1970s. Many feminists would rather quickly decide to condemn Beauvoir to the dustbin of history, despite having once turned to her for inspiration. Germaine Greer was one. She declared her 'repellently male-oriented', although, in *The Female Eunuch*, Greer had all but paraphrased her – it was Beauvoir who first saw femininity fashioned as 'intermediate between male and eunuch.'[219] In the cruel combat conducted by feminists in France, the Lacanian Antoinette Fouque referred to

Beauvoir's 'feminism of non-difference' as 'the master trump card of gynocide'![220] Irigaray said much the same thing. Only a generous soul, like Angela Carter, would more gently tease Beauvoir with her 'thinking woman's' question: 'Why is a nice girl like Simone, sucking up to a boring old fart like J-P?'[221]

For my purposes here, exploring the transmission of generational experience in both the personal and political realm, returning to Beauvoir's legacy seems essential, despite her coming from a cultural context distinctly different from the Anglo-American one prevailing in Britain. This is not only owing to her singular impact on my generation, but also because of her own enduring interest in the role of identity and attachments in sustaining lives of political commitment. She expressed both a lifelong resolve to seize the moment, living fully and freely in the present, deploring hypocrisy, injustice and exploitation, while at the same time a determination to chronicle all the 'enthusiasms and disappointments' of her life, in the hope that they might provide a model and resource for others.[222]

In so doing, she highlights the difficulties of any such project, including my own, of using autobiographical reflection to ponder the mutability of radical passions. She lived her politics so personally, yet so publicly: frequently self-critical, forever engaged (at least from her thirties onwards) in exposing and supporting those struggling against colonialism, exploitation and cultural denigration, emphasizing (from her forties onwards) that much that she wanted to say was linked to her 'condition as a woman', throwing her weight behind Women's Liberation and all its activist campaigns when it took off in the 1970s (by this time, already in her sixties). She also wrote poignantly, from early on, of her fears of the fate of the ageing woman. How puzzling once again, it might seem, that the very women most indebted to Beauvoir's insight and fortitude would later become so critical of her. Lessing became cross with feminists, who echoed her own criticisms of men and their mores, but feminists became cross with Beauvoir, who had virtually founded and later signed up to their cause. Why? Primarily, because of all the contradictions she so unashamedly exposed when making her private life public. She was much too close for comfort. Yet these are the very contradictions that sustained her intellectual endeavours and political engagement in the first place.

Movement between exposure and evasion, documentation and delusion, haunts any attempt to make the personal political, or to describe political life personally. But the contradictions in Beauvoir's biography, which she barely acknowledges, leave her especially vulnerable to attack. The woman who valued her 'independence' above all else, urging women not 'to take shelter in the shadow of men', was resolutely determined to see herself as the subordinate half of a couple: 'far from feeling embarrassed at the thought of [Sartre's] superiority, I derived comfort from it.'[223] The expounder and zealous critic of the symbolic subordination of the 'feminine', more or less uncritically idealized the 'masculine', cherishing the esteem of men.[224] It is this tireless labour of alliance with Sartre, displacing all impediments to unity with her chosen double, which underwrites both her power and her pain, leading others to suggest that her apparently rigorous self-examination itself helped her sustain a kind of self-evasion, becoming an exercise in concealment.[225]

Absence and evasion there surely is in Beauvoir's memoirs (which focus more on Sartre than herself), yet it was a strategy that served as constant motivator for her life's work. Beauvoir does not want to *be* Sartre, she does not ever compete, but believes she must *have* him. Fantasizing completeness through him (knowing and not knowing the infantile, illusion-ridden nature of that fantasy), it worked for her, although not without anguish at his infidelities and neglect. The 'betrayal' that confounded many feminists in Beauvoir's devotion to Sartre as the bulwark of her life, 'masculine' self-sufficiency as her ideal, has to be placed alongside the strength she derived from it: the courage to write and to act in conditions requiring extraordinary levels of bravery.

Beauvoir called for sexual information and abortion rights for women in the 1940s, at a time when one woman was guillotined for performing the operation and others jailed for providing contraceptive advice. Three decades later, with abortion still illegal in France, she allowed her home to be used as premises for the practice.[226] The publication of *The Second Sex* in *Les Temps Modernes* in 1949 (the magazine founded by Sartre, Beauvoir herself and Merleau-Ponty in 1945) detonated thunderous blasts of obscenity against her throughout France.[227] In the 1950s, she and Sartre were isolated and attacked, facing bomb threats, for their staunch support for Algerian independence and exposure of the rape and torture of its militant supporters by French officials. Only in the 1960s could she rejoice, as calls and marches calling for 'Peace in Algeria' finally gained widespread support in Paris: '… how good I felt! Solitude is a form of death, and as I felt the warmth of human contact flow through me again, I came back to life.'[228] So hell is not always 'other people', whatever her loyalty to Sartre and his aphorisms![229] What intrigues me about Beauvoir is that her radicalism increased with age. She spent the last fifteen years of her life fighting primarily for women's rights, though her sustaining fantasy – of oneness with Sartre – continued to the end.

If the power and authority Beauvoir felt she gained from

her sense of merging with Sartre would puzzle later feminists, it was only after her image as independent woman had already inspired women the world over. I was certainly one of them, and though I never had her photo pinned to my wall, I was always pleased to see her there in the homes of my women friends. As she suspected, it was her autobiographical texts that women read most avidly.[230] *The Prime of Life* sold 40,000 copies in advance of publication, in 1960. Seeing her hurtle from unlimited passion for universal freedom and full humanity into recurrent despair at the state of the world and the vicissitudes of life, I want to know what else sustained this exemplary activist and intellectual woman? At fifty-three, in the late 1960s, Beauvoir completed her third memoir with words full of anguish, devastated by her long-held fears of ageing: she loathed her appearance, grieved over the absence of a man (while watching a succession of plentiful young lovers competing for Sartre), had lost hope of ever again 'feeling any new desires'. If this is to last, she laments: 'how long it seems, my short future.'[231] It did not last. Ten years later, she had no new man, but she had found new joy, a new love, a new sense of unity even (with a woman, Sylvie le Bon, thirty-three years her junior), new projects and a new identification, with feminism. 'Today I've changed,' she would say, 'I've really become a feminist.'[232] She had pulled it off again, identified her ageing self with the otherness of the youthful other, partially escaping the plight of the old she now worked to expose and decry.

Eyeballing her horror of ageing, Beauvoir embarked upon her second major piece of theoretical research for her book, *Old Age*, published in 1970. Again she contrasts the marginalized Other (the old) with the norm (the young and male). Once more, she insists the disparaged meanings attached to this abject Other are not fixed in the body, but a product of cultural neglect and disparagement: 'man never lives in a state of nature.' Yet, still too, she (like Sartre) reveres and identifies with youth. On the one hand: 'We must stop cheating [and] recognize ourselves in this old man or that old woman.'[233] On the other, she loathes the ageing body, especially the ageing female body, particularly her own. She portrays the older, abandoned woman with little sympathy in her novels; she imagines herself always and only as a young woman; she works, even in sleep, to deny her age: 'often in my sleep I dream that in a dream I'm fifty-four [which at the time she is], I awake and find I'm only thirty. "What a terrible nightmare I had," says the woman who thinks she's awake.'[234] Tellingly, whereas Lessing in her fiction pours scorn on young women's dreams, Beauvoir reprimands the ageing woman for her delusions.[235] However, just as Beauvoir's culturally disdained female self did not confront but rather insisted upon her unity with a man, so her ageing one will not criticize youth but instead establish a new unity with a younger generation (a woman and a movement), making her also young, as well as old:

> The better I knew Sylvie, the more akin I felt to her ... There is such an interchange between us that I lose the sense of my age: she draws me forwards into her future, and there are times when the present recovers a dimension that it had lost. [236]

This avatar of women's autonomy was the last person who could live unpartnered; this polemicist against the plight of the elderly surrounded herself with youth; this feminist, who enjoyed the friendship and love of women, never spoke openly of her lesbian experiences (though she publicly supported lesbians). She needed and found close friends, her alternate 'family', and functioned best with a small group or social movement to support her. This was the source of her intellectual and political strength. She muddled through her contradictions, exposing rather than denying them, much like the rest of us, but better than many. Having been idealized, discarded, often embraced anew, the paradoxes that sustained Beauvoir's passions demand our attention, still.

Temporal belongings

I have come full circle. Reviewing Sheila Rowbotham's *Promise of a Dream*, the writer and critic Jenny Diski (echoing Lessing's ageing disillusionment) saw in it no more than evidence of banal generational conflict: to be young is, ineluctably, to be opposed to the old. Meanwhile, she suggested as her own lasting lesson in disenchantment, the world takes 'not a blind bit of notice' anyway, but goes on its way impervious to the struggle between age groups, whose 'cycle of anger, action and failure is as inevitable as hormone fluctuation.'[237] She could hardly be more wrong. The world takes all too much notice of generational stirrings, ever watchful for ways to contain and commercialize the creative resistance of its young critics.

As I tried to illustrate in earlier chapters, when the women's movement ran with the slogan of the American New Left, 'the personal is political', it had excellent reasons for doing so. Hidden cruelties and violence were rife in the domestic 'haven', hypocrisy endemic to sexual life. The 'freedom' masquerading as 'revolutionary' was blatantly sexist (while veiling a host of other embedded pecking orders). There was little that was unchallenging about centring attention on personal life and intimate experience when most women had yet to learn that their bodies, sexuality, intellect and inclinations were not inherently ludicrous, unless hidden or mimicking those of men. Women who had wanted to get a sense of themselves as autonomous agents in the world of the 1960s had, in our fantasies, to switch sex to do so. Moreover, women's new collective concern with their own lives was not primarily any encouragement of individual self-promotion, something which was usually moralistically disdained. Its purpose was rather to enable women to participate more fully in the political arena, broadening its concerns in preference to abandoning politics for a retreat into private life.

Personal narratives of political journeys are valuable because they may help us translate the insights of men and women in one cultural moment, rendering them more intelligible for those in another. While political parties hand down memories (albeit often self-serving and distorted), non-aligned activists and thinkers have only our snatched and fleeting reconstructions of seizing the moments when change seems possible. The transmission of generational histories can foster ways of communicating as times change. Older radicals and younger rebels have equal need of such history. Looking out for intergenerational affinities can curb the stabilization of stereotypical age roles: the frequent anger or cynicism of young critics; the common resignation or disillusionment of old-timers. Moreover, such affinities are not necessarily as difficult to construct as we are led to expect. Since identifications are largely phantasmatic, we can be – in a sense, we cannot avoid being – young and old at the same time. Lessing rejected politics, partly, as I see it, because she turned her back so determinedly on any affirmative identifications with a younger generation. Beauvoir, in contrast, launched herself into just such identifications and affiliations.

Interestingly, Sheila Rowbotham points out that in 1969 just a few women who were much older came to very early women's liberation meetings, such as Lucy Waugh, who as a young girl had come across that famous first-wave suffragette and socialist, Sylvia Pankhurst:

This generation were like political grandmothers to us, closer to our wavelength than the political mothers – the left women in the generation that preceded ours ... They had their own struggle to be independent, political activists and saw the 'women' tag as restrictive; to us it was liberatory. [238]

Whether we like it or not, Seventies feminists are the grandmothers of today, so perhaps we had better get to grips with cyber-culture, creating our own dissident blogs. Older people's identification with the young is often disparaged as a 'disavowal' of ageing. But we can, and we do, have a more complicated relationship with time than this.

6

When sexual warriors grow old

I have been cautioned by some of my friends to avoid even thinking, let alone writing, of my generation – the over-fifties – as 'old'. Others disagree. They see benefits in ageing, making us (or some of us) more self-knowing, open, tolerant and patient, offering skills of continuity and survival to the young, when pondering the fears and fulfilments of growing old. Moreover, if generational categories are ambiguous, age divisions are even more elastic, their flexibility throughout any lifetime affected by the imprint of class, ethnicity, economic options, just for a start. In prosperous settings today, the freedom of youth often extends well into people's thirties, as they face the world child-free, hedonistic and single (many, especially young men, still residing in their parental home). The idea of middle age keeps lengthening, moving on from the fears once attached to reaching thirty, to accompany many travelling effortlessly through their forties and others who find themselves working harder than ever in the workplace in their fifties. Indeed, it is a tag that remains with some of us, we like to think, contemplating diverse futures at sixty.

However, the lengthening of age divisions is itself a sign of the cultural force of age anxieties, routinely surfacing as blatant gerontophobia. In cultures that fear signs of

deficiency and despise dependency, we are encouraged to
remain 'forever young', even on reaching three score years
and ten, once definitive of old age and immanent mortality.
At seventy, the British TV presenter Joan Bakewell launched
a column in the *Guardian*, 'Just 70', reflecting the fervour of
the Zeitgeist with her sense that she is no older than she
feels: 'which is young'.[239] It ran for two years. Today, there are
serious moves to heed, rather than merely evade, the old – so
long as they assert their youth. Just a few cultural figures in
Britain are famous for having always been old, such as Philip
Larkin and Alan Bennett (it helped that they were still young
when their elderly predilections were spotted). I note their
gender, and wonder what change, if any, has occurred in the
thirty-odd years since we could have read, but almost
certainly did not, Simone de Beauvoir's most neglected
book, *Old Age*. It was everywhere a forbidden subject, she
found: 'What a furious outcry I raised when I offended
against this taboo ... great numbers of people, particularly
old people, told me kindly or angrily but always at great
length and again and again, that old age simply does not
exist!'[240] With the two words too unpleasant to mention, she
was told that some people are simply 'less young' than
others. Her book at first appeared in English, with the
euphemistically blurred title, *The Coming of Age*. Old age,
Beauvoir insisted, was always evaded, except when
discussed as a problem, which is precisely what makes it a
cultural as much as a biological matter. 'How can we ever
have thought we age by nature alone?' self-styled North
American ageist resister, Margaret Gullette, asks
rhetorically.[241] 'Growing old is mainly an ordeal of the
imagination – a moral disease, a social pathology – intrinsic
to which is that it affects women much more than men,' her
compatriot, Susan Sontag, had protested three decades
earlier.[242]

Before beginning this book, few things held less appeal for me than looking at life through the prism of age – any age – though childhood's magnetism in retrospect always seems the most seductive, even when conditions were painful. This was not just the usual evasion of the biological fate awaiting us, however much we learn to dread and avoid the topic, but extended to dislike of feminist celebrations of women's journeys through life. In its heyday, feminist homage to women's 'life-cycles' typically conjured up a very precise normative course, even while challenging the existing regimes for regulating it. The stages continued to unfold in counterpart with our reproductive potential, and their associated familial patterns: before, during, and after our menses; our lives as daughters, mothers, wives, grand-mothers, sentinels of hearth and home. Here the toil, excite-ment, anxiety devoted to our jobs, politics, friendships, even sexual interests, remain in the wings, especially as we age. My fear of mapping these maturations of 'womanhood' and their customary ties expresses both the cultural dread of female ageing and, perhaps, a distinctive personal inheri-tance.

Cultures of ageing

Wherever we look, inwards or outwards, whether calling upon literature, psychoanalysis, feminism or demographics, fear or denial of ageing is ubiquitous, but especially fears of the ageing female. So much activity is needed, Colette once wrote, 'to hide that horror – the old woman.'[243] Colette herself underwent the brutal process of a face-lift in the early 1920s.[244] This was over sixty years before bodily reconstruc-tion techniques were refined, with plastic surgery now a massive industry feeding off women's – and to a lesser extent men's – fear of ageing, making it almost a form of compulsory grooming for many in the affluent world today (over ten million cosmetic plastic surgeries were performed in the USA alone in 2005).[245] 'You have no idea how terrible it is to be an old woman', my own mother said when in her seventies, in a voice of unrelieved gloom to my male partner at the time, lamenting that she was living alone. '*What* is terrible, being old or being a woman?' my lover queried, with his characteristic insistence on precision. 'Both, both,' she moaned, 'both are terrible!' It is more acceptable, I've thought, for old age to 'burn and rage', than for it to raunch and rave. And yet Hollywood has little problem with *Grumpy Old Men* – Walter Matthau and Jack Lemmon got even grumpier with every sequel. So perhaps I'm wrong, but only, it might seem, when it comes to men. These cantankerous, crusty old males are feuding over the affections of beautiful young women; in other movies the ageing stars will marry them. Yesterday's Man is Tomorrow's Dad, as Michael Douglas or Jack Nicholson testify. Their female contemporaries were jettisoned decades earlier from any romantic leads, as Diane Keaton noted, in her surprise at being offered a romantic role at fifty-eight, with the significantly older, but still accepted romantic lead Jack Nicholson, in *Something's Gotta Give*. Signs of change? We have yet to see.

Men and women face the fears, challenges and losses of ageing at much the same time. I have no wish to deny or diminish the anguish men experience with the losses of ageing: 'I think the anxiety that death arouses ... torments men more than women,' the French psychoanalyst Jean-Bertrand Pontalis has suggested, seeing women as more resigned to their lot.[246] Nevertheless, cultures of ageing are unquestionably gendered. This has a special significance for those straight women who, in earlier days of militancy, fought for (and helped secure) women's claims to sexual pleasure and more supportive intimacies. The double standards, disparagements and sexual harassment we had met in our youth could mockingly mutate into enduring disregard in the disparities appearing in the sexual options of women and men as they age.

In much of his compelling writing, that remarkably astute, reliably conservative observer of the human condition, Philip Roth, once delighted in portraying this particular inequality in contemporary urban America. He skilfully evokes the plight of the older woman who, having successfully 'democratized the entitlement to pleasure' in her youth, suffers the 'chronic insomnia' and 'compound of disappointments' so common in the biographies of professional women now living alone in their apartments from their forties onwards: 'evening meals more often than not are delivered to the door of their Manhattan apartments in a plastic bag by an immigrant.' His compassion for such women merges with his triumphant bravado at the ease with which a successful older man (such as himself) can seduce a certain type of much younger woman. These are the women who make it clear to him that 'to give yourself over intimately to a much older man provides [her] with the authority of a kind she cannot get in a sexual arrangement with a younger man ... both the pleasures of submission *and* the pleasures of mastery'; which is, as he sees it, exactly what men want.[247] Fortunately, despite the multiple doppelgängers he loves to let loose in his fiction, all men are not Philip Roth, but more now share a sense of his possibilities and entitlements. Older women, even when powerful and rich, especially when powerful and rich, lack a parallel sexual allure. Neither women nor men can easily escape what one psychotherapist from the USA sums up as our culture's 'almost visceral disgust for the older woman as a physical being.'[248] Demographically, the documentation verifying the flight from older women as sexual objects, at least by men, is overwhelming.

Here is one raw statistic, increasingly true the world over: women living alone are the fastest growing household unit, but – less well known – only lone *older* women. This is not merely due to differential mortality rates affecting mainstream heterosexual populations, as some believe, since it emerges well before the age when they commence and the longevity gap between the sexes is narrowing. Nor does living alone appear to be something women are simply choosing. When younger, in their twenties and thirties, women are far less likely to be living alone than men. In figures available from Australia and the USA, single men outnumber single women until their fifties, after which there is a rapid reversal, with roughly sixty per cent of people living alone from the age of sixty-five being women.[249] In Britain, men living alone outnumber women almost three to one between the ages twenty-five and forty-four, but there are twice as many single women as men over the age of sixty-five.[250] Divorce statistics in Britain reflect the same pattern. Up to the age of forty, divorced women are as likely as men to remarry, but over that age men are more likely, and definitely more able, to find a new partner.[251]

Matching evidence of older women's thwarted aspirations for intimacy is evident in a host of other studies from the USA, all revealing that women and men both chose sexual intimacy as the single main ingredient of 'happiness', though almost fifty per cent of women over forty reported having no sexual contact in the previous year, compared to only twenty per cent of men.[252] Even making allowances for male braggadocio, it would seem that these older men must be sexually connecting with younger women.[253] Here in the UK, the British Household Panel confirms the picture, gathering information annually throughout the 1990s from

10,000 adults in 5,000 different households. Its studies show women faring less well than men following marriage or partnership break-ups, with women who remain alone thereafter having the worst mental health of all groups surveyed. Serial cohabitation, rather than marriage or remarriage, proved most conducive to men's mental health. However, like other studies, strangely – though not inconsistently – they also suggest that women are more adept at living alone than are men, with those who have *always* lived alone emotionally healthier than other women, or lone men.[254] Certainly, the data from such demographic research lacks the nuanced complexity of studying life histories. But it does provide a rough sketch of the social background, the 'objective conditions', for locating the dilemmas of many an ageing woman, whether or not they were ever touched by, indifferent or even hostile to feminism.

Hazards of autonomy

Unsurprisingly, however, one knee-jerk reaction to the older women's predicament is to blame feminism: look where women's foolhardy search for independence has got them – more women facing old age, unpartnered and alone! As proof, they could point out that women with more work experience and earning capacity face a greater risk of divorce in this recent research, although they are also more likely to remarry, at least until they are, hazardously, 'older'.[255] More surprisingly, perhaps, what sounds like a gleeful backlash against feminism today was already appearing as gritty feminist realism in some popular women's novels of the 1970s.

The importance of challenging the centrality of men in women's lives was the theme unequivocally advocated in Marilyn French's *The Women's Room*. Her heroine leaves her unhappy marriage, declines to follow in the footsteps of her lover and ends up, at forty-four, facing the challenges of life alone, having in the meantime learned to value her women friends and her intellectual work. This book was described by the equally popular British writer, Fay Weldon (then a self-declared feminist) as 'a book that changes lives', and was seen by all its readers, I recall, as a positive feminist text, its heroine learning to face the world free from all illusions.[256] Yet, seemingly at odds with its emancipatory message, it begins and ends with its newly-fashioned feminist heroine voicing her loneliness, even wondering 'if she's going mad', while trying to console herself with the observation, 'I don't think it's all my fault that I'm lonely.'[257] Not her fault, because men need to change before any woman could find real happiness with them. In a new introduction to the book twenty-five years later, French repeats her moral mantra that women must not depend on men, while still delineating the same bleak context for women, without them: 'A woman may endure, but suffering never ends.'[258] Her consolatory words this time sound even less reassuring: 'as [women] grow older ... "Love" moves to a secondary or even tertiary portion in our universe.'[259] That's not what I hear, it's not what I feel; nor, listening to women voice their desires in late middle age, is it what researchers find.

I never accepted French's pessimism about men, nor her suggestion that women's struggles for greater independence and fulfilment in the world at large are inescapably at odds with happy heterosexual lives. I was drawn instead to other feminist voices, such as the gleeful optimism of Angela Carter. Carter celebrated 'the sense of limitless freedom' she could sometimes experience, satirizing women who exalted the self-righteous suffering of blameless women: 'who remain grumblingly acquiescent in a fate over which they believe they have no control.'[260] She knew it was the first time in history that women such as her, from wealthy western countries, could now enjoy an active sex life with men, with access to contraception, as well as to the gynaecological care, that would keep them strong and healthy enough to 'to write big, fat books.' I read all her big fat books, including *Nights at the Circus* and *Wise Children*, where she wrote with wicked wit, demythologizing all the 'extraordinary lies designed to make people unfree.'[261] However, she was also sufficiently astute to realize that by enabling more women to make bolder choices in pursuit of recognition, love and new commitments to others, the twin forces of feminism and reproductive freedom had initiated social changes whose effects were as yet unknown.

Unknown to Carter herself they would remain. Together with her many fans, I was left to mourn the loss of her razor-sharp irony as those new gender patterns unfold today. She died, tragically, at fifty-two, her son still young, her career flourishing, her life still politically active and enthusiastically bohemian. But, even with the invaluable support of knowing herself part of a loving family, the cultural condescension towards ageing women had already begun niggling at her life. Reporting her physical discomfort and pain to a young woman doctor a few years before her death from lung cancer, Carter felt rebuked when told that she had reached a period when 'she would simply have to accept ageing'.[262] The confidence feminism had nurtured, enabling at least some women to dream of different futures, even for themselves and not just their daughters, grew shakier for many of us, most especially if and when we found ourselves living alone in late middle age.

As women are everywhere reminded, the cultural marker of this phase, understood as a strictly biological affair, is the menopause. 'How come you've never written anything about the menopause?' Angela Carter phoned to ask her dynamic older friend, Grace Paley, on reaching fifty.[263] Surely, she must have thought, her professional comrade from America, who could write with such playful tenderness about love, relationships, mothering, even ageing, should have something useful to say on the dreaded 'change of life'. I read of this exchange, because I too was checking up on the thoughts on ageing of Paley, as another enchanting feminist warrior of the strictly pacifist brigade, who was several decades my senior. Paley pondered her literary silence on the matter in an article written a few years after her friend's query, pointing out that, born in 1922, she was more than twenty years older than the movers and shakers of Women's Liberation. The menopause and the movement arrived together in her life, in the late 1960s and early 1970s. This meant, she later reflected, that she bonded anew with so many women friends, having moved on from the waning civil rights and anti-war work of previous decades, to link up with the 'wild, delighted' activities of women's liberation:

> We could laugh, because the years were lively, energetic, risky, hopeful; lots of politics, literature, friendship, love … The high anxious but hopeful energy of the time, the general political atmosphere, and the particular female moment had a lot to do with the fact that I can't remember my menopause or, remembering it, haven't thought to write much about it … I've asked some of my age mates, old friends, and they feel pretty much the same way. We were busy. Life was simply heightened by opposition, and hope was essential … If I were going through my menopause now, I think I would remember it years later more harshly.[264]

It may have been more than good timing, or eponymous naming, that enabled Paley to age with grace. She has always thanked the women's movement for enabling her 'to cross the slippery streets of indifference, exclusion, and condescension' more cheerfully, while still celebrating the perils and pleasures of women's desire for men. Paley reflects often on all she has gained from her lifelong passion for women's independence and sexual freedom, giving her an enduring sense of political purpose – though now quite unwell, she continues, even as I write, to express solidarity with peace movements, near and far. The recognition Paley has received for her sparkling, sporadic writing has no doubt also helped sustain her apparently boundless generosity and exuberance. Yet, it is her special good fortune, she also emphasises, to have stayed married, the second time around, in a mutually loving partnership with the architect and writer, Bob Nichols, without whom, she suspects, even with her political commitments and her literary recognition, 'real life would be smaller and probably sad'.[265]

The bonds of loss

Smaller and sadder is how I and quite a few of my women friends sometimes think of our lives today, when living without sexual partners, though we may be fortunate in many other ways, physically fit, socially active and doing work that we value. About time too, some may think, of the hubris that emboldened a women's vanguard in the late 1960s and early 1970s to try to live our lives as if we were entitled to similar sexual options as the men we related to, and would still end up in secure relationships. From the beginning, this was spelled out as a woman's right to define and determine her own sexuality. And from the beginning, the unique difficulties of maintaining what felt like appropriate, valuable sexual and loving attachments could easily fall hostage to feminist uncertainties, or worse, prescriptiveness.

A good man was always hard to find, which is a major

reason some feminists ended up having or raising their children without one. Invented kinship, whether in collective households, the enduring support of female friends, or the camaraderie of political attachments, usually kept the most corrosive assaults of loneliness at bay. But feminist suspicion of 'romance' and 'love', seen as traditionally leaving women submissive to and dependent upon men, was sometimes replaced by an all-too-fleeting bravado. 'Sleeping Beauty wakes up and doesn't need her prince any more,' the Dutch writer Anja Meulenbelt celebrated in her bestseller of the late 1970s: '"Darling when I need you, I'll call",' she wrote.[266] And he'll be waiting? Perhaps not. I was asked to review this early feminist memoir for *Spare Rib*, on its publication in Britain in 1980. My review was largely favourable. I was clearly more pleased than irritated by the expedient bravado of its heroine, with her determination 'to be someone who is visible', who does more with her life 'than just endure it as a natural disaster'.[267] (Surprisingly, over two decades later, I encountered Meulenbelt in Israel's occupied territory in the West Bank – in 2004 – in her current role as senator for the Socialist Party in the Netherlands, working for justice for Palestinians. Sexual politics was at that moment far from uppermost in our minds.) However, as one of the initiators of the Dutch feminist movement, Meulenbelt was for many years in the forefront of attempting to trade in old romantic illusions for new feminist ones: any woman can replace her desire for the love of a man (deserving or undeserving) by sensibly beginning to love herself. She even wrote her own instruction manual, *For Ourselves*: 'A number of women [have] learned to live alone, and discovered that there is more eroticism to be found in our daily living than from the odd fuck which used to have to satisfy all our needs,' it began. Many colourful illustrations followed on the joys of masturbation and 'how to make an orgasm'.[268] This time I was more critical, unkindly mocking Meulenbelt's brash prescriptions.[269]

In the embattled feminist terrain of sex and politics I never fell for any such solipsistic sleight of hand. Beyond the mechanistic framings of the sexological imagination, and with or without Jacques Lacan, it seems obvious that desire is always a longing to be the object of the desire of another, that very particular other whom we can manage to cathect. As another French psychoanalyst, Jean Laplanche, notes, this explains its basic affinity with passivity, however often, however anxiously, disavowed in men's sensual life. Desire is culturally manipulated, but it is never, simply, consciously willed, never easily malleable. It was illogical, in the silliest sense, to imagine that in our most intimate longing for the love of another we could simply substitute ourselves. For the joy of coupling, surely, has something to do with escaping from oneself, whether we lose ourselves in the process or feel recreated anew in the eyes of another. So, I persevered in the traditional search for passionate and reciprocated hetero-sexual love. 'I wish you'd fall under a bus!' I screamed at the lover who was leaving me for another in the late 1970s, after pulling his long, tousled hair. 'You're a tyrant, an emotional tyrant!' he responded. We both survived to love again, to love better. He, several partnerships later, remains with the charming companion of his late forties, around ten years younger than him. My perfect partner, the one who turned my forties and early fifties into the most romantically cosy and individually productive years of my life, has just started a family with another.

Whether we are coupled or alone, despondent or cheerful with our lot, older feminists can be proud that, mostly because of us, the situation of the lone woman today is very different from the spectre of the spinster, or 'old maid', as depicted throughout most of human history, even as recently as my own childhood. 'She won't die wondering,' was the quaint euphemism applied then to an unmarried woman whom people suspected might not be a virgin. But she would live facing the pity or scorn reserved for the older woman on her own. Back in the 1950s even a divorced or widowed woman who remained single, was often not much better off, though her husband might well have died bravely for his country. After his father was killed in battle in 1943, the British cultural theorist, Alan Sinfield, recalls his mother's hard life throughout his childhood: 'the disability of not having a husband, moved Lucy, decisively, to the bottom of the pile ... Her social life shrank almost to nothing.'[270] Janet Hobhouse opens her autobiographical novel, *The Furies*, with a similar description of her early loneliness as the daughter of a divorced mother, where both of them, for a very long time, 'lived such a precarious life ... [one] in which all men were ominous lurkers or heartbreakers.'[271]

Nowadays, we are far less likely to humble single women as mere victims. We would mostly assume that older women living alone had probably led sexually active lives when younger, perhaps choosing to leave their partners, unless – unusually – they had simply preferred not to engage in any sexual activity. Post feminism, there is a new cultural respect for female friendships, as well as much personal affirmation of the significance of love between women – whether or not it is sexual. With women almost as likely to be as successful, glamorous, worldly and knowing as men, there is less and less force to the derision once reserved for women's worlds. We boast about our female friends, we gain real strength from each other. When forty-two per cent of women over eighteen in the world's leading nation – the USA – are now single (divorced, widowed or never married), it is hardly surprising that word is out to reclaim spinsterhood: 'we should be swaggering about, dictating the future mindset of the advertising and marketing industries ... scaring society, not letting it pity us. Pushing to the front, not whingeing on the shelf,' columnist Barbara Ellen writes in the *Observer*.[272]

Even so, in heterosexual arenas, feminist victories can be double-edged. They have a haunting shadow. For certain, many western women live independent, fuller, freer lives when living alone today, often far from devoid of intimacy. Yet, just because of this, it has proved easier for a man to choose to move on from one woman to another as he ages, at a time when similar choices (once shared and perhaps indulged by his former partner) start to close down precipitously for her. Indeed, ironically, the more successful the woman, the less the moral guilt the man feels in leaving her, and the more likely she will end up living alone. However, visibly successful or not, what remains less easy for many an ageing single woman, despite cultural shifts, is to beat back a looming sense of failure and diffidence in social settings as she struggles to elude the way she fears others still look upon her. 'I feel shame,' one of my best, most feisty of friends tells me, her husband of many years having left her to make his life anew in a different country. Another of the early Women's Liberation activists who lived in my house in the 1970s depicted her loss of nerve when interviewed in the following decade by the writer Liz Heron, despite having achieved significant literary acclaim in the meantime. From her late teens, she reflected, she had never been without a male lover, never imagined 'being without a guy', till finding herself alone in her forties:

> The bad things are loneliness, and a sense of failure. Because for a single person it's really hard not to feel a failure ... [to feel] that you don't matter that fantastically much to any other person ... And the social thing is really difficult. I think it's much easier socially for a single man, just to go around and be

accepted. And be chased by women. But for a single woman, certainly over a certain age, even if other people aren't thinking all sorts of things about you, you're thinking them about yourself.[273]

Pondering her decision not to take HRT, feminist activist Sue O'Sullivan reflected in her fifties that it was sad and maddening, if all too understandable, that 'feminists, so confident in their youthful twenties and thirties about the ephemeral nature of "attractiveness", and its male-defined meanings, began to waver and lose confidence in their forties and fifties.'[274] From my experience, I would suggest that single women's unease does not reduce to issues of 'attractiveness' and its meanings, but rather to the ontological insecurity always lurking when lacking the routine recognition offered in unconditional intimacy: 'Do I exist, if nobody really needs me?'; 'What is the point of my existence?' As I've noted, cultural climates are also implicated in experiences of ageing. Like all social aspirations, political struggles encourage us to be forward-looking, even if their motivation is a longing for real or imagined conditions of the past. Women's Liberation, in particular, with its reaching out to others to create a fairer world, seemed to promise that we would always have meaningful work to do, and never be alone. But the waxing and waning of the feminist movement occurred in tandem with the expanding and shrinking of social and emotional ties more generally for many of its activists.

In the 1970s, I read all the books of another pioneer of Women's Liberation, the American author Alix Kates Shulman, who launched herself as a writer into the rising tide of autobiographical fiction – women's coming-of-age stories as young rebels: 'At last, to be identified!/At last the lamps upon thy side/The rest of Life to see!' were the stanzas from Emily Dickinson serving as the epigraph on one of her early novels, *Burning Questions*.[275] I didn't note then the hubris of Shulman detaching these lines from Dickinson's religious mysticism, 'Except to heaven, she is nought; Except for angels, lone', though I did detect something of the fragility of the book's mildly narcissistic boasting.[276] Two decades later I would read her memoir on ageing, *Drinking the Rain*, recording the crisis she experienced in her fifties, as the decline of the women's movement and her own ageing came together in a single sense of personal loss, inflected by the world's insidious opinion of ageing women:

> I was dismayed by these feelings, even ashamed, having
> always assumed that a good feminist would beat this rap ...
> but now my complacency gave way to astonishment that this
> obsolescence was happening to me, alternating with sorrow
> and, when I lost confidence to write, dread.[277]

'I am nobody, who are you?' is the better known line from Dickinson that encapsulates Shulman's anxiety at this point in her life.

Shulman went on to reclaim her serenity, and certainly her authorial voice, learning to transcend her loneliness in a deserted cabin on a windswept beach. There she embraced the sensual delight of meditative solitude, feeling herself in tune with the rhythms of the plants and animals she tended, as one of her older mentors, May Sarton, had earlier sought to accomplish.[278] This spiritual renewal of hope and confidence via meanings assigned to the natural world also served to realign Shulman with contemporary eco-politics, by now more fashionable than feminism. Such a transcendental search has long been a favoured way of confronting the fears of ageing and mortality, when even the most committed materialist may begin to lapse, whether turning to the mythological archetypes and counselling of Carl Jung, who promoted the importance of the 'afternoon of life' for its inner spiritual journey, or other comparable forms of sustenance.[279]

However, the call of the wild also highlights certain privileges of the affluent. It is hardly a compelling option for the more typical urban nomad, such as myself, feminist or not. Vivian Gornick shared the same time and place of generational excitement as the slightly older Shulman, and her books too have multiplied on my bookshelves. Having once flung herself exuberantly into the rise of Women's Liberation, finding joyful emotional shelter, as well as her voice as a writer, in its collective embrace, Gornick also saw its community life receding and the movement fragmenting from the 1980s. Suddenly, she was not only living on her own, but having to keep busy each day trying to curb her anguish through the discipline of work: 'existential loneliness ate at my heart ... A fear of lifelong solitude took hold of me.'[280] Gornick finds little joy in her self-sufficiency, listing the pressures and growing eccentricities that can befall those who live alone: 'Thirty years of politics in the street opened a door that became a floodgate, and we have poured through in our monumental numbers, in possession of the most educated discontent in history.'[281]

Her words resonate with those of others I hear around me this side of the Atlantic. It may seem a bitter harvest that women who worked so hard to build more open, equal and responsible intimacies with lovers, who showed solidarity with those fighting injustice near and far, and supported so many who had yet to find a voice, are often themselves today living, unexpectedly, alone. With her usual poetic eloquence, Denise Riley speaks for many of us:

> ... No, what I
> really mean to say instead is, come back

won't you, just all of you come back, and give
me one more go at doing it all again but doing it
far better this time round – the work, the love stuff.[282]

The sex stuff too.

Yet, if in the end some of us may not seem to have fared
much better in our love lives than those before us, I suspect
we have not fared worse, and most of us embrace life itself
more fully. Our mothers' unheeded depression, the bitter,
resentful, argumentative, atmosphere that many of us recall
from our childhoods has not been reproduced in the lives of
my friends and acquaintances today – whether single or
coupled, mothers or childless. Some, like Gornick, speak of
past relationships ended because they had begun to feel in
marriage 'more alone than when alone'.[283] Every ageing
feminist I know, to a woman, agrees on the importance of their
old friendships, often from the heyday of the women's
movement. While not always sufficient to keep loneliness at
bay, they 'matter immeasurably', as Liz Heron reports, taping
a conversation between five old friends in the mid-1980s:

> Not just having friends, but having them round the corner, a
> short walk away. I can walk to L's flat in five minutes, to R's in
> less than ten, in the opposite direction. The three of us crow
> about how fortunate we are and we have other friends too in
> the neighbourhood. We couldn't contemplate moving. What a
> difference it makes. With a quick phone call we make instant
> arrangements, dropping in for a cup of tea, a swim on the spur
> of the moment, a walk in the park. A plea for help sometimes –
> come around, I feel awful. We urge the other two to consider
> moving so we can all be together. What safety.[284]

Moreover, celebration of female friendship has moved on
from the heartlands of feminism to the mainstream of media
endorsement. In *Sex and the City*, to take an obvious recent
example, the celebration of female friendship was at every

moment also a rehearsal of female fears, above all alarm over the 'very small pool, very shallow pond' that heterosexual women heading for middle age will be left to fish in for a sexual partner, or potential father for a child, increasingly competing with younger women. These fears are valid, even though they are diligently promoted by conservative forces always eager to highlight disquiet in the successful, solvent and female; blaming feminism (or indeed any form of progressive struggle) for secretly worsening the lives of those they have fought so hard to improve.

The brakes on love

The ubiquitous narrative of 'age-as-decline' not only keeps afloat massive profits for the commodities, treatments and surgical interventions marketed to delay our ever-looming decay, but also works to silence the diversity of other stories that could be told about experiences of ageing. These tales would register continuing pleasures and satisfactions that do not vanish over time, even as we mostly mourn the attractive, lovable creature we – only in hindsight – believe we once were. Sometimes, indeed, our skills at handling the fears and vulnerabilities that linger on, almost from the start, improve with age, including greater clarity in facing lack while sharing loss, still fishing for love, sharing wisdom, wit and laughter, while ageing together. But, in 'fishing for love', it is the obstinacy of sexual desire and its all too familiar search for objects and recognition that I have seen, and felt, placing older women in jeopardy.

As I described in the last chapter, old age haunted Doris Lessing from an early age (her late thirties). She could brilliantly depict her pain, and its pathos. 'Don't imagine for one moment that I am this old hag you see here, in this chair, not a bit of it, *that* is what I am really like': this is what older

women are secretly saying, she suggests, when they display
pictures of their youthful selves prominently before
visitors.[285] 'A woman is her mother. That's the main thing,'
Anne Sexton declared, unsuccessfully battling her own
demons.[286] Her capacity to empathize with her vision of old
age seemed to make her battle harder, as her poetry captured
just before she committed suicide, at forty-six:

> What are you doing?
> Leave me alone!
> Can't you see I'm dreaming?
> In a dream you are never eighty.[287]

Of all the things feminists have evaded when and if framing
a new sexual politics for relationships with men, none has
proved harder to confront than the differential odds facing
older, reluctantly single women and men, beyond
denouncing an ageism that is far harsher in its treatment of
the former. I know, because a feminist I respect has accused
me of just such evasion, the Canadian literary scholar Lillian
Robinson, when reviewing my book *Straight Sex*. One
problem, at least in my experience, is that when you are
happily coupled, it is just too hard, too frightening, to believe
that the fulfilment it offers could close down, seemingly
overnight, if women over fifty find themselves suddenly on
their own again.

'Doctor I'm suffering from a serious case of mind-body
problem … My head agrees with Segal, but my heart and my
mind have already been shut out of her narrative … my sexual
isolation is not being addressed in these otherwise exciting
books,' is how Robinson ended her generally positive review
of *Straight Sex*. My account of the possibilities of women
finding pleasure and power in sexual relationships with men
excluded her, she indicated, making her feel sad and guilty,
reading of a place she now seemed forbidden to visit:

> I am 53 years old, feminist, heterosexual and celibate ... I am
> not celibate and proud or even celibate and resigned. I am
> celibate and ashamed, ashamed of my involuntary condition
> and ashamed that it is involuntary. I feel the desire that inhabits
> me is a disease ... I do my work as mother, scholar, teacher and
> writer. I do it well and authentically. I live – abundantly – all
> other kinds of love that are given me to experience. But no man
> desires me, and that makes the pages before me assume the
> shape that they do, as I avidly scan them for something that
> isn't there, wondering whether I have the right to be
> disappointed at its absence.[288]

She does, of course, especially as I am a mere year or so
younger than Robinson. I regret that I did not address her
sense of exclusion, other than to deplore the sexism
combined with ageism that haunts older women, before
racing onwards to affirm – from my own reflections, and in
the words of others – that older women can and do enjoy
'undiminished, post-menopausal sexual pleasure'.[289]
Robinson was not alone in her feelings. Two female friends,
with much the same grievance, cornered me crossly in the
women's loo the very night of the launch of *Straight Sex*, in
late 1994. Even so, I still do not know what strategies to
suggest that directly address the desert of sexual opportuni-
ties complained of: 'How did that single aspect become a
fixed – if regrettable – context, rather than being part of the
world "we" have to change?', Robinson chides me. It is not
my fault, I limply plead.

'The world "we" have to change' can't be changed by
legislative decree, nor trade union struggle, nor any other
obvious form of effective collective demand, though we
could try, I suppose, unfurling a brand new Post-Fifty
Female Fighter's Flag, silver thread emblazoned on the red:

> A woman's flesh can still be roused, though she is fifty years
> and more.

Her need for love is as before, men must keep knocking at her door.

Here, of course, we face the danger of confounding physical intimacy and sexual encounter: it always being far from clear whether intimacy is desired in order to enable sexual expression, or sexual encounters are desired in order to reassure us (perhaps deceptively) of our significant ties to another. These differing aspects of intimacy have never been easy to unpick: the shakier the attachment, perhaps, the stronger the desire for sex; the securer the coupling, the less the clamour for sex. I foresee further protests to my new feminist pitch from younger women, who sometimes tell me that they too can't 'find a man', the 'right man', asking why their situation is any different from that of older women. Demographically, it is true, the odds look rosier for the bachelor girl in her twenties and thirties, but individually it must feel much the same, possibly worse, if she is worrying about having a child, and perhaps in employment that leaves her little time for pursuing relationships. Furthermore, such heterosexual demands would prove irritating to lesbian feminists, all over again, for sidelining what they may see as their far 'better' alternative. Nor have we the means, given the obstinate persistence of sexist cultures, to wipe the smirk off men's lips, or to eradicate the rapist's last laugh. Meanwhile, those straight women who do say they are giving and receiving the hugs, kisses and physical attention they desire, could still be accused of boasting. It is not my fault, I repeat, a little less hesitantly.

'I only feel old when I look at you,' a man is overheard saying to his wife, without rancour.[290] What is the perceptual adjustment that would be needed for the older man to look, with unthreatened desire, at the older woman, without fearing her as the Medusa who can turn him to stone? What, indeed, is the adjustment needed for we ageing women to be able to look at ourselves without alarm in our eyes, as sags and wrinkles appear: 'I despair of ever being able to reconcile my overall sense of well-being, self-confidence, achievement, and pleasure in the richness of the present with the image I see in the mirror,' Vivian Sobchack writes.[291] However culturally implanted, in our visions of the 'monstrous harridan' of folktale, the grotesque ghouls of horror movies, the 'smothering mother' of formulaic Freudianism, the 'matronly dragon' on hospital wards, the 'scorned woman' at large, the 'management bitch' mocked in today's new workplace, women's social confidence can be hard to sustain. The older man, when dapper, fit and solvent, does not lose his erotic power quite as fast – at least in certain female eyes – as a woman knows she does in the eyes of men, and therefore, usually, in her own eyes too. Carol Ann Duffy captures the mythic Medusa lamenting her fate, confronting her hero, the man who once loved her, the man she loves still, who is not only rejecting her for younger women, but forcing her to face abjection:

> I'm foul mouthed now, foul tongued,
> yellow fanged.
> There are bullet tears in my eyes.
> Are you terrified?
>
> Be terrified.
> It's you I love,
> Perfect man; Greek God, my own;
> But I know you'll go, betray me, stray
> From home.
> So better by far for me if you were stone.
> ...
> wasn't I beautiful?
> Wasn't I fragrant and young?
>
> Look at me now. [292]

Look at me! Why do older women report that men no longer 'see' them, let alone desire them? The answer is popularly perceived as underpinned by biology, evident in the enthusiastic promotion of evolutionary psychology in fashionable science journalism. Returning us to the late-nineteenth-century polarised images of gender and sexuality, the male of the species – any species – is seen as driven by genetic imperatives to impregnate as many young females as possible; while the female waits, restrained and selective, cautiously seeking out older males with 'resources' to protect her reproductive task of successfully nurturing offspring to reproductive age.[293] Of course we are all biological creatures, but evolutionary stories have constantly been used, politically, to misrepresent the remarkable complexity of our embodied existence and its entanglement, at every moment, with the world it inhabits.[294] Contradicting the predictions of evolutionary psychology, for instance, in recent times both men and women in more affluent societies have inexorably chosen to have fewer children. Women have been delaying motherhood, if they have children at all, until they are older. The pursuit of diverse forms of non-procreative sexual activity has become ever more prominent. Erectile dysfunction is said to affect a huge swathe of men. With almost no aspect of human sexual practice conforming to reproductively driven dictates, there is little reason to presume a primarily genetic origin for the only area of sexual conduct that can be aligned to fit its supposed purview: men in middle age having more access to new female sexual partners compared with women of the same age. Even here, the abundant evidence that post-menopausal women do still *desire* sexual partners fails to fit the putative reproductive underpinnings used to explain our sexual practice, while cultural shifts are clearly evident in the age at which women are thought to be no longer sexually alluring and marriageable across time and place, lengthening by almost two decades in modern times. One thing that has been clear for a very long time is that human sexuality does not reduce to any reproductive compulsions, Darwinian or otherwise.

Look at me now! Well, not if you have turned into my mother, the psychoanalyst might suggest. It is Freud who emphasized that the battle to become a man means escaping from mother, or at least appearing to do so. Although, with or without depth psychology, we already have a cultural basis for the opposed erotic sway of men and women as they age. Women from the beginning have always been encouraged to eroticize the more distant, more powerful, father figure (even grandfather figure, as ageing Robert Redfords impact upon our imagination) in order to authenticate their femininity, in ways that reverse for men, shielding their masculinity. Nevertheless, Freud's emphasis on the peculiarities and perversities of sexual desire, so often at odds with what is prudent, available or reproductively efficient, might suggest he could perhaps offer us a richer story of the life of desire, accompanying ageing. But no, as his biographers have noted, Freud's own morbid dread of ageing, decrepitude and death, from his early forties onwards, meant that he ignored old age, when not disparaging it, as a time of uncreative inflexibility, of little interest to psychoanalysis.[295] Merely reprising mythic fears that turn the ageing female into the grotesque and abject, Freud wrote:

> It is well known, and has been a matter of much complaint, that women often alter strangely in character after they have abandoned their genital functions. They become quarrelsome, peevish, and argumentative, petty and miserly; in fact they display sadistic and anal-erotic traits which were not theirs in the era of womanliness.[296]

From such foundations it might seem just as well that

Freud's followers have, for the most part, made the topic 'virtually a taboo area'.[297] The taboo holds, even in the deliberately subversive, alternative trajectories of psychoanalysis, incorporating queer theory and a diversity of poststructuralist perspectives, all stressing the sliding, ambiguous meanings at play in erotic encounters, where fantasy provides a space for multiple, contradictory identifications.[298] Here, special attention has been given to the project of rescuing homosexual and other forms of dissident desire from the normative psychoanalytic disparagement traditionally framing them as essentially narcissistic, immature or pathological. 'Perversion Is Us', New York psychoanalyst, Muriel Dimen, applauds.[299] These Freudian iconoclasts aim to support and give power to those who have been collectively denigrated or marginalized, exploring how to shape new cultural mythologies to sustain them.[300] Yet, in a recent text aiming confidently to wed the psychoanalytic and intellectual avant-garde, *Bringing the Plague: Towards a Postmodern Psychoanalysis*, the dilemma of ageing, male or female, receives not a solitary mention in any of the essays addressing the concerns of 'the postmodern subject'.[301] The postmodern subject, her plasticity interminable, has yet to age. She, too, remains forever young.

Women are going to have to become the most talented mistresses of invention to resist this concerted cultural neglect of their ageing libido. 'It's every woman's tragedy that, after a certain age, she looks like a female impersonator,' Angela Carter wrote in her final novel, *Wise Children*.[302] Pondering this, feminist publisher Ursula Owen suggests, 'I don't think the sexual liberations of the past thirty years have much altered women's experience of ageing.'[303] It seems easier for older women, especially if they are feminist and single, to sidestep the treacherous world of bodily passion altogether, bonding instead through shared resignation, disavowal or proclaimed transcendence of sexual needs. All these options have been tried, especially the last two. Indeed, in age's coming of age, they are finding a new market niche.

Age comes of age

Despite the sexual enthusiasm flaunted in her spectacular entry into print, *The Female Eunuch* (1970), thirty years later Germaine Greer was once again one of the first feminist writers to put her ageing body on the line, this time to celebrate the chaste joys of the older woman. The timid female eunuchs Greer had tried to ignite in her youth, she spied once more, irritating her all over again, among the 'gallery of grotesques' who were now 'pathetically' still trying to please men – seeking to stay young by any means possible. Wanting to encourage women to age with more female grace and dignity, she castigated the venal misogyny behind the Masters of Menopause who had aggressively marketed hormone replacement therapy (HRT). Disengaging from the whole disruptive arena of sex and relationships was the strategy she advocated now, whilst, ever the exemplary public optimist, assuring her female readers: 'To be unwanted is to be free'; 'I never knew such strong and durable joy before ... I lay in the arms of young men who loved me and felt less bliss than I do now ... I would never dream of bartering an hour of a spring morning to lie in bed.' No longer at the beck and call of others, it is the deep delights of the natural world that contribute to the many ways of enjoying 'the peculiar satisfactions of being older.'[304]

I only mildly doubt the all-embracing satisfactions Greer reports from her commingling with the natural world. But yes, perhaps, 'someone should give [me] a slap', as she once said, because I also detect disavowal and denial accompanying her rituals of transcendence, assisted by the ancient powers of the eccentric, carefree Crone. There is the telltale silence on any experiences of loneliness, envy, regret or anger in Greer's bulletins from her post-menopausal world, as she celebrates the innocent delights available to the older woman, free at last to reclaim the imagined joys of her pre-pubescent integrity: 'You were strong then, and well, and happy, until adolescence turned you into something more problematical, and you shall be well and strong and happy again.'[305]

A fantasized return to innocence may be one way of trying to keep lonesomeness and feelings of abandonment at bay, and certainly it is important to register that being coupled does not guarantee healthy companionship. But I find the suggestion that the decline of our raging oestrogens can be celebrated as the end of heartaches about as convincing as its opposite, HRT as comprehensive panacea. I detect similar disavowal in other mainstream literary feminists, as in Eva Figes' version of the liberation women should find in invisibility, grey hair and wrinkles: 'She may be alone, but she is no longer lonely, since her body no longer craves what she cannot have.'[306] Well, the bodies I know have minds of their own, at odds with this fixing of their nature. A matching feminist high-mindedness is mirrored in the writing of another forerunner of second-wave feminism, Betty Friedan in *Fountain of Age*, published in 1993, with strong media and even US government endorsement.[307] However, just a few other famous Americans of her age group, also wanting to revalue the ageing process, such as Susan Sontag, have attacked the double standard that renders women sexually obsolete long before men.[308] At odds with the resolutely heterosexual retrenchments of all the feminist voices I have mentioned so far, Sontag's own apparent sexual confidence, right up until the time of her death in 2004, may perhaps not be unconnected to the fact that she had enjoyed a ten-year companionship with another bold and beautiful woman, the photographer Annie Leibovitz, in between other relationships with women in the second half of her life. Sontag never highlighted her lesbianism, but she did occasionally refer to the pleasures of her love of women: 'As I've become less attractive to men, so I've found myself more with women. It's what happens ... And women are fantastic. Around 40, women blossom. Women are a work-in-progress. Men burn out.'[309]

So let me point out, just one last time, that minds and bodies are not separable, and the mind that inhabits an older woman's body is quite as likely as it ever was to crave companionship, affection and the confirmation of being desired and needed – feelings most commonly associated with and fulfilled through the physical endearments of 'sex'. Nevertheless, as Sara Maitland notes, it may be extremely helpful for older women to try to cloak their bodies with a story that denies this: 'To acknowledge and address the sexual desire of women who can no longer bear children is to expose the whole structure; it is better to act as though they did not desire, and if they do it is peculiar, tasteless and neurotic.'[310] As feminists objected over thirty years ago, 'the whole structure' sustains the view that the infinitely puzzling domain of intimacy and desire reduces to sex, itself seen in terms of reproductive imperatives, with men as prime movers. Yet, even if we do try to ignore – as though we could – all the psychic investment in bodies and the discourses that allow us to speak of them, the sexual cultures of ageing reflect as little about the actual biology of the male body as about that of the female. Biologically speaking, men are also subject to a steady decline in fertility from the age of forty, or before; they experience a sharp drop in penile sensitivity even earlier, accompanying a dramatic increase in rates of impotency (as the soaring sales for Viagra attest), with little accompanying cultural chatter that they no longer desire women.[311]

Unexpectedly, my suspicions about denial, at least in Greer's case, are confirmed. A decade later, another volte-face, and Greer declares, at sixty plus: 'I'm still very susceptible to men. Boys even more,' announcing this on the British and Canadian airwaves in 2000. Indeed, she added, she was attracted to 'everything' about them, 'sperm that runs like tap water', for one thing; and yes, she was in love again, she confessed, with 'a boy'.[312] Back to her ballsy roots, a new book appears, in which Greer now complains rather than celebrates that older women are seen as no longer sexually desiring: 'The erotic interests of girls and older women are seldom acknowledged by mainstream culture.'[313] Since she is always one of the first to detect which way the wind blows, we can be sure that mainstream culture is also up and running ahead of her, already noticing the sexuality of older women. Only yesterday, there were next-to-no films in English-speaking cinema about women over fifty having flings with sexy young men – Hal Ashby's cult classic, *Harold and Maude*, the rare exception. Overnight, it seems, that is changing. Or is it?

In the British film *The Mother*, scripted by Hanif Kureishi, a newly widowed, timid grandmother, approaching seventy, finds escape from her resentful, dysfunctional family and a resurgence of long-abandoned sexual pleasure in the arms of a bohemian builder half her age. Kureishi, who loves to shock, was delighted with the discomfort of audiences viewing an old woman having sex: 'In the cinema in Cannes, there was a young woman sitting near me and when the old woman started having sex, she covered her eyes,' he reported: 'It's shocking. Our mothers aren't supposed to be sexual; their bodies belong to us.'[314] Kureishi's calamitous finale in *The Mother* is replaced by a fairytale ending in

Nancy Meyer's Hollywood comedy, *Something's Gotta Give*, where the fifty-eight-year-old Diane Keaton ends up not only winning the heart of ageing roué Jack Nicholson (after he's had a heart attack), but also that of the handsome thirty-six-year-old, Keanu Reeves, whom she chooses to abandon for her older lover.

On screen, as in life, Nicholson is famous for his romantic couplings with much younger stars. On screen, as in life, things have been very different in Keaton's career. One critic has written hopefully of an emerging genre of 'older bird' movies arising, detailing the sexual awakening – awakening? – of middle-aged women, embarking on new sexual adventures.[315] But that may be a step too far. No sex, but taboo-breaking partial nudity, appears in the British film *Calendar Girls*, with its dozen fifty-plus female stars; while in the French-directed *Swimming Pool*, Charlotte Rampling also briefly appears naked. Another telling French film, *Heading South* (*Vers le sud*) raises the latest contentious issue of women's sex tourism, again starring Rampling, who currently personifies the fashionable face of female ageing. *Heading South* is a cautionary tale addressing the pitfalls of sexually needy older white women paying for the services of young Caribbean men. It was showing in cinemas in London in the summer of 2006, just before a play with the same theme, *Sugar Mummies*, written by Tanika Gupta, opened at the Royal Court, also in London. The play deplored the self-delusions of the western women seeking sexual consolation with young Caribbean 'beach boys', as well as the mutual exploitativeness characterizing their interactions.

Meanwhile, back in the Hollywood mainstream, there is little change in male/female casting. Indeed, film buffs indicate that there are fewer roles for older women nowadays than there were between the 1940s and 1960s, even if the tough roles regularly handed out to older stars, such as Joan Crawford and Bette Davis, were rarely free then from misogyny and ridicule, their 'lost' beauty becoming the trigger for horror, as in the archetypal *Whatever Happened to Baby Jane* (1962). 'Old age ain't no place for sissies,' is the quote attributed to Bette Davis.[316] Older women's sexual flings, at least on home ground, may still prove more wishful than otherwise, as the demographers suggest, but more talk about their possibility seems here to stay. In the USA, the widowed schoolteacher Jane Juska wrote a much-hyped book about the plentiful sexual encounters she had in her late sixties after placing an ad in the personal columns of the *New York Review of Books*, hoping to escape from a life with no 'touching in it', a life that increasingly felt 'just a little like dying'.[317] It was not plain sailing – Juska put up with considerable levels of humiliation and rejection, remaining single, but still hopeful, at the book's close.

As so often, we have to look to lesbian literature, where age barriers are said to be less rigid, for something a little more inspiring. 'After forty, femmes turn butch, we would repeat laughingly,' Joan Nestle writes in her mid-forties. She depicts her now differently gratifying ways of making love to a much younger woman, in the essay 'A Change of Life'.[318] In this playful arena it becomes just a little easier, she and other lesbians suggest, for women's actual age to disappear as they fancy themselves at many different ages, while in the loving arms of another. Nestle's voice is just a little sadder in her next book, written after she has been fighting colon cancer in her late fifties and recently separated from her much younger lover. She wonders how she is 'to love when I keep failing … to be brave when I am so fearful … to protest injustice when I am so tired … to embrace difference when I do not even trust myself.' Nevertheless, with a body often racked by pain, she can still write of loving sexual encounters, while asserting, with all her old conviction: 'I find this to be a time of great passion in my life, a time of deep commitments to the forging of fragile solidarities that, if of the body, may last only a night, and if of a more sweeping kind, carry me more humbly than ever into the historic processes.'[319] Nestle has always agreed with Victor Serge that the meaning of life is 'conscious participation in the making of history', although she transforms the project in ways undreamt of by that dissident Marxist. Her historical research includes chronicling narratives of intimacy, bodily pleasures and personal anguish.[320]

And I? Having juggled to have it all, in love, work and politics, sometimes winning, and then again losing, where am I now? This book is not written as a confessional narrative, but rather as a personal political journal of my life and thoughts attempting, with others, to meddle in the ways of the world. But as its stories hopefully illustrate, feminist journeys breach the barriers between public and private, with personal lives part of the baggage we open up and puzzle over. So where am I now? All too privileged, in many ways, partly via a ladder feminism helped provide, as the old universities eventually caught up with a demand for gender specialists. I love my work, and receive enormous, largely undeserved pleasure, when students sometimes express gratitude for what they get from my teaching. I believe that my political activities, where and when I manage them, are exercised with greater openness, tolerance and practical reflection: 'Coalitions are the things you stay with, even though you want to leave,' Judith Butler shares a joke that captures our new-found wisdom.[321] I feel capable of loving better, when and if I have the chance, as I seem to again at this moment. But, with neither resignation nor denial to assist me, I have till very recently lived for a number of years with the fear that I would never again be lucky enough to form another lasting erotic tie, though

keeping my eyes wide open and my fingers crossed. It is by
other women, rather than by men, that I more often feel
myself desired nowadays. Out of the blue, or so it seems, I
am currently blessed with the joy of finding myself loved
again, desired and desiring anew. But having grown used to
that physical wilderness always threatening to enclose the
older woman, it is all too recent and unexpected for me to
know our future, if we have one. My fingers, if not always
my legs, stay crossed.

As I suggested earlier, the attempts some feminists once
made to live another way, seeking new patterns of
household intimacy, have rarely survived the passing
decades. But some still ponder the possibility, or live, as I do,
in looser forms of shared housing, coming into and out of
each others' lives as and when we want to. In Manhattan a
few years ago, Vivian Gornick called a meeting of all her old
feminist friends to discuss their fears and hopes for the
future. Despite huge differences 'in temperament, interests,
and finances,' she reports, 'every woman in the room that
night agreed that isolation of the spirit was the thing she
most feared about old age.'[322] Many meetings, and a small
core of people later, an ambitious utopian project was born,
called THEA – The House of Elder Artists. Money is being
raised for the building of conjoined apartments, to include
common dining-rooms, exhibition, lecture, film, reading
rooms, and more. I have heard of one or two less ambitious
projects in Britain, with more than occasional talk of buying
neighbouring houses or apartments, here or in some warmer
clime. Most, however, are wary of how they would ever
tolerate living with any new people, more aware of their
own and others' sedimented eccentricities.

I still live in my large four-storey home, its rooms housing
visitors for significant chunks of the year, its garden, at least
in my eyes, now beautiful all year round. The lawn is no

longer a weed-strewn wilderness, only partially hiding the naked bodies of the women who used to sunbathe in its long grass, decades ago – when I once spotted a man risking life and limb on a high roof nearby to spy on us all. The longest-lasting other resident living in the basement of that house today is my sharply witty, endearingly contrary friend and lodger, Éamonn, with whom I laugh regularly, as we try to support each other in our parallel lives as best we can. Upstairs another old friend seems here to stay, at least in the foreseeable future, working out how to hold on to his past emotional ties, but from a distance. Another of my closest gay friends, Alan Sinfield, asked by me how he sees the outcome of our three decades of militant movement politics, replies with his habitual laconic precision:

> I think when I turned 50, it dawned on me that the transforma-tion for which I had been looking was not going to occur in my lifetime. A difference of time scale. Futility of individual life. Less a crisis than a disappointment; perhaps I had known all along really.[323]

Perhaps we all had. But that does not mean that our dreams were fruitless. For the most part, I enjoyed pursuing them. We had significant partial victories, especially in building greater tolerance for dissident sexualities and wider recogni-tion for issues once downplayed as distinctively women's concerns. But it has become harder, overall, trying to combat the further entrenchment of economic inequalities, while an ever more unregulated corporate capitalism builds a culture of disdain for all those who are never likely to be winners in its competitive milieu.

Since it was reading Beauvoir's words on how one 'becomes a woman' that many feminists launched themselves into politics over three decades ago, let me conclude this chapter with her reflections on the closing years of such journeys:

> There is only one solution if old age is not to be an absurd
> parody of our former life, and that is to go on pursuing the ends
> that gave our existence a meaning – devotion to individuals, to
> groups or to causes, social, political, intellectual or creative
> work ... One's life has value so long as one attributes value to
> the life of others, by means of love, friendship, indignation,
> compassion.[324]

A sombre note, perhaps; or perhaps not. Solidarities thrive
through acceptance of responsibilities, shared humour,
admiration, moments of joy and, above all, the sense of
belonging to some sort of community. The more diverse and
open the community, the more likely it is that the identities
we present can loosen, stretch and modify themselves,
escaping the age constructions and inevitable futilities of
individual lives. For adults, as the most imaginative have
noticed (in this case the psychoanalyst Donald Winnicott),
'are not just their own age; they are to some extent every age,
or no age.'[325] This may seem a confusing message to live by,
but it is the nearest I can get to a feminist sexual politics of
ageing. Turning backwards – often a rather useful direction
to face when grappling with age – we sometimes find there
latent identities which, discounted hitherto, begin to unfold
in ways that make efforts of retrieval a form of reinvention.
Such has been the case for me, anyway, as a political swerve
engaged me, for the very first time, with issues of Jewish
identity.

7

As a rootless cosmopolitan: Jewish questions[326]

'I live between hope and despair,' my Israeli friend says on the last night of my first trip to Tel Aviv, a few years ago. 'I know that's a cliché, but things have been so terrible for so long.' Her words get gloomier and gloomier. I listen in bewildered horror. Then we both start laughing, realizing we are talking at cross-purposes. 'I am sorry things are so hard at present, do you think they will get better?' I had asked. But my words on the difficulties accompanying the joyful arrival of her baby son had criss-crossed with other conversations we'd had on the escalating violence in the ongoing Israel–Palestine tragedy. The personal has its political dynamics, but fortunately not quite so entwined as this, even for Jews, even in Israel.

Who's a Jew?

Jewish identity is a perplexing issue, its implied myths of origins, 'race', religion, shared culture or context, arousing even more than the usual muddles, which is, however, just one of the reasons I've only thought about it recently. In all of my formative adult identifications, as a libertarian, socialist and feminist, in my day job also, as an academic, women from Jewish backgrounds were prominent, especially in the women's movements of the 1970s. Mostly secular, often socialist, we were rarely vocal 'as Jews': 'Our Jewishness went unarticulated and unsung,' as Jenny Bourne commented the following decade.[327] Given some of the corrosive notes struck with the rise of 'identity politics' at the close of the decade, this was perhaps just as well. As indicated in earlier chapters, rival claims for recognition and influence were part of the unravelling of the women's movement in the 1980s, along with the defeat and retreat of the Left. I was not only dubious about the tactics of asserting competing claims of injury often associated with identity politics, but felt especially distanced from the particular Jewish feminist voice that had emerged in opposition to the fierce condemnation of Israel's military aggression in Lebanon in the early 1980s.

Twenty years later, it was not any change of mind that drew me to Israel as part of an international delegation organized by two groups I now support, *Jews for Justice for Palestinians* (JFJFP) in the UK, and *Faculty for Israeli–Palestinian Peace* (FFIPP) internationally. Nor was it a sudden search for roots. I am unable to trace even my grandparents' origins, as they moved around Europe just over a century ago, let alone map out their lineage to some genetic material I might conjure up as prehistoric 'ancestors'. Nor, in the remarkably diverse ethnic hierarchies and differing religious and secular factions that divide Jews in Israel, did I find – or expect to find – echoes of my own cultural history as a second-generation Australian living in London. (Although in Tel Aviv I did notice more people than I usually do who looked a little like my paternal uncles and aunts, who hailed from somewhere near Vilna, in Lithuania.) Tellingly illustrative of its ethnic hierarchies, on the very first night I arrived in Tel Aviv I was marched off to a meeting of Mizrahi women (a slightly confusing term, used for Jews from the Middle

East and North Africa, once known as Oriental Jews) speaking bitterly of their exclusion by privileged Ashkenazi/'white' feminists. For all its rhetoric of unity, racism begins at home, in this Homeland, where some say the external threat is all that manages to unite the Jews of Israel.

What had taken me on that quite extraordinary journey to Jerusalem and Ramallah was a call to arms from an old socialist feminist friend, Irene Bruegel. After visiting Palestine in 2001, Irene contacted some of her former comrades from activist days, who happened to be Jewish, urging us to join her in resisting the daily harassment, humiliation and worse of Palestinians in the West Bank and Gaza by the Israeli army. Protest against Israel's military actions in support of Jewish settlements and its continuing territorial invasion into Palestinian areas in the West Bank and East Jerusalem, she suggested, would be all the more effective if we spoke out as Jews. It was with this identity that we could have most impact on both Jews and Palestinians working, against appalling odds, for reconciliation and an end to conflict. For what is so distressing to those of Jewish descent who think as I do is that whether we like it or not, and we most surely do not, it is literally in 'our' names too that Israel's Law of Return (passed in 1950) asserts its right to keep its borders open to millions of Jews worldwide. We are encouraged to leave our homelands to settle in Israel, while the right of return, compensation or even recognition for all they have lost, is denied to Palestinians and their children who were born within its borders, but forced to flee their homes in my lifetime. The small group who initially met to form JFJFP, in February 2002, came together primarily as old socialists and feminists identifying, as best we could, with an open-ended, universal notion of justice and solidarity, transcending specific affiliations. Nevertheless, this contingency would, paradoxically, draw me towards exploring a very particular 'identity', hitherto unmarked, wondering in what way, if at all, I might think of myself as 'Jewish'.

I thus discovered I had a new strategic 'identity' for engaging with a now rather old problem – the continuing calamity of the Israel–Palestine conflict. 'Proud to be ashamed to be Jewish', my orthodox Jewish friend, Stephen Frosh, tells me those with my views are called (although, complacently, I've always been rather pleased to be Jewish, just that little bit different!). A SHIT (Self-Hating, Israel-Threatening) Jew is the toxic tag attached to a photo of me, alongside 7,000 other Jewish folk on a website of the Israeli Right, for daring as Jews to criticize Israel. Acquiring so many new identities at a stroke made me all the more curious about Jewish questions, beliefs and belongings, while also returning me to my personal history in unimagined ways. There is no doubt also something in the nostalgic culture of the times that, together with the effects of ageing and the loss or imminent loss of parents, encourages us to look backwards, pondering perhaps anew the world that, as radicals, we once thought we had escaped, the world of our parents and its impact on our actions and outlook. However, unlike my parents, one thing I was not seeking to escape or protect myself from was anti-Semitism, never having knowingly experienced it. All the same, aware how strongly others have felt anti-Semitism shaped their own lives, what I did decide to do was to pursue some research into my own family history.

History lessons

The earliest Jews to arrive in Australia were the small number sent out as convicts on the First Fleet from Britain in

1788, adding up to some 1,000 by the time transportation ended in 1852.[328] Those Jews who chose to leave Britain for Australia after the 1820s were mostly young and middle class, joining a few arriving from parts of Germany. Official Jewish histories covering the lives of these early settlers in one of Britain's farthest flung colonies all report that they experienced minimal anti-Semitism and, despite its continuing prevalence in Britain and Europe, they faced no official discrimination in Australia (although they had to fight – eventually successfully – for full religious equality). Many were soon flourishing in business, politics, the judiciary and public life generally.[329] Indeed, so well assimilated were they that the major fear facing the community (with around one in three Jewish men marrying gentiles) was its disappearance as a distinct group. As Paul Bartrop points out, there 'was never a possibility that Jews would accept the status of "Other" in Australian colonial society.'[330] That place was reserved for the indigenous Australians, the Aborigines, who were from the beginning dehumanized and degraded in ways that, if not officially genocidal in intent, in effect amounted to the indifferent annihilation of a people.[331]

By 1895 there were 14,500 Jews in Australia, most of them moderately – if not notably – prosperous, including both my maternal grandparents, whose families had been settled by then in New South Wales for some years. These English Jews saw themselves first and foremost as loyal to Crown and Empire, different from other white Australians only in their religion. When the first attempts were made to raise money for resettling Jews in Palestine in the 1860s, an Australian newspaper of the day reported:

[Many] Jews ... declare that no greater calamity could come to them than to be obliged to repossess themselves of that very undesirable country known as the Holy Land ... The Jews do not desire to be evangelized and they do not wish to go back to Jerusalem.[332]

However, mirroring what was happening in Europe and Britain at the time, the arrival of many more Eastern European Jews from the late 1890s, and increasingly thereafter, was perceived as a threat by both its Christian settlers and the existing 'westernized' Jews of Australia (later to be disparaged as 'effete', 'non-vibrant', English 'gentlemen', hostile to Zionism). A recurring feature of Jewish life in modern times has been the deep divisions that formed, first of all, *within* the Ashkenazi community, between the highly assimilated elite from 'Northern Europe' and the more conspicuously 'foreign' or 'Orientalized' Jews (the Ostjuden), on their arrival in any western metropolis from Russian and Eastern European backgrounds.[333] Fleeing pogroms, persecution and conscription, these 'foreign Jews' were used to seeing themselves, and being seen, as a people apart, with their own dynamic but more insular communities. (My father's family reached Sydney, via South Africa, from this poorer, Yiddish speaking, Lithuanian background in the early twentieth century.) Yet, even those Eastern Europeans, arriving penniless and facing more initial anti-Semitism, gradually prospered; few, however, quite as spectacularly as the Russian Jew, Sidney Myer, landing destitute in Melbourne in 1899 but, within a few decades at the pinnacle of Victorian business and cultural life, drawing 100,000 people onto the streets to mourn him on his death in 1934.[334]

Imbued with the strict skin-colour hierarchy of colonial settler-societies, Australian Jews remained assertively 'white', never assuming the pariah status reserved for Aboriginals, Maoris and neighbouring Pacific Islanders; nor were they essentially part of the 'yellow peril' – Indians,

Afghans or, 'worst' of all, Chinese – whose geographical closeness was seen as particularly threatening to this vast, under-populated, 'lucky country' in the southern hemisphere, reserved for 'white' settlers. Nevertheless, as fascism spread through Europe in the 1930s, with tens of thousands of European Jews seeking sanctuary in Australia (or any other safe place), some Jews came to be racialized as 'Asiatic' or 'black', depending on their skin colour.[335] Even then, as historian Alan Crown notes, 'the Australian government remained anxious to receive Jewish immigrants from Britain.'[336]

I never knew my grandfather, Alfred Harris, nor did my busy, restless mother speak of him. But today I am proud of his legacy. As mentioned before, throughout most of the first half of the twentieth century he was the editor of Australia's main Jewish paper, *The Hebrew Standard*. There he was increasingly embroiled in a battle over Zionism, along with his friend and adviser, Sir Isaac Isaacs (who became Governor General in 1931) and the leading Australian Rabbi of the 1930s, Francis Cohen. Reflecting sentiments common amongst Jews in much of Western Europe, they were critical of the World Zionist Organization, founded in Vienna in 1897 by the secular Jew, Theodor Herzl. Prominent British opponents of Zionism at the time, such as Claude Montefiore and Edwin Montagu, believed that Herzl's plan to create a separate Jewish state was *itself* 'a child of anti-Semitism'. In their view, those who supported the plan, Jews and non-Jews alike, were abandoning the struggle to defend the right of Jews to stay in Europe, living free from persecution in the differing homelands they had inhabited for hundreds, if not thousands, of years. They were hardly wide of the mark. The leading non-Jewish supporters of Zionism were indeed often motivated by anti-Semitism, including Arthur Balfour who had pioneered the Aliens Act of 1905, specifically designed

to keep Jews out of Britain, before later signing the Balfour
Declaration agreeing to 'view with favour' the establishment
of a homeland for the Jews in Palestine in 1917: Jews, he
warned Parliament, 'remained a people apart'.[337] Herzl
himself was contemptuous of what he saw as the servility of
European Jewry.[338]

Deeply worried about the rights of the overwhelmingly
Arab population of Palestine if a Jewish state were to be
imposed on the land they had lived in for fourteen centuries,
The Hebrew Standard supported moves to find alternative
Australian sites to establish a Jewish homeland for those in
need of shelter as discrimination against European Jews
heightened. Sites were suggested on land in the Northern
Territory and later in Western Australia, but both attempts
foundered, unsurprisingly, because the Australian government refused to allow the formation of an autonomous
Jewish state within its territory.[339] However, *The Hebrew
Standard* continued its opposition to a Jewish state in
Palestine, my grandfather's editorials insisting that such
moves would inevitably fail to allow 'due weight to the
spiritual aspirations of the Christians and Moslems'. To
ensure justice for all three religious groups, he backed the
formation of a Palestinian state. Zionism, his editorials
summed up, was 'unjust, dangerous to a degree, even cruel
in its inevitable consequences and, after all, unattainable.'[340]
He was proved wrong, all too soon, on only that last, crucial,
point.

Faultlines of memory

'Who can say "I am Jewish", without a shudder of the
tongue and mind?' Hélène Cixous asks, in her homage to her
friend and mentor, Jacques Derrida.[341] I can, and always
have, is my instant reaction to her query. Is this sheer insensi-

tivity, complacency, disavowal? Or is it, as it seems to me, a simple statement about my own experiences in the world I have known, as an altogether secular Jew? In my life, my wholly Jewish ancestry has just never attached itself, however fleetingly, to any form of anxiety or opprobrium. Quite the contrary. I am willing to agree at once that perhaps I never appeared 'Jewish enough' to elicit disdain; no doubt my parents, all too aware of the recent horror of anti-Semitism, had successfully 'whitened' their children, in their ostensibly successful assimilation at the expense – as some would see it – of passing on any strong sense of Jewish heritage.[342] But I know too that in all the spaces and places I have been, overt expression of anti-Semitism – any insinuation of dislike of Jews – was *the* hallmark of 'prejudice', a sign of vulgar ignorance and stupidity. I must have picked this up from my cultural milieu in the 1950s. It was not incompatible, for sure, with residual covert expressions of anti-Semitism connected to the epoch's still confidently expressed racism, officially endorsed as the 'White Australia Policy'. However, as I've said, Jews were for the most part seen as 'white', more so than the generally poorer immigrants arriving from Southern Europe, especially southern Italians, treated throughout my childhood with abiding contempt as 'stinking dagos'. Class overrode ethnicity in the circles I knew. The devastating details of recent Jewish history in Europe were energetically evaded in the post-war boom years, as Jewish families, for the most part, integrated more successfully than ever before into their differing homelands.[343]

At least, this was the situation for Jewish families such as mine who had escaped from Europe well before Hitler's devastation. Those fleeing at the eleventh hour, arriving from fearful hiding or, most haunting of all, surviving slave labour camps in Nazi-occupied Europe, were usually treated, at best, with distancing pity. 'Be thankful you were born in this wonderful country ... They're making them into lampshades over there,' the Australian writer and poet, Fay Zwicky, recalls her mother saying to her as a child in the 1940s, following her daughter's recoil from one such crushed survivor in Australia, her piano teacher. Portraying her own negation of anything so unbearable, she writes: 'I had laughed, but shrank from the grotesque absurdity of the statement.'[344] We all did. We all did. The lampshade was a fantastic, yet far from absurd metaphor; soap stood in for the then unspeakable in my own recollections. But it is impossible here to unpick anti-Semitism from the more familiar psychological recoil, turning away from those whose suffering is too challenging to face.

Conflicting currents remained, but as a girl growing up in Sydney in the 1950s I was not alone in picking up more positive than negative associations with Jewish identity. Indeed, writing of that time, Germaine Greer records her own 'intense yearning to be Jewish'. She fantasized till late in life that she might be partly Jewish, imagining a hidden Semitic background for her father, even deciding to learn Yiddish and preferring to date Jewish men. Many 'sensitive children' of her post-war Australian generation, she wrote, 'grew up longing to be Jewish': 'I did not know if I had any Jewish blood or not [she discovered she did not], but I felt Jewish and I went out with Jewish boys.'[345] A certain cultured intelligence, a more sophisticated European elegance, were the glamorous qualities some came to believe (not wholly inappropriately) Jews had brought to the backwoods of Australia. (It was rather different, so Irene Bruegel tells me, growing up at this time in the significantly Jewish suburb of Golders Green, in London, where Jews – being neither 'exotic' nor 'unknown' – seemed far from sophisticated![346] Their post-war experiences were different.)

By the 1950s a self-righteous liberalism that was above all ostentatiously *against* anti-Semitism was the official order of the day in the western metropolis. The genocidal finale of European anti-Semitism, with Hitler's systematic extermination of six million Jews, was to be expunged by alternative stories of the courageous Allied defeat of fascism and Germany. In the orchestrated forgetfulness of post-war consciousness no one reflected publicly upon the decades in which western governments had remained inactive in the face of the rise of fascism in Germany, Spain and Italy, had suppressed information available on Hitler's execution of his 'Final Solution' and, above all, had done far too little to assist the escape of Jews fleeing Europe, the USA least of all (with its immigration restrictions between 1929 and 1948).[347] Nor were people prepared to encounter the shattered worlds of Jewish survivors of the genocidal nightmare, except as grateful new citizens. One version of innocent Jewish suffering that would prove compatible with the new mood of liberal tolerance, however, was celebrated in the popular marketing of *The Diary of Anne Frank* in 1952. Although it too was initially rejected by at least ten publishers, and early editions sold relatively few copies, Anne Frank would eventually become the personification of the Holocaust, with her words translated into fifty languages and selling over twenty million copies to date, making it, apparently, the most widely read book in the world, after the Bible.[348] Young girls still identify with the courage and hopes of the now unforgettable teenage diarist, although the enormity of the horror that destroyed her obviously does not appear in the diary itself.

I was not one of the twenty million and more who read Anne Frank's diary, identifying with its author. Nor did I read any of the other immensely popular Fifties books of wartime heroism. Those of ex-bomber pilot, Paul Brickhill, with his tales of mass escape from a German prison camp, were the favourite amongst my school friends, alongside the autobiography of the British wartime hero, another bomber-pilot, the legless Douglas Bader.[349] Having a lifelong squeamishness about anything painful or distressing, I hated even the thought of acts of war, a disposition that had yet to be articulated as a principled pacifism. I now have altogether new reasons for heeding the dramatic shifts in the recounting of wartime memories as well as for pondering the politics of memory. Today heroic narratives of Allied Aryan officers escaping from the relative comforts of imprisonment in Stalag Luft III have been replaced by a growing interest in the trauma narratives of Jewish survivors of Nazi death camps. Only a full generation and more afterwards did the embarrassed silence on the enslavement and massacre of European Jews turn into the confident clamour of commemoration, with the belated emergence of 'Holocaust piety'.[350] The shift itself tells us so much we need to understand about the deceits and betrayals dictating cultural interest in the truths of memory.

While survivors of the Nazi death camps displayed the palpable marks and tormenting psychic effects of the carnage, and some, despite feelings of shame and horror, wanted desperately to talk about their harrowing experiences, nobody – Jews or gentiles – wanted to listen. It was much the same the world over. Those who analyse the politics of the current summons to remember the Holocaust point to the paradox that it serves, incongruously, as a form of *forgetting*. Memory work is evident everywhere, but modes of denial are its ubiquitous shadow.[351] Today's fervently embraced memorials to the Holocaust (a term that would not be used until the 1960s) have mushroomed *only* with the fading of public responsibilities towards those caught up in the catastrophe and its immediate aftermath.

Tellingly, Holocaust Memorial Day was first officially observed in London in January 2001, almost sixty years after the 'liberation' of those still alive in Auschwitz-Birkenau, in 1945. When Primo Levi first tried to publish *If This Is a Man* in 1947, describing his year of slavery, starvation and torment in Auschwitz, it met only rejection slips. When eventually published, it was for years barely read; a similar fate greeted his other books on the death camps.[352] In France, it was fifty years before Paul Steinberg would dare to conjure up the two years he spent as a teenager in Auschwitz, beginning with the ghostly homecoming imposed, he recalls, upon all camp survivors:

> The family and friends I came home to stopped up their ears. Those who could avoid me fled ... I could not avoid the chasm between us. Drawing the obvious conclusion I held my tongue. I severed all my ties to the camp ... That went on for forty years.[353]

In Holland, a country proud of its five centuries of 'tolerance' towards Jews, three out of four Jews perished under Nazi occupation. Amongst those few who returned, Greet van Amstel wrote of her pain *after* surviving Auschwitz, now doomed to live between the 'fungi of misunderstanding' and the lingering 'needles of hate'. For a while after the war, Jews were daily advised 'to remain as invisible as possible to avoid anti-Semitism,' as Dutch historians report some four decades later.[354] We really do need to realize that it is almost always the compelling desire *not* to know that is the cultural truth of disaster in our midst, especially towards human cruelties we might have helped to prevent.

One of the first to comment publicly on the earlier collective global indifference to the Holocaust was the Polish Marxist, Isaac Deutscher: 'It is an indubitable fact,' he wrote

in London in 1958, 'that the Nazi massacre of six million
European Jews has not made any deep impression on the
nations of Europe ... It has left them almost cold.'[355] It would
be over thirty years before historians, almost all of them
Jewish, began analyzing this indifference, and its impact on
Holocaust survivors.[356] Survivors' children have also started
recording their parents' experiences. Almost fifty years after
arriving in Britain from Auschwitz, the mother of the British
journalist, Anne Karpf, interviewed by her daughter,
recalled: 'No Jewish organization in England ever
approached us to offer help ... We wanted other people to
know [our experiences] ... [But] for many years people
weren't interested at all.'[357] Even in Israel, especially in Israel,
aversion rather than the desire to remember was the first
main reaction greeting survivors. Astonishingly, old anti-
Semitic imagery, disdaining the rootless, submissive Jew,
without ties to his 'native' soil, resurfaced in Zionist perspectives.[358] In his impressive chronicle of the impact of the
Holocaust on Zionism, Tom Segev reports the overwhelming
disdain for Hitler's victims expressed by the 'new Jews' in
Palestine, at least until – post-1967 – the Holocaust began to
emerge as the definitive justification for Israel's war with its
neighbours and continuing dispossession of Arab
Palestinians.[359] As the Israeli writer, David Grossman, recalls
of his time at school in the 1950s, 'we learned more about the
French revolution than we did about the Holocaust.'[360]

It is as important to remember this grimly enforced silence
as it is to recognise the significance of all it suppressed.
Personally, it helps me understand why my parents were so
unwilling to foreground their Jewishness; politically, it
makes it easier to see something of the complex forces that
have to be confronted in my recent engagement with people
working for peace in Israel and Palestine. Adding to Segev's
account, Israeli historian Idith Zertal explores the creation of

'the new Jewish Man', always armed, ready and eager to defend his land and his people. This image of Zionist Man is founded precisely on its negation of Diaspora Jew, representing those who went 'like lambs to the slaughter'.[361] Israeli psychologist, Yosef Grodzinsky, corroborates accounts of Ben-Gurion's initial insensitivity towards Holocaust survivors, his discomfort with them only reversing as Holocaust memory came to serve him as a tool both against Israel's Palestinian and Arab opponents, and against any other critics of Israel's aggressive policies. The process was perfected during the trial of Adolf Eichmann in Jerusalem in 1961 for crimes against the Jewish people.[362] (Eichmann was the mastermind behind the 'efficient' deportation of three million Jews to extermination camps.)

The politics of Holocaust memorial is thus not what it seems, simply a call to remember. Having once worked angrily to end the decades of silence, Anne Karpf today conveys her new discomfort at the shift from evasion to obligation, as the Holocaust is ceaselessly evoked, but only certain things can be said. Participating in a celebration of 'survivors' in London, she writes anxiously of the unproblematic sense of 'moral superiority' in the words of second-generation 'survivors', each one clapped as they rose to speak: 'This is the apotheosis of feeling good about feeling bad.'[363] Echoing the thoughts of historian Paul Novick, Norman Finkelstein, whose parents were also enslaved by the Nazis, berates the even greater hypocrisy in moves from complete indifference to crass exploitation of the Holocaust in the USA.[364] Detached from its historical context, the Nazi genocide has been reduced to a 'fairytale of good and evil', the writer Eva Hoffman judiciously concludes about the latest stories from children of 'survivors', with their now captive audiences.[365] We avert our eyes from actual victims, but indulge a vicarious identification when times change.

Denial is ordinary. Few things are easier, it would seem, than for most of us to avoid seeing what we don't want to see, avoid recalling what we don't want to know, as Stanley Cohen summarizes in his painstakingly researched book on the topic: 'the ability to deny is an amazingly human phenomenon, largely unexplained and often inexplicable, a product of the sheer complexity of our emotional, linguistic, moral and intellectual lives.'[366]

The sole Holocaust survivor I knew in Sydney, my friend George Molnar, that irritatingly unflagging talker, never once referred to his life as a ten-year-old starving in the cellars of Budapest, so emaciated that his colour vision disappeared.[367] But for many today, unlike yesterday, the new focus on Holocaust has a type of ontological significance, its deferred effects and traces the key to salvaging a sense of Jewishness, especially for those who adhere to minimal (if any) religious practices or beliefs and are, for the most part, at least as well integrated into the wider world as the next person. On the one hand, as individuals, most 'Jews' resent attempts to categorize them, however well intentioned. On the other, many seem to feel, as a group, that there must be something special, even redemptive, in asserting one's Jewishness, signifying all the suffering they have faced simply for being Jews. Moreover, threatened adversity, exile and dispossession, is at the core of rabbinical Judaism, especially after the Crusades: the most humble and devout of God's people suffer just because, eliding multiple paradoxes in both man and God, they *are* His 'chosen people': in man, humility doubles as hubris; in God, punitiveness doubles as preference. Threatened harm easily becomes the phantasmatic glue when even the minority of Jews today who, interestingly, in increasing numbers, are deciding to align themselves with 'Orthodox' Judaism, or pursue Talmudic study, in practice no longer follow any classic Jewish orthodoxy. Instead they resort to secular rather than rabbinical courts, rejecting most of its pre-enlightenment theological tenets – the resurrection of the dead, messianic redemption and final judgement. More disorienting again, for any who want to grasp some essential core of Judaism, the majority of Jews feel more distanced from particular manifestations of it (such as the Hasidim) than they do from many non-Jews.[368]

Such unfettered diversity may be just what we might expect when trying to ground *any* collective identity in the shifting, deracinated contexts of contemporary modernity, where those who identify as Jews neither share the same religious outlook, culture, ethnicity or 'race', nor any genuine equivalence of historical suffering. There have been multitudes of ways in which Jewish communities have survived and often thrived, both despite and even because of the prevalence of anti-Semitism.[369] 'Today the Jew is indefinable,' Esther Benbassa and Jean-Christophe Attias conclude, scrutinizing the rich diversity of Jewish existence across time and place.[370] It is this very indeterminacy, however, which underlies the *power* of shared injury: the role of adversity in binding Jewish identity as much as, and probably more securely than, any other common practices or constructions of underlying sensibility, intellect, humour or pride (Yiddishkeit) as Jews. As some scholars of Judaism are noting, occasionally with regret, it is Holocaust remembrance itself that has gradually become, except for the most orthodox Jews, a vital ingredient for identification as Jewish.[371]

The hidden powers of injury

Why should this bother me in the way it does? Confronting persecution is certainly a morally compelling reason for affirming collective identity, as well as a powerful way of sustaining it. 'As long as there is a single anti-Semite in the world, I remain a Jew' seems an admirable stance for any progressive person of Jewish descent.[372] Such defensive identification, via past calamity and potential persecution, is hardly surprising for a people who have many times over faced catastrophe, cruelty, injustice – for two thousand years the paradigmatic scapegoats and quintessential outsiders within Christian creed and consciousness. Yet such identification has become as problematic as it is compelling.

As others have noted, the perfect enemy is the one whose threat exists primarily in fantasy.[373] Just as anti-Semitism, with its irrational fantasy of the Jewish menace, has served so well in the past to instil a sense of unity in western communities, the reverse is also true. The invocation of anti-Semitism, as the perennial danger from without, has helped to maintain its prey, securing a sense of Jewish identity and superiority. Being so open to violent manipulations in the service of power struggles, identity and community maintenance (both conscious and unconscious), means that at the very least we need to be constantly attentive to, permanently curious about, the precarious and shifting relations between the actual and the imagined threat securing the Jew as modernity's archetypal scapegoat and victim.

It is more than three hundred years since Baruch Spinoza suggested that Jews 'are preserved largely through the hatred of other nations.'[374] In those pre-Enlightenment times when breaking away was impossible, or Jews lived almost entirely within their own closed religious communities, adversity from without heightened the force of Jewish tradition and solidarity within.[375] Two centuries later, post-Enlightenment and its 'emancipation of the Jews', yet in the wake of the Holocaust, Jean-Paul Sartre echoed aspects of Spinoza's analysis in his influential *Anti-Semite and Jew*

(1946): 'It is the anti-Semite who creates the Jew,' he argued, producing the situation that shapes Jewish existence as scorned outsider, whether he mixes only with his own community or is thoroughly assimilated, urbane, sophisticated and patriotic, within his European homeland.[376] (Simone de Beauvoir, of course, soon reworked this analysis, analysing the words and ways of men in creating the subjugated identity of women – as *his* quintessential other.)[377] The 'authentic' Jew, Sartre said, is the person who can recognize his condition as one of the persecuted, feeling solidarity with Jews everywhere and knowing that there is little escape from the damaging perceptions of others; Hannah Arendt similarly referred to the intellectual Jew as a type of self-aware 'pariah'.[378]

Sartre was later condemned for his failure to locate any positive core of Jewish identity, yet on publication his essay was received with joy by many Jews around the world: 'my very way of walking in the street was transformed by the reading of *Anti-Semite and Jew*,' the then twenty-year-old Claude Lanzmann recalled twenty-five years later.[379] He was not alone. 'We were astonished, even stunned, for what we were used to was hatred and contempt,' Robert Misrahi similarly evoked the immense impact of Sartre's words on French Jews, as their nightmare ended and the world simply expected survivors to carry on as though everything was normal.[380] Despite the Holocaust, for a few years after the war, while many surviving European Jews remained displaced refugees or newly migrant, the world did seem little changed from its pre-war, anti-Semitic normality – notwithstanding fierce denunciation of Hitler and all things German (continuing to this day, in familiar reflex jingoism). Joseph Goebbels' Nazi propaganda, invoking the intellectual, rootless Jew, stirring up trouble, resurfaced during the Cold War witch-hunts, when over fifty per cent of those hauled before McCarthy's 'House of Un-American Activities Committee' (HUAC) were Jews.[381] The same spectre of 'Jewish traitor' hovered over the trial and execution of the Rosenbergs as spies in 1953, even though both judge and prosecutor were also Jews. Roy Cohn, the ruthless Republican prosecutor, determined to ensure the joint death penalty, offers a preview of the rapidly shifting role of Jews in the USA – a rising mainstream within the conservative establishment.

Fifty years later, during the paranoia around security after September 11, 2001, it is no longer Jews who are feared as enemies of the state. Until at least the 1950s, the Left in the United States (as elsewhere in the west) was largely upheld by the commitment of Jewish people – despite, and doubtless partly because, the Marxism that loosely underpinned it aspired to a universal equality that paid no special attention to Jews. After that decade, the ties between Jews and the Left gradually weakened internationally, through the triple dynamic of increasing Jewish prosperity, declining anti-Semitism and the emerging role of Israel.[382] Without reflecting upon it, my generation was busy reading Jewish novelists, playwrights and critics. These quickly became the most vibrant voices from the 1950s onwards, both as cause and outcome of the decline in anti-Semitism, despite secret quotas restricting Jewish applicants apparently remaining in place in many educational and other elite establishments for another decade in both Britain and the USA.[383]

The daringly foolhardy, all-male heroes and antiheroes of Bellow, Roth, Miller, Mailer or Heller were the imprimatur of the 'Jewish Fifties' in the USA, all so beguiling precisely because of their ambivalent relation to their colourful immigrant roots; Woody Allen, Tom Lehrer and other comedians made New York humour all but synonymous with Yiddish sentiment; while Jewish newcomers studded every nook and cranny of Hollywood and popular broadcasting.[384] Late in life, Leslie Fiedler, having written so much about American Jewish culture, reflected that he had 'profited from a philo-Semitism as undiscriminating as the anti-Semitism in reaction to which it originated.'[385] Even in Britain's more staid cultural scene, Jewish émigrés were soon prominent in intellectual life, especially in higher education, publishing and the arts.[386]

As always, the flip side of this triumphant assimilation into the mainstream was a parallel waning of the old Jewish communities from which the rising celebrities had emerged. This leads some critics to suggest that Jewish assimilation arrives only in exchange for the silence and invisibility of Jewish community life within western democracies. It is an assertion, however, which says as much about the flux of *any* affiliations in modernity, with their shifting ties to influence and respectability, as it does about anything uniquely Jewish. Revealingly, although many Jews were again prominent in student radicalism of the 1960s, the only one to lose his job in the USA was a Jewish rabbi at Columbia University, fired *not* by the university authorities but by the Jewish Advisory Board, who ruled that by opposing the war in Vietnam, he had 'abandoned his co-religionists'.[387] As Naomi Schor, a voice from the following decades' feminist protest movement concludes: 'Today's Jew is no longer as he was for hundreds of years, the paradigmatic stranger, the unassailable Other. That role has been reassigned today to the immigrant, notably the members of Islam.'[388]

Is she right? Historically, we know, the image of the clever, cunning, conniving Jew has held such sway within the western imagination that it is hard not to believe it remains still prevalent today, at least unconsciously, within shared fears and fantasies – although currently jostling alongside a grisly array of denigrated others.[389] Yet it is difficult to assess the symbolic power of the alien Jew, the Svengali figure, when it has mutated so dramatically in different contexts and constituencies. Classic anti-Semitism has been borrowed in recent times to incite Judeophobic sentiments in Arab countries, with their ongoing hatred of Israel's role in the Middle East. It also flourishes prominently still in hubs of Nazi sympathisers around the world. Their poisonous hatred is disseminated most efficiently in certain websites in the USA, such as 'JewWatch', although the effects of such chilling hate speech in that superpower remains – at present – politically ineffective.

Whatever our thoughts on the prevalence and significance of contemporary anti-Semitism, overt or covert, we can hopefully all agree that at present its broader context is quite distinct from that of any earlier period. Jewish people, overall, are more than averagely prosperous the world over, as well as freer than ever before from personal degradation, harm or discrimination from any reigning western government, social or cultural elite. Anti-Semitic attacks still occur in Europe, on the rise especially in France. They are utterly repellent, whoever their instigators, yet such assaults display more discontinuities than continuities with the past. In France they are nowadays sometimes the work of right-wing extremists in the 'Front National', but overwhelmingly more often they are perpetrated by marginal, disaffected Muslim youth, targeting the presumed 'Zionist enemy' – their occurrence rising and falling with reported levels of repression and resistance in Israel's occupied territories.[390]

In Britain too there has been a horrifying increase in attacks on synagogues and other symbols of Judaism, including appalling instances of personal assault. Nevertheless, the now routine comparison of these occurrences by some of the Jewish establishment to

Kristallnacht in Germany in 1938 (when Jews were systematically arrested, murdered and their property looted on orders from the Third Reich) is in every way unhelpful.[391] It does not mitigate the crime of anti-Semitic attacks to point out that racism and xenophobia are on the rise generally at the moment, with Europe's Arab and Muslim inhabitants overwhelmingly its first targets. It does, however, place them in a clearer contemporary perspective. In British crime statistics covering 1999 to 2004, for instance, there were well over 100,000 racist incidents reported, the number rising year on year, of which anti-Semitic attacks – including leafleting and verbal harassment – went from 270 to over 310.[392] That figure kept rising, with 375 incidents in 2003 and a record 532 in 2004, but fell again to 455 incidents in 2005, when the number of anti-Semitic attacks reported from around the world dropped significantly.[393] Terrible as these are, in the hierarchy of hatreds, they remain the same extremely low (roughly 2 per cent) proportion of race attacks overall (compared to 32 per cent against people of African and Caribbean origin, 30 per cent against Indians, Pakistanis and Bangladeshis, and 22 per cent against white Europeans).[394] Defending against any increase in attacks is crucial. Indeed, there could be growing anti-Semitism, given the current intensification of global conflict, especially in the Middle East. But in attending to actual anti-Semitism and reactions to it, past and present, it is crucial to neither embellish nor distort the particular patterns of prejudice, discrimination, violence and neglect all around us. Those Jewish groups who accuse the government and media of inaction mislead us. Attacks against Jews and Judaism are widely reported and robustly condemned, with police protection usually very evident when requested.[395]

The real anomaly of the present situation is that evocation of Jewish victimhood and castigation of widespread indifference to alleged burgeoning anti-Semitism in Europe and the USA have increased in parallel with the strongest condemnation of any manifestation of it in all echelons of power. Outside the Middle East, Ethiopia or Central Asia it has never been easier to shout one's Jewish identity from the rooftops, with pride – at least for those untroubled by the actions of Israel. This is all the simpler if you are a secular, socialist or humanistic Jew, as I am, on whom Judaism makes little, if any, demands; only marginally more challenging if you are a member of one of today's typical Reform or Orthodox schuls, which are mostly inclusively pluralistic.[396] The ease with which we can proudly proclaim our Jewishness today has everything to do with the willingness of the powerful to recall the victimization of a people no longer in any real need of shelter and protection, as they once were when Jewish immigration was severely restricted in the first half of the last century, with Jews then the only significant immigrant ethnic-faith community on the move. Today's immigration restrictions, along with the bulk of western prejudice, are directed against those people who are newly dispossessed and on the move, especially the Muslim population, arriving since the 1950s, and now seven times larger than the estimated Jewish presence.[397] Fifty years may be a short while, I know, to shrug off the habits of two millennia of intermittent persecution, at least for Ashkenazi Jews.[398] Nevertheless, times change. Naomi Schor is right. Muslims have replaced Jews as Europe's quintessential outsiders.

While he was Britain's Chief Rabbi, Lord Jakobovits celebrated the end of the twentieth century with these words: 'For the first time in 2,000 years of the Jewish experience, there is not a single Jewish community anywhere in the world where Jews are officially persecuted *because they are Jews.*'[399] Yet, it is just since that moment that we find an intensification of opposing claims, insisting that a 'new' anti-Semitism is on the rise. 'We see the spread of the wildest anti-Semitism,' Ariel Sharon announced in July 2004. The leading alarmists of the new catastrophe facing the Jews are predominantly voices from Israel and the USA, but their claims are echoed around the world. Sharon had his expedient reasons for urging Jews the world over to leave behind homelands where they face negligible personal threat for the only country in the world today where they are in the midst of the most tragic conflict over territory. Among the panic peddlers in the USA is radical feminist Phyllis Chesler, who once directed her hyperbole elsewhere and now writes of a new 'war against the Jews' being waged 'on all continents'.[400] Her compatriot, Abraham Foxman, goes further, insisting that Jews, wherever they are, now confront a threat as great 'as the one we faced in the 1930s – if not a greater one.'[401] Greater? No mere genocide! Several other books have repeated the apocalyptic titles and tone. In this country, as in the USA, it is clear that the 'new anti-Semitism' is all but synonymous with criticism of Israel's actions in its occupied territory, arising in concert with the last Palestinian Intifada following the breakdown of the Oslo peace accords in 2000.[402] In stark contrast with the anti-Semites of old, we are told that the new threat comes from those generally most committed to promoting justice and compassion, Left liberal elites, the media, trade unions, progressive churches and universities.[403] Defenders of Israel's military actions insist that they are not opposed to 'fair' criticism of Israel. However, since it is they who presume to judge what is and is not fair comment, they feel free to condemn all weighty criticism of Israel as 'excessive' or 'one-sided'.

This takes me straight back to the beginning of my recent encounter with Jewish concerns, to attitudes to Israel, in which the worst use of Holocaust memory serves to forestall censure of its current policies. We are here in the most troubled waters. For alongside often shared histories of brutal suffering and loss, one of the most visible ways Jews have united as Jews in recent times is in support for the State of Israel, accepting its right to see them all as its potential citizens.

According to a recent survey of thousands of British Jews (self-selecting, as those already wanting to affirm their Jewishness), more than seventy-eight per cent say they 'care deeply' about Israel (against only five per cent who do not).[404] Many were troubled by reports of Israeli military aggression in Palestinian territory, but they were far more 'disturbed' by what they saw as 'biased media coverage' attacking Israel. In actuality, media bias works the other way, as the Glasgow Media Group reported recently, with the authorities consulted and language used powerfully favouring Israeli government views over Palestinian accounts. Despite the much higher Palestinian death rate, the emphasis primarily on Israeli casualties meant audiences typically viewed Israel as responding to Palestinian violence.[405] In the USA, an even larger survey of over 50,000 Jewish households revealed a clearer religious-secular split, with only the majority of religious Jews strongly attached to Israel.[406] Nevertheless, there have been huge confrontations on US campuses, with critics of Israel accused of inciting anti-Semitisim – most forcefully in recent times by Larry Summers, when president of Harvard University, and by Jewish students at Columbia. At Columbia security men spent the final month of 2004 at the university gates, braced with a fire hose, after violent conflict arose from a group calling itself the David Project, who demanded the removal of most of the university's professors of Middle East Culture for their attacks on Israel.[407]

Critical connections: Jews and the Israeli–Palestinian conflict

I find myself increasingly caught up in this heated crossfire, insisting upon the dangers of identifying criticisms of Israel's messianic dreams with anti-Semitism. The dispute, already such an old one, was once entwined with my family history, but is now, unexpectedly, linking me directly with peace activists in Israel and Palestine. At no period since the inception of political Zionism in nineteenth-century Europe have all Jews supported its goal of secular nation-building, at odds with orthodox notions of awaiting messianic redemption, the arrival of the Messiah to return his chosen people to a homeland of their own, to live in eternal peace, truth and happiness.[408] Political Zionists have themselves never been of one mind on the exact nature of their goals, the type of state they wished to build, how they should build it, or where its borders should be.[409] There have always been significant Jewish voices pointing out that political Zionism, with its rejection of non-violence, adulation of tough manliness and zeal for building the strong state, was not only a renunciation of two thousand years of European Rabbinic Judaism but also, in a paradoxical but familiar swerve, an internalisation of Aryan, anti-Semitic culture. It was therefore *itself* a form of Jewish self-hatred, as Peter Loewenberg concluded his psychoanalytically informed history of Theodor Herzl and his followers: 'In this sense Herzl was a Jewish anti-Semite.'[410] His views have been strongly supported in the work of fellow Jewish American scholars exploring the intersections of Judaism, nation-building and anxieties over manhood: whether in the historical explorations of the late George Mosse, the witty Talmudic scholarship of Daniel Boyarin, or the colourful Jewish ethnography of Jonathan Boyarin, to name just a few of the most significant.[411] Zionist man, they all noted with regret, would be a 'tough' Jew, no longer the gentle guest in another's land, ready to turn the other cheek. With her own powerful fusion of Judaic theology, psychoanalytic theory and historical research, British literary theorist Jacqueline Rose similarly explores the enduring lethal contradictions of Zionism.[412]

From Martin Buber and Gershon Scholem over eighty years ago, to a minority in Israel today, there have been powerful Jewish voices questioning the founding myth of Israel, the idea that the land in Palestine belonged to the Jews, rather than to the predominantly Arab population who lived there. The research of those called the 'new historians' over a decade ago, Avi Schlaim, Simha Flapan, Benny Morris and Ilan Pappé, exposed once again (for any willing to know) how much has been denied in Israel's short history. This includes the prolonged 'ethnic cleansing' of Palestinians, especially in the 'Nakba' of 1948, with the destruction of hundreds of villages, thousands of homes and several massacres, leaving 700,000 Arabs driven forcibly from their land.[413] As Rose's *The Question of Zion* illuminates, it is this information that is acknowledged by the global network of Jews working for peace and for some form of justice for Palestinians still trapped in that historic sequence of violence and repression.[414] We also highlight the denial of full civil rights and land ownership to one million or so Arabs who remain inside Israel's 'democracy'. Sadly, any awareness of the politics of the region reveals the continuing deceptions in Israel's equivocal engagement in 'peace negotiations': on the one hand, promising Palestinians a state; on the other, overtly or covertly, promoting more land seizure and illegal settlements in what remains of Palestinian territory – with the recent withdrawal from Gaza the single case of withdrawal and so far serving only to deepen the geographical imprisonment of, and attacks upon, its inhabitants.[415]

Yet it is no great secret, even in Israel, that there can be no lasting peace so long as the massively armed, dictatorial Israeli military machine keeps over three million Palestinians living under virtual detention in its occupied territories, in the land seized in 1967. A few years ago, the Israeli politician, Shulamit Aloni, publicly lamented: 'The truth is that no one in the government wants peace with the Palestinians.'[416] The same point is made by historian Idith Zertal, comprehensively documenting the ways in which every Israeli politician who has worked for peace has been personally vilified in the right-wing press, likened to Hitler's appeasers or themselves labelled 'Nazis'. Yitzak Rabin was murdered a month after Sharon and Netanyahu spoke at a right-wing rally in October 1995, indicting the Oslo Peace Accord supporters as criminal 'Judenrats' (Jews carrying our Hitler's orders).[417] Lacking genuine sovereignty, freedom of movement, or even control over their water supply, Palestinians in Gaza and the West Bank live confined to a few overcrowded detached enclaves in only fifteen per cent of what was once mandated Palestine.[418] Daily confronting, even as he condemns, 'the long path of humiliation and despair' that lies behind the creation of a 'terrorist', the Palestinian psychiatrist Eyad El-Sarraj grieves that the struggle of many Palestinians is now 'how not to become suicide bombers'.[419] This is the man who is chair of joint Israeli–Palestinian group I work with, FFIPP, but his voice, like those of other prominent Palestinian community leaders denouncing violence, is rarely heard by the wider world.

Western guilt at its own inability to prevent the destruction of two-thirds of Europe's Jewish population helped secure the success of the Zionist political dream to found a modern nation state in Palestine in 1948. The catastrophe this brought to its resident Arabs is not best seen as the fulfilment of any messianic promise to the Jews so much as the betrayal of civilization in Europe. Writing with genuine sympathy for and apprehension about Israel, Isaac Deutscher pointed out a generation ago that Jews in Europe had thrived, wherever they were allowed to, not as nation builders but as diasporic cosmopolitans. Paradoxically, he concluded, the final founding of the Jewish state was another Jewish tragedy: 'a monument to the grimmest phase of European history, a phase of madness and decay.'[420] It is hardly the first nation state to be built upon continuous dispossession and elimination of its indigenous people. Nevertheless, it is not only specious to assert that criticism of Israel is anti-Semitic, but it also demeans the reality of the long history of Jewish persecution. According to all who have seriously studied it, the political struggle in that region does not involve opposing Israel *because* it is Jewish; it stems overwhelmingly from opposition to Israel's continuing dispossession of the Palestinians and its failure to pursue fairer, or even genuine, roads towards a peaceful settlement.[421]

Tragically, fanning fears long embedded by Jewish histories of displacement and catastrophe, anti-Semitic stereotyping and propaganda does appear in criticisms of Israel (made all the more likely by Israel's insistence that it represents all Jews). The recent frightening rise of Islamic fundamentalism, perversely fed by the US-led, British backed, 'war on terror', encourages a virulent anti-Semitism. It is expressed in the public sale and media airing of the notorious tsarist vilification of Jews contained in *The Protocols of Zion*, the hoax text from the 1890s supposedly detailing a Jewish plot to take over the world. This accompanies fanatical death threats issuing from maverick imams against 'the USA', against 'Jews' and, as I write, fierce anti-Semitism and denunciations of Israel from at least one head of state, the religious fundamentalist, Mahmoud Ahmadinejad, the current leader of Iran.

The rise of religious fundamentalism, whether Islamic, Christian or Jewish, is alarming, although its relation to Zionism and Israel is very complex. On the one hand, some of Israel's strongest backers today, the leaders of the Evangelical Christian Right in the USA, are fiercely anti-Judaic, believing, along with Jerry Falwell and Pat Robertson, that all Jews must return to Zion, whereupon Armageddon will occur: Jews will either convert to Christianity, or be destroyed.[422] On the other, some of Israel's strongest critics, a few of whom I now know and love, are committed to a peaceful future both for Israel and for Jewish people generally.[423]

It is Israeli dissenters, including some calling themselves Zionists, who have long been active in dozens of grass-roots struggles and cross-border activities, working tirelessly for peace, whether in Ta-ayush, Btselem, in campaigns to prevent Israeli demolition of Palestinian homes and olive groves, working for refugee rights or joining the courageous multi-faceted women's peace movement – perhaps in silent vigil with Women in Black, or monitoring the deliberate harassment of Palestinians within Machsom (check point watch). I have met people from all these groups; they encourage and inspire me, both despite and because of their small numbers and all the impediments they face as they insist that the future of Israeli Jews and Palestinians is together, living and working in harmony. In her always eloquent, largely unpublished writing, my friend Mirjam Hadar, who is an activist in the peace group New Profile, daily bears witness to the brutality accompanying Israel's refusal to work for peace and reconciliation with the Palestinians, or with its neighbours:

> Here in Jewish-Zionist Israel the national ethnic family silences
> the suffering – recollected as well as ongoing – and the fear at
> the roots of its existence. It does so forcefully, through
> cultivating a society that puts its faith and the best of its
> resources, both human and material, in brute force. With so
> much emphasis on survival, there is a feeling that we cannot
> afford to reflect, to look at our own weaknesses.[424]

Meanwhile, the majority of diasporic Jews, Zionist or not, show little desire to claim their biblical land rights, 'reissued' with much help from terror squads committed to notions of death and martyrdom (so like the Palestinian nationalists whom Israelis claim to find incomprehensible today).[425]

Fearing that his country today itself poses a danger for Jews, the Israeli journalist Akiva Eldar comments: 'It is much easier to claim that the entire world is against us than to admit that the State of Israel, which arose as a refuge and a source of pride for Jews, has not only turned into a place less Jewish and less safe for its citizens, but has become a genuine source of shameful embarrassment to Jews who choose to live outside its borders.'[426] He exaggerates. The same mechanisms of denial and projection are often at work in the minds of diasporic Jews. They too are adept at turning potential shame into anger, and the greater the condemnation, the fiercer the anger. There remains an ever-increasing defensiveness, on the one hand, and ever-growing despair, on the other (with only occasional glimmers of hope), amongst Jews wanting a resolution to the Israeli–Palestinian conflict. For people like me, so often flooded with despair, it is of course the absence of even minimum human rights for Palestinians living in the Occupied Territories that triggers anguish – whether it is the right to work, to travel, to be educated, even to keep their bodily integrity, as Palestinian homes are bulldozed, orchards destroyed, civilians bombed, teenagers incarcerated to be recruited as spies, children 'inadvertently' shot.[427] For some time, Palestinian life has evoked that of Jews in the worst periods of anti-Semitism in Europe: living in increasingly isolated geographical ghettoes, subject to collective punishments, harassed, humiliated, deprived of their means of livelihood, impeded in their efforts to maintain civic infrastructures or assert political agency.

The ruthlessness of Israeli enclosure has reached its terrifying climax with the construction of the steel and concrete 'security fence' or Wall, through the West Bank. Appropriating or destroying even more Palestinian property, depriving thousands of adequate access to healthcare, education and even water, the Wall shuts down the livelihoods of some Palestinians, cutting them off from their olive groves and other forms of employment. As the American psychoanalyst, Joel Kovel mourns: 'Zionism has negated what was done to the Jews in Europe, but recreated its own past, with a different set of masks'.[428] Afif Safieh echoes the thought, 'we the Palestinians, have become the victims of the victims of European history, the Jews of the Jews'.[429] Both are reprising the famous words of Primo Levi to an Italian newspaper in 1982, after the massacres at Sabra and Shatila, when he accused Begin and Sharon of bringing shame on the name of the Jews: 'Everybody is somebody's Jew. And today the Palestinians are the Jews of the Israelis'. Recalling my journey through the checkpoint out of Ramallah in January 2004, after a FFIPP meeting attended by the leading Palestinian spokeswoman from Ramallah, Hannan Ashrawi, I experienced the gravity of these words. Our passage through the checkpoint felt like encountering a stage-set for hell. I was travelling with, among others, a woman who worked for the UN, and had spent time in the trouble spots of Kosovo and East Timor. However, queuing in the rain as the light faded, pushed backwards time after time, surrounded by apparent chaos, barbed wire and lines of young soldiers with guns, she was soon shivering, on the point of collapse: 'I have never seen anything so frightening, anywhere,' she replied, when I suggested that surely she must be used to this. For me, the situation was so grotesque it did not seem real.

Can we hope for better times, or is the conflict now interminable? It is hard to be hopeful. As I return yet again to this chapter as the end of the summer of 2006, the situation remains as bad as ever in Gaza and the West Bank. Israel's renewal of war in the Lebanon, in massive retaliation for the Hizbollah movement's capture of two IDF soldiers and the killing of several others, has only sewn the seeds for further conflict in the uneasy truce that follows so many civilian deaths and so much physical destruction inflicted by the familiar Israeli strategy of bombs not negotiation. On the Palestinian side, President Mahmoud Abbas, leader of the Palestinian Authority and uncompromisingly opposed to the use of violence in his subjugated enclaves, searches for points of agreement with the Islamic Party Hamas, over-whelmingly elected to power in the Palestinian Legislative Council at the beginning of 2006. With Hamas written off by Israel (and the US) as a terrorist organization, members of the Palestinian parliament are now regularly arrested by Israel. There are certain positive initiatives, as Fatah (linked to the President) and Hamas move towards a united programme involving peaceful recognition of Israel to accompany the establishment of an independent Palestinian state, much in line with the Saudi peace plan of 2002 which some Arab states are talking of reviving. However, whether the Israeli government will help to foster these moves, rather than continue, as hitherto, to pursue punitive policies that fuel the fundamentalists on both sides eager to overthrow any possibilities for peace, we have yet to see.

Despite all the ongoing chaos, there is still near-unanimous agreement from all voices committed to justice and peace in this conflict on the only way to achieve it. Yet we see no movement in that direction. The majority of the Palestinian people, including Hamas, would have to believe that there is some hope of obtaining nationhood (an autonomous, contiguous and, above all, viable state) through peaceful means, if they are to back away from the violence and martyrdom their desperate struggle – and the dark side of their ideology – has bred. It would take massive pressure on the Israeli state for it to abandon policies it has pursued from the beginning: policing, isolating and restricting access to Palestinian communities, wherever they are. Tragically, what we see instead is the reverse. George Bush Jr is offering increased financial backing for Israel's continuing military aggression as part of his floundering wars to create a 'New Middle East' in the service of American geo-political interests. US strategy is fully supported by Britain, while the European Union equivocates – withholding funds from Hamas for its failure to recognize Israel, putting no pressure on Israel to uphold international law by ending its annexations and occupation of Palestinian territory.

In this political gridlock, it will also take the most skilful use of power and intense persuasion to end Palestinian violence against Israeli civilian targets. This has proved as counter-productive as it is morally wrong. Along these lines, Edward Said argued a few years before he died, that Palestinians and Arab intellectuals must engage openly and courageously with Israeli audiences:

> What have years of refusing to deal with Israel done for us? Nothing at all, except to weaken us and weaken our perception of our opponent ... we need to rid ourselves of racial prejudices

and ostrich-like attitudes and make the effort to change the
situation. The time has come.[430]

The time has come to change the situation. This is not just to
provide peace for Palestinians and Israelis. It is also because
the failure to settle this brutal conflict strengthens warlords
and military hawks on all sides, whose deadly strategies are
creating the global insecurity and curtailment of democratic
and human rights that now threaten us all. There are few
reasons for hope. But that does not preclude us supporting
the efforts people make, against all odds, to foster the
conditions to nurture them.

Dissident affiliations

'But where does it all place you, after foregrounding your
Jewishness as you recently have?' my few observant Jewish
friends wonder and my secular friends worry. I hardly know.
I could, of course, shrug off such confusion with a cheerful
nod to fashionable theorizing of our fluid and fragile identities in 'liquid modernity'.[431] When I became a feminist there
were soon disputes over the nature of 'femininity',
squabbling over how this 'socially constructed' notion
should be rejected, subverted, reclaimed or transcended.
Nevertheless, it seemed clear enough that we remained
women, despite the distinction being drawn between a
certain affirmation of the 'female' and refusal of aspects of
'femininity'. In time this distinction too would be subject to
fierce conceptual interrogation. However, if moving between
identity and politics remained fraught within feminism, it is
altogether more dubious around 'Jewishness'.

Of course, those identifying as Jewish are keen to be
counted within an identifiable historic lineage, especially
one including Marx, Freud and Einstein, contributing so

decisively to the evolution of modernist thought and sensibilities. (It is this mantle of enlightenment that lies behind Ashkenazi Israel's enduring disdain for its surrounding Arab states.) Interestingly, in Portugal today there are apparently more self-declared Jews than officially recognized ones, telling us much that is often denied about the decline in personally injurious anti-Semitism, as well as the apparent need nowadays to affirm some – almost any – distinct and special identity.[432] Personally, thinking through so much recent Jewish history suggests to me many ways in which specific forms of dislocation, and my parents' eagerness to transcend them, fed into tensions and ambitions shaping my own sense of self. Nevertheless, without any obviously shared genetic, ethnic, religious or cultural characteristics, it remains persistently puzzling what exactly it means to identify oneself as a Jew.

Perhaps this doesn't matter. Identities are often experienced as significant and meaningful when no longer either our inescapable fate or some shared and timeless inheritance. In the nomadic western metropolis, identities are largely fictitious ways of aligning ourselves with others, searching for similarities and downplaying differences. Such 'tribal' belongings (not so unlike supporting a football team) establish an imagined space with those whose tales of triumph, waves of woe, daily tussles, we feel able to experience vicariously or to learn from. Alongside any narcissistic gratification, such affiliations provide ways of giving to others and, above all, of establishing communities, even as they serve to exclude people and – especially when under threat – all too easily trigger hatred towards them. The very fact that identities are far from stable frequently makes their assertion only the *more* brittle and strident.

So let me confess, finally, to certain pleasures I have found in exploring my specific Jewish roots, noting some of the contrasts between the shifting aspirations, desires and dangers faced by Jews in Britain, the colonial world, Europe, Palestine and the USA over the last century. There is something more here, though I know I partly dream it up and project it. When I feel a special closeness to one or two Jewish people, it feels a valuable closeness, for all its narcissistic conceit and selective recognition. Can forms of disidentification, as psychoanalysts might say, also function to affirm identity?

It has indeed been passionate criticism of Israel's intransigence towards recognizing Palestinian rights that has sufficed to bring more than one lapsed Jew back to affirming their Jewish heritage, in critical engagement with messianic Zionism. We can draw upon one particular Jewish legacy which, moving beyond shtetl and synagogue, freer of fierce national ties and (selectively) more sensitive to intolerance and discrimination, put its faith in universal emancipation and enlightenment. Here, being a 'good' Jew meant cherishing the stories of the struggles, sacrifices and successes of one's forebears by holding progressive social values (if not necessarily, although in greater numbers, embracing Marx and Freud, alongside commitment to radical causes).[433] More incongruously, it has given some of us friends in Israel, a place I once never wanted even to visit. But now I find myself connected to some within that embattled, small minority working for peace in the region, their children sometimes facing jail as Refuseniks, their jobs perhaps on the line, watching glumly as their country becomes an ever more militarized zone, responsible for daily atrocities. I even briefly acquired a kind of surrogate son, Misha Hadar, who came to live with me for a few months, escaping to London before returning home to face (mercifully short) imprisonment as a young Refusenik.

So yes, in this picture, and very personally, once again a

type of dissidence is serving to ground a critical sense of belonging, though echoing earlier strands of Jewish radicalism from the days when Jews faced the contempt, or worse, of the powerful. Like many of my friends, as someone long distanced from my place of birth, forming such critical attachments has often seemed like a way of coming home: an enduringly, critically rooted cosmopolitan, one might say. This thought was also expressed by my American friend, Bruce Robbins, who with his daughter Sophie joined me on that academic delegation to Israel I mentioned at the opening of this chapter. Along with his former academic rival, Alan Sokal, he initiated 'An Open Letter from American Jews' in 2002, opposing the historically unprecedented US military aid sustaining Israeli expansion and brutality in the West Bank and Gaza (to the tune of more than three billion dollars annually).[434] He too writes of 'being critical as a *way* of belonging', also noting the paradox that 'dedication to universal rights', including justice for Palestinians, 'seems to have offered many of those "lost children" (Jews by birth but little else) a means of belonging *as Jews*, something they can proudly affirm about their difference from others and about their sameness with others.'[435]

Who's a Jew? I asked at the beginning of this chapter. I am little nearer to knowing at its close, other than to stress the cultural diversity of histories that might connect and, as often, divide 'us'. Neither the old anti-Semitism that united Jews in adversity, nor the new Zionism that moves many to defend Israel today, can underpin Jewish identity. As Judith Butler writes, 'the "Jew" exceeds both determinations, and is to be found, substantively, as a historically and culturally changing identity that takes no single form and has no single telos.'[436] We are defined by our particular familial, cultural and political histories, in which Jewishness may at times be foregrounded, although it may also often remain barely discernible. And though we may be drawn to criticize the actions of the Israeli state from certain identifications we make, or receive, as Jews, there is more at stake here.

First of all, the move towards embracing identity categories for political ends is for many of us part of the collapse of hopes in a more open and inclusive Left project, committed to tackling all entrenched injustice and inequalities. Given the deepening hierarchies of wealth and wellbeing, the only new communities most of us seem able to envisage nowadays are no longer confidently utopian, but instead benevolent versions of more traditional affiliations.

Secondly, conjoining identities with politics (whether as Jews for Justice, Women for Peace, or whatever) produces categories that need to be kept at least analytically distinct, each term endlessly rethought, even as they serve to sustain each other. On the one hand, collapsing the two into one threatens to create chauvinistic identity stances which are, if not altogether oppressive, likely to become nostalgically complacent. On the other, disdaining all personal identifications for the comprehensive embrace of universal goals has in the past, although it need not, often produced political stances that themselves congeal into inflexible identity work, unassailable dogma and the morbid sectarianism of the party hack.

It is, after all, the lethal ties of politics to national, religious and ethnic identities, disguising struggles over trade, territory, economic exploitation and, as significantly as ever, battles over manhood, that fuel the worst forms of fundamentalism today. It was also, as we've seen, the politicising of Jewish identity into a form of colonial nationalism (consolidated by the climate of murderous anti-Semitism in Europe) that created the cadres for political Zionism. That mutation of Jewish manhood, from scholar to soldier, has now shifted again into an even more dangerous version of 'religious Zionist'. At the very least, these transformations tell us that while we can battle to preserve different images of Jewishness, we will never agree on its definitions. Fighting for justice 'as Jews' (whether in some psychically rooted or primarily strategic way) is entering a battle for justice, not one to redefine Judaism. Nevertheless, the affiliations this provides, fraught and fragile, perplexing or pleasurable, as they may be, are likely to prove pressing for quite some time.

8

Ways of belonging

It is not only looking at old photographs that we sometimes feel an irresistible urge to see the future in the past.[437] It is easy to trace out threads running through a life, our own or another's; easy, that is, once we are working backwards, selecting out (or placing in) precisely what we are seeking. For the patterns in a particular life, the ways we leave our mark on others, are never either pre-ordained or even loosely predictable, evolving only within the happenstance of time and place. The most credible memoirists know this, unsettling comforting vanities and reassuring loyalties. 'A life is such a strange object,' Simone de Beauvoir sighed, labouring valiantly to register the significance of every move she made, 'at one moment translucent, at another utterly opaque, an object I make with my own hands, an object imposed on me ... how heavy it is and how inconsistent: this contradiction breeds many misunderstandings.'[438] Not least, as we have been sharply warned of late, in surveying ourselves, if inattentive to the fact that we use favourite recipes when serving up our 'raw experience'. That octogenarian political chronicler, Eric Hobsbawm, echoes Beauvoir's reflections; glancing backwards at the 'buried stranger', the 'remote and unfamiliar child' he once was, he writes of himself: 'had he lived in other historical circumstances nobody would have forecast a future of passionate commitment to politics.' However, for a clever, brooding, Jewish boy, entering adolescence in the Berlin in the 1930s, 'political innocence was impossible.'[439]

Entering adolescence in any of the developed capitalist countries a mere thirty years later, things could hardly have looked more different. Despite enduring inequalities, the options before my post-war generation were often quite exceptionally rich and diverse. This was, Hobsbawm pronounced in his Olympian survey of the last two centuries, 'the golden age of capitalism'.[440] As I have suggested in previous chapters, it was for this very reason that so many of us tended to look hopefully forwards, never wistfully behind us. We echoed the distrust of those two masters of modernity, Marx and Freud, wary of all the dead generations still weighing so heavily upon the minds of the living; although not, as we saw it, on our own. This was a time when the imagination of radical youth, discovering Reich, reading Laing (or home-grown variants), cavalier about its own future in the disdained mainstream of society, was stirred by the starkly contrasting plight of those most excluded from it: the mentally ill, the incarcerated, the unemployed, the homeless, any people at all we saw as displaced, despised, destitute or dispossessed.

The terrible irony now is that it is precisely these groups of needy people whose numbers have soared in the last two decades, just as many of their champions have scattered. Those former campaigners, now in settled careers, may even resurface at the centre of once-derided institutional agencies, as the modern state learns how to co-opt some of its leading critics, providing them with limited powers to contend with the social problems they once hoped to eliminate. In every statistical survey of the state of the nation over the last two decades mental health has deteriorated and prison rates have rocketed. Living standards have risen for many, but wage inequalities have deepened and relative poverty became more entrenched in the closing decades of the twentieth century. The romance of dispossession has long fled, with any sense of security, whether in the workplace or in relationships, harder to maintain. The world in general appears a far scarier place than it seemed a mere few decades ago. Neither increased knowledge of the casualties in our midst, nor distant body counts and injuries, necessarily encourage concern, never mind solidarity.

'I just can't see any light at the end of the tunnel,' my mother would say at the close of her life, refusing, as ever, to look behind her. Her fear of monsters lurking there kept her facing always, and only, towards the future. I often feel much the same. Backward glances are not necessarily more radiant. But they can be personally gratifying. They may prove more rewarding still, if the stories they spark manage to find receptive audiences, able to understand, share in or perhaps merely mull them over, as time goes by. The purpose of this book, as I said at the start, was to shine a light backwards on my own political journeys, and those of others who were part of it, however distantly. As women, more of us travelled further than ever before on our own personal march through the institutions of power, usually ending up, once on the inside, closer to if not wholly absorbed into the bourgeoisie we had once mocked and loved to frighten. We did, however, engender many reforms from within, even while noting those still in difficulties without. To take just one instance, there is today widespread recognition of the frequency of sexual and physical abuse of women and children (as radical concern with the outcast or those deemed 'mad' shifted to those trapped in brutal domesticity), yet its incidence, despite all the attention feminists have brought to the matter, remains obstinately high, its occurrence still under-reported, its immediate remedies far from clear.[441] Only a limited audience is taking note of the continuing rise in domestic battery and abuse, noting the way in which it mirrors the dismantling of welfare, a correlation that is most evident in the USA.[442]

As a member of that shrinking audience, I find that politics is still a part of the glue that attaches me to others, although any engagement I have with differing campaigns for justice, social equality or a share of the good life ebbs and flows, each remaining rather distinct from the other. That youthful search for an all-inclusive political ensemble, trying to make relationships, work, pleasure and political endeavour flow cheerfully together, is long gone. Yet the traces it has left do not strike me as the totalitarian nightmare some now like to paint of any such attempted synthesis, but more a resolve, wherever possible, to keep friendship, warmth and sociability alive in political work.

Generational transmission

However, if local deprivations, not to mention global depredations, suggest old radicals might individually and collectively stand accused of having been ineffectual in many political arenas, the space for renewed imaginative resistance and solidarity never altogether closes down. Indeed, at just this moment of accelerated warfare, national-istic and ethnic violence, with heightened security threats globally, significant protest movements have been reappearing. More aware of the ways in which struggles wax and wane, the stories of those with lengthy histories in oppositional politics provides material for these new idealistic voyagers, although I hardly know whether our most generous hopes and inclusive visions will afford inspiration or amusement today. All retrospection will not only be filtered through its creator's particular, perhaps shifting, place in the world, but also reflect far more idiosyncratic proclivities, whether affable or belligerent, optimistic or gloomy, patient or rash, always slanting the stories we tell.

'I, for one, never accepted that desires for more money, more freedom, more individual expression, were legitimate and ceaselessly renewable,' writes Sarah Benton, characteristically, rebuking herself for her failure to anticipate the appeal of Thatcher's shredding of the social democratic consensus and trade union rights in the 1980s. She also has rather dismal memories of Left debate (which many share): 'It goes without saying that it was a fractious and disputatious world, that floated on unspoken arrogance.'[443] However, it hardly needs qualifying, others on that scene saw things differently. I recall another socialist feminist friend, then known as Angie Weir, sharing Benton's allegiance to the Communist Party at the time (although soon in a different faction of it), bewildering me with her passing desire to be driven around in a big flashy American car, while thriving on the rhetorical skills she acquired in spirited debate – later put to exemplary use in the media and other mainstream forums. Both of these feminists are still politically active, both writing and campaigning for the rights of women, gay men and lesbians. But the latter, a gay and lesbian spokesperson, now has an OBE, and the ear of some in the current Labour cabinet, light years away from the situation of her old comrade. Each recalls her past in differing ways. But it is just such multiple viewpoints and differing structures of feeling that we need to understand if we want to know what encourages political bonds, and their duration, as people either hold onto or move away from earlier convictions and engagements. In pondering their inconsistencies, gaps, overlap and possible insights, political memories just might become richer cultural resources, whether it is the past or the future that is on our mind.

Nonetheless, generational transfer is something that is characteristically problematic for the radical spirit. 'I'm not a vegetable, I don't have roots,' one of my close Turkish friends who entered adulthood as a Marxist in the Sixties likes to say. In fact, in these ignominious times for old Lefties, he is busy collecting 'revolutionary' memorabilia from its glory days. The rise of radical thought and action involves, at the very least, the resolve to change things. The desire to be the generation that makes a difference, disrupting life as they have known it, is voiced all the more strongly by the young, when time is on your side, and transformations perhaps beckoning from the horizon. The downfall of radical thought and action is usually that change, if and when it arrives, mutates at once – with certain troubling continuities reappearing in new moulds. The shedding of former aspirations can prove all the more mournful, when time is speeding up and options already closing down. Almost by definition, then, communication between generations, stress on continuities and tradition, seems to align itself more readily with classic conservatism than with radical activism. In the archetypal conservatism of Edmund Burke, it is always 'pernicious to disturb the natural course of things.'[444] All societies must involve a contract or partnership 'between those who are living, those who are dead, and those who are to be born.'[445]

The job of the conservative is thus to pass on a sense of the past to the future, not prioritise the living over the dead. The job of the radical appears almost the reverse, to try to escape the stranglehold of tradition, rejecting any sentimentalizing of the past, or 'pie in the sky' promises about the future. Hence the importance conservatism attaches to the family, the nation, religion, and all the other structures of tradition that capitalist modernity has, all along, been so dramatically disrupting. And there's the rub. For one minute the radical stands on her soapbox, deploring the present and exhorting change. The next minute it becomes clear that much that she condemns is an aspect of change itself. One minute men are never at home to help her with the childcare and other domestic tasks. The next, she's no longer there herself, but chained to the office, although what she had fought for had been less, not more, of a separation between workplace and household. This is not life as she finds it today.

Those who, in the footsteps of Karl Marx, analyse its nature, know that it is capitalism itself that it is the most 'revolutionary' force of all, destroying everything in its restless wake. (Burke, of course, foresaw this too; indeed, his objection to the French revolution of 1789 was primarily a defence of the aristocracy and clergy against the unbridled materialism of a new merchant class, which would in time rip down all that stands in the way of its profits.) The power of corporate capital, wherever given free rein, will inevitably work to tear down whatever cannot immediately be incorporated to serve its ends, at the very same time as it props up anything at all that helps secure its global reach. When securely grounded in the US State Department, for instance, this has meant, for a time at least, supporting Osama Bin Laden, Saddam Hussein or, currently, allowing certain US conglomerates to back specific Islamic fundamentalist Chechen warlords, in order to destabilize the Caucasus (attempting to undermine Russian control of the pipelines being laid to secure the rich oil supplies in the Caspian Sea).[446]

It is thus not so surprising that those who struggle collectively for better times sometimes notice that it is we who are battling to defend the value of traditional attachments and belongings, whether our own or the livelihoods and communities of others. Even when radicals do look back in horror at the nightmare of history, knowing the barbarism that has been perpetrated (or tolerated) by all the dead generations, in the name of Church, class, ethnicity, religion or nation, we also call upon our own particular political ancestry to help forge future hopes. However, for us, holding on to the past, whatever its configuration, will be important for its role in helping us to refigure the future anew, searching for more equitable, inclusive, peaceful ways forward.

Looking back critically, yet still starting over, time and again, without either wiping out or disowning the past, has to be the paradoxical nature of any radical tradition worth preserving. That much at least we can be sure of, whenever we try to turn again to confront the tyranny or defeats of history, our own as much as those of others. This thought has for some time been the focus of the stirring poetics of that intricately identified feminist veteran in the USA, Adrienne Rich, writing as a socialist, lesbian, Jewish, pacifist, still politically engaged, after all these years. Beginning again, while keeping hold of different ways of assessing where we have come from just might, in her words, produce the 'midnight salvage' that keeps both passion and politics alive. Rich, whose poetry is always rooted in feminist politics, who registers that 'capitalism lost no time in re-arranging itself around "feminism",' who sees that 'one period's necessary strategies can mutate into the monsters of a later time' (calling for a moratorium on her own once favoured words, like the 'body'), laments her earlier forms of blindness, while still, stubbornly, preserving her own oppositional imagination: 'A politicized life ought to sharpen both the senses and the memory.'[447] She is one of the genuinely radical feminists who can help persuade me of the importance of neither disowning our political past, nor glorifying it, but rather of keeping on the move, while still remaining as generous as possible to our earlier selves.

Oddly, having recently acquired yet another contingent identity (as dissident Jew), at present this is something I do not find hard to do. There are also a host of other writers, thinkers and activists, not to mention friends and even a few neighbours, who inspire me in much the same way. Some, based in the USA, are especially useful in forestalling lazy inclinations to simplistic anti-Americanism. They are all the more significant for me when coming from very different places in Left trajectories, thereby transcending the turf wars within academia, where differing perspectives are often pointlessly polarised: class and economic analysis versus cultural enquiry and subjective identifications.[448]

Emblematic of 'high theory' in feminism in the 1990s, Judith Butler has recently been publicly discussing possibilities for an 'international feminist coalition' to think through and act upon the global dilemmas women face. She has also begun addressing critical Jewish thinking to explore the shifting nature of Jewish identity, in particular its ambivalent relation to Israel. Sharply critical of Israel's denial of its own long history of brutality towards Palestinians, she writes of the complex legacies of the Zionist past, in search of other ways forward to a 'post-Zionist' future.[449] The Hegelian and deconstructive pathway Butler navigates in defence of the global egalitarian, pacifist stance she takes is not one that would be popularly accessible. It begins with the need for historical and cultural translation to understand the role of the 'other' in the formation of any identity category: 'I am nowhere without you. I cannot muster the "we" except by finding the way in which I am tied to "you", trying to translate, but finding my own language must break up and yield in order to know you.' [450] Few will master Butler's demanding art of translation in the formation of subject positions, or realize that 'the human comes into being, again and again, as that which we have *yet to know*.' Fortunately, as I have often heard Butler point out in her lectures, 'various routes lead us to politics, various stories bring us onto the street, various kinds of reasoning and belief.' When not triggering envious attack, it is of course her academic celebrity itself that now moves her audiences, me included, as she urges their political engagement, while allowing studious fans to project their best selves onto her intellectual aura and radical political stance.

From the plain-talking opposite end of the same feminist spectrum, archetypal 1970s socialist feminist Barbara Ehrenreich inspires me still, as she did in the beginning, when she stirs audiences with her astute grasp of everyday cruelties. Leaving philosophical analysis and theoretical abstraction to look after itself, a short while ago she took on whatever menial jobs she could, recording her experiences among America's most exploited female workers with such fiery humour in her book *Nickel and Dimed* that it became a bestseller in the USA.[451] Ehrenreich deploys much the same political insights and supportive vigilance today as she did almost forty years ago, remaining attentive to the welfare of the whole of humanity, not merely those closest to home. Back then, she travelled the world to record the first upheavals of student protest in the 1960s. Today, with Arlie Hochschild, she records the voices of 'global woman', in particular immigrant domestic and sex workers, leaving their own homes and children behind, forced to ease the 'care deficit' in richer countries far afield (just as once poor women had been the maids or even wet-nurses of ladies of leisure, living nearby).[452] Speaking today to audiences larger than she has ever seen before, Ehrenreich participates alongside the tens of thousands of campaigners currently flocking to the Social Forums that have been held internationally since they were initiated in Seattle in 1999, all seeking new ways of working together from their very diverse positions to prove that 'a better world is possible'.

Facing up to the very bleak beginning of the twenty-first century, knowing all that stands in the way of any progressive causes, it is clear to me that there remains a Left spirit that is more than the home of lost causes, more than a repository for forsaken beliefs and impossible loyalties. Having never been a united body, the Left is not the cosiest place to be, and far from the 'coolest', yet the provenance of progressive politics in sustaining the radical imagination is growing again. Left formations are always most creative when most inclusive, attending to the multitude of voices working collectively, usually independently, inside their umbrella. Although they were defeated, we saw the diversity of forces in the enormous opposition to the re-election of Bush Junior in 2004. Two years later many have returned, trying to encourage grass-roots resistance to his policies and the damage they have caused, both at home and in the Middle East. 'We're sorry,' friends and strangers sent around the Ethernet, with Bush reinstalled in the White House. Sadly their regret can find few more effective channels as democracy atrophies under the weight of corporate capitals' control of the dominant airwaves and those elected to Capitol Hill.

I have been suggesting throughout this book that it is never possible to isolate quite why it is that some people find matters of political conviction and allegiance have an inescapable hold on their lives, while others do not. Surveying my personal past, I can point to intimations that might be seen in the vulnerabilities of a sickly, over-sensitive, outgoing young girl, in an inherently eccentric if superficially conventional but palpably unhappy family, or in the peculiarities of our largely disowned Jewish heritage that took the form of a fiercely rationalistic atheism, or in a host of other individual and cultural particularities that made me especially receptive to dissenting voices, as quickly distressed by noticing humiliation and cruelty as by the merest thought of receiving it. However, it was my encounter with particular historical conjunctures that provided the pattern for that journey: propelling me into the wave of radical protest in the Sixties, onwards into the upsurge that became Women's Liberation, before alighting on the softer shores of pedagogic feminism and a continuing critical, if often rather limited, engagement with calls to support those battling to confront what seems most amiss in the present. Political identity derives neither from one's specific background, nor from good theory, as my friend the gay theorist Alan Sinfield illustrates in all of his compelling writing: 'It derives mainly from involvement in a milieu.'[453]

Oppositional consciousness is thus never simply a product of individual experiences, whether in families or broader culture, but the embrace or refusal of possible group allegiances. Yet, however contingent such commitments, I am sure that the more we try to understand and accept both their continuities and transformations, the easier it becomes to welcome, rather than fear, those who may follow us. 'The young are on the way up. My natural enemies!' declares the once famous, long fading composer, in one of Julian Barnes' brilliant portrayals of the bitter, corrosive egotism of the ageing artist.[454] Political journeys, if we manage to keep travelling, can help to soothe our envy of the young, as my contact with a few of the young Refuseniks from Israel has most recently underlined.

Fragile endings

'Your garden is too beautiful, and your life is too good,' yet another recent Israeli visitor protests, only half joking. This arresting man, now living in California, is the central cog keeping afloat the particular Israeli–Palestinian peace initiative I have been involved in of late (FFIPP). Elaborating on his teasing regret, he adds, 'You won't want to work,' or at least, he thinks, I won't want to work hard enough to advance his political goals. He dedicates his life now to toiling for peace in the Middle East, almost every demanding, waking minute, unwilling to slow down until he sees a total end to Israel's control over Gaza, the West Bank and East Jerusalem – 'I haven't been to the cinema for twenty years,' he tells me, in one e-mail. It is true. I could not do that.

Second-wave feminists in the 1970s had mostly scorned the Leninist cadre, the tough-minded 'dead man on leave', believing he (or sometimes she) should subordinate personal life to political struggle, Brecht's grim militants who in laying the ground for friendships, could not themselves be friendly. Our feminist disdain looks wise in hindsight. At the time, the British 'working class', to whom these cadres dedicated themselves, for the most part wanted neither their lives, nor even their leaflets. Such self-denying revolutionaries are poor at inspiring others with visions of a better life, however correctly they sometimes harness anger at an unjust world. Nevertheless, to have a sustained impact in any politics of resistance lined up against a corporate capitalism now so rampantly unconstrained, not to mention armies aggressively on the move and eco-systems threatened, it is necessary for some people to have the sort of dogged dedication, discipline and strategic planning that feminists often viewed with suspicion. Again, notwithstanding certain exhilarating cultural theorists who romantically disdain the process, it is no less essential that any appropriately distrustful and rebellious 'multitude' find the wisdom and tolerance to unite tactically wherever possible.[455] This means seeking out conduits for working with any sympathetic representatives who can be found on the inside of national governments and international confederations, within existing circuits of power. The political formations I have been closest to, now strongly represented at the new Social Forums, have never found this easy.

Expressive of the way feminism brought personal reflections to political lives, the South African born feminist writer, Gillian Slovo, has written of the pain and resentment she and her sisters often felt as the daughters of two of the leading white anti-apartheid revolutionaries (both themselves Jewish immigrants in South Africa), knowing that they were always second in importance to their parents' political work: 'In most families, it is the children who leave home ... In mine, it was the parents.'[456] Nevertheless, she is immensely proud to be the daughter of those parents, who inspire her ambitions to understand and oppose brutality and injustice in her own literary and theatrical productions. The world simply looks too grim at present for the optimistic jubilation with which some feminists once liked to echo, 'if I can't dance, I don't want to be in your revolution,' attributing the sentiment to Emma Goldman.

Whatever our habitual concern or indifference, there is no way of getting the balance exactly right if we to try to weigh up the ways in which we affect those who directly depend upon our attention, love and support against too great, or too little, identification with the predicament of others near and far. Or rather, there is no rational way of specifying what this would mean, of finding the ethical scales for balancing intimate dependencies, on one side, and opposition to injustice and unnecessary suffering, on the other. Nevertheless, accepting a necessary disjuncture between the spheres of the personal and the political is very different from the traditional Left's disregard for when and how they do connect. It is not just that combining women's rights and sexual freedoms generally with attention to basic economic and material needs (with which they often intersect) has become increasingly significant in human rights movements globally. In far more complicated ways, it is more necessary than ever to analyse the varied gendered investments in warfare and conflict. We are nowadays more aware of the lethal binding of certain masculinities to acts of spectacular violence, which intensify or diminish according to time and place. The power of virile metaphor is the ubiquitous accompaniment of states of war and spreading militarization, with violence against women being declared a 'global epidemic' of the twenty-first century, reaching immeasurable levels of brutality and cruelty in many situations of conflict.[457] However, deliberately overlooked, although these days clearly visible, is the presence of women combatants inflicting sexual humiliation in western militias, as in Abu Ghraib, or serving as avenging wives and mothers on Islamic suicide missions.

Being drawn to feminism, as a woman, brought politics back into my personal life in the 1970s. But then, being drawn to politics has kept me attached to wider loyalties and commitments, allowing at least some escape from the self-doubts and disappointments that shadow individual lives. Indeed, it is the volatility and fragility of our personal lives and attachments in today's world (one where most of us, much of the time, must defer to the demands and upheavals of market forces) that make us the more compulsively driven to consume capitalism's own flimsy authorizations of authenticity, its marketing of our ever-vanishing heritage, whatever that heritage might be. As I like to see it, staying personally political means keeping hold of some narrative of the self that is consistent enough to enable old radicals to remain at least partially rooted, however critically, in the specific attachments we have formed, yet flexible enough to facilitate our seeing beyond them. If we are lucky, we may form new solidarities as time removes or erodes former bonds, all the while refusing to abandon some sense of connection to that volatile category, shared humanity.

It is on the world's stage that it is easiest to see the permanent nature of political struggle, as (oddly) I was taught in my very first political awakening, amongst the Sydney Libertarians. We never simply win; but then again, we never simply lose either. If we cannot manage to change all that we would like to change in line with a heart's desire for greater justice and equality in the world, we might at least attempt to understand it. But if we bother to attempt to understand it, we might at least puzzle over what changes might be for the better, and play what part we can in the possibilities and perils of promoting them. Since the world will not stop changing, it makes sense to promote the least bad outcomes, always wondering along the way whether we are for the moment winning or losing. Hope must live with apprehension, either way. Politically, it remains possible to find continuities that help me weave anew differing trajectories across time and place: whether noticing the gendered and racial dynamics entwined in the brutal and brutalizing battle over territory in the Israeli–Palestinian conflict, or attending to the voices of those working to expand shrinking democratic spaces, or threatened public resources, locally or globally. Personally, these solidarities can help to shrink familiar generational divisions and to bridge formidable temporal discontinuities. This happens, at the best of times, and when it does, it feels good.

Notes and references

Prologue

1 Communique 9, dug up from scraps in my personal memorabilia.

2 I obtained this information through a friend, John Gibson, then working at the Islington Law Centre, who visited Jake's prison in an official capacity.

3 David Papenoe, *Disturbing the Nest: Family Change and Decline in Modern Societies*, New York, Aldine, 1988; David Blakenhorn, *Fatherless America: Confronting Our Most Urgent Social Problem*, New York, Basic Books, 1995.

4 Sheila Rowbotham, *Promise of a Dream*, London, Penguin, 2000, p. 214.

5 Maureen Freely, *What About Us? An Open Letter to the Mothers Feminism Forgot*, London, Bloomsbury, 1996.

6 There were similar though not identical patterns for women and men. Elsa Ferri, John Bynner and Michael Wadsworth, *Changing Britain, Changing Lives*, London, Bedford Way Papers, Institute of Education, University of London, 2003, pp. 264–8.

7 Edmund White, 'On the line', New introduction to *A Boy's Own Story*, London, Picador, 2000, p. ii.

8 Carolyn Steedman, *Dust*, Manchester, Manchester University Press, 2001, p. 77.

9 For an excellent overview see Roger Luckhurst, 'Traumaculture', in *Remembering the 1990s: New Formations*, no. 50, Autumn 2003. For examples of some of the bestsellers in this 'survival of trauma' genre, see Dave Pelzer, *A Child Called It: One Child's Courage to Survive*, Deerfield Beach, FL: Health Communications, Inc, 1995; Dave Pelzer, *A Man Named Dave: A Story of Triumph and Forgiveness*, New York, Dutton Books, 1999; Anthony Godby Johnson, *A Rock and a Hard Place: One Boy's Triumphant Story*, New York, Signet, 1994; Torey Haden, *The Tiger's Child*, New York, Avon Books, 1995; Ruth Picardie, *Before I Say Goodbye*, Harmondsworth, Penguin, 1998; Oscar Moore, *PWA: Looking AIDS in the Face*, London, Picador, 1996. In the art world Tracey Emin, Nan Goldin, Gillian Wearing and Tracy Moffat are among the best known imagists of wounded bodies; see Julian Stallabrass, *High Art Lite: British Art in the 1990s*, London, Verso, 1999; Hal Foster, *The Return of the Real: the Avant-garde at the End of the Century*, Cambridge, Mass., MIT Press, 1996.

10   Frigga Haug, 'Sexual deregulation or, the child abuser as hero in neoliber-
      alism', *Feminist Theory*, vol. 2, no. 1, 2001, p. 56. From a different political
      moment, Haug had coined the term 'memory work' for a type of
      Foucauldian methodology used to unpack the complex meanings and
      charged discursive contexts shadowing the words we use for naming
      bodily attributes, enabling people to reflect upon their corporeal pasts,
      while trying to 'wriggle free of the constraints of purely personal and
      individual experience', Frigga Haug in Haug, et al., *Female Sexualization: A
      Collective Work of Memory*, trans. Erica Carter, New York, Verso, 1987, p. 36.

11   J.-B. Pontalis, *Love of Beginnings*, London, Free Association Books, 1993,
      p. xiv.

12   Clifford Geertz, *Works and Lives: The Anthropologist as Author*, Stanford,
      California, Stanford University Press, 1988, p. 79.

13   Roland Barthes, 'La Lumière du Sud-Ouest', Roland Barthes, Incidents,
      trans. R. Howard, University of California Press, 1992, pp. 3–9.

14   As Carolyn Steedman has again historicized so well in much of her
      writing: Carolyn Steedman, *Strange Dislocations, Childhood and the Idea of
      Human Interiority, 1780–1930*, Cambridge, Mass., Harvard University
      Press, 1995; *Past Tenses: Essays on Writing, Autobiography, History*, London,
      Rivers Oram, 1992; 1995; Dust, Manchester, Manchester University Press,
      2001.

15   This was simply a familiar attribution to Dutschke, I never knew its actual
      source.

16   See Stuart Hall, 'The "First" New Left' in *Out of Apathy: Voices of the New
      Left 39 Years On*, London, Verso, 1989.

17 · The first essay I ever published, which accompanied Sheila Rowbotham's
      Beyond the Fragments: Feminism and the Making of Socialism, London,
      Islington Community Press, 1979, later expanded and published by
      Merlin Press, 1980.

18   I have tried to assess the theoretical progress of feminism, and its political
      significance, many times before, in *Is the Future Female? Troubled Thoughts
      on Contemporary Feminism*, London, Virago, 1987; *Straight Sex: The Politics
      of Pleasure*, London, Virago, 1994; *Why Feminism? Gender, Psychology,
      Politics*, Cambridge, Polity Press, 1999.

19   Gareth Stedman Jones, 'History and Theory: An English Story' in
      Historein: *A Review of the Past and Other Stories*, vol. 3, Athens, 2001, p. 110.

20   Adam Phillips, 'On Translating a Person' in *Promises, Promises*, London,
      Faber, 2000, pp. 126–7.

Chapter 1

21 Simone de Beauvoir, *The Second Sex*, London, Picador, p. 528.

22 Richard Wollheim, 'Germs: A Memoir', *London Review of Books*, vol. 26, no. 8, 15 April 2004, p. 5.

23 First published in 1918, the beautiful drawings in May Gibbs' tales made them all the more compelling.

24 See Suzanne D. Rutland, *Seventy Five Years: The History of a Jewish Newspaper*, Sydney, The Australian Jewish Historical Society, November, 1970, p. 64.

25 All quotes taken from Rutland, ibid., pp. 53–5.

26 Isaac Isaacs, 'Alfred Harris: An Appreciation', personal copy given to me by my uncle, Dr Louis Harris.

27 Anne Coombs, *Sex and Anarchy: The Life and Death of the Sydney Push*, Harmondsworth, Viking, Penguin, 1996, p. 239.

Chapter 2

28 I made this comment in *Straight Sex: The Politics of Pleasure*, London, Virago, 1994, p. 69.

29 Germaine Greer, 'The Strongest Influence on my Life', radio talk for BBC Radio 4, aired 28 May 1975.

30 Anne Coombs, *Sex and Anarchy: The Life and Death of the Sydney Push*, Harmondsworth, Viking, Penguin, 1996, p. 245.

31 All quotes in this paragraph taken from D. J. I. 'Futilitarianism – A Libertarian Dilemma?', *The Libertarian*, no. 3, 1960, p. 21.

32 It was not until 1971, helped by the election of the Whitlam Government at the end of 1972, that there was an effective end to federal censorship of explicit discussion of women's or gay sexuality.

33 James Franklin, 'The Push and Critical Drinkers', in his *Corrupting the Youth: A History of Australian Philosophy*, Sydney, Macleay Press, 2003, p. 176.

34 Bob Ellis, written in 1973, quoted in Coombs, op. cit, p. 305.

35 Coombs, p. 40.

36 Ibid., p. 60. Confirmed later in conversation with Roelof, who offered much useful advice and commentary on this chapter.

37 Ibid., p. 65.

38 See Susan Varga, 'Twice the Man: The Two George Molnars', *The Sydney Morning Herald*, 9 August, 2003 (http://www.smh.com.au/articles/2003/08/08/1060145848387.html as retrieved on 13 March 2006).

Chapter 3

39   'I Got out of Bed on the Right Side' is a promotional clip from one of Esther Williams' films, *Dangerous When Wet* (1953).

40   For information on the Angry Brigade, see Gordon Carr, *The Angry Brigade: The Cause and the Case*, London, Christie Books, 2004; Stuart Christie, *Granny Made Me an Anarchist*, London, Scribner Books, 2004.

41   Milan Kundera, *Identity*, London, Faber, 1998, p. 43.

42   The quotation is an often-used phrase originally used by Marc Bloch, writing on the importance of unwritten evidence in historical observation, from his classic *The Historian's Craft*, first published in 1953.

43   Notes taken from recording in conversation with my reading group, 1 February, 2003; Sally Alexander, in Michelene Wandor, *Once a Feminist: Stories of a Generation*, London, Virago, p.85.

44   Audrey Battersby, Janet Rée, Val Charlton, Sue O'Sullivan, all interviewed in Michelene Wandor, ibid., p. 113; p.97; p.161; p.218.

45   Alison Fell, 'Everyday Offensive: Notes on Ideology', *Red Rag*, no. 6, 1973, p. 18.

46   See Lisa Baraitser, 'Oi Mother, Keep Ye' Hair On! Impossible trans- formations of maternal subjectivity', *Studies in Gender and Sexuality*, vol. 7, no. 3, pp. 217–38, 2006; Naomi Wolf, *Misconceptions: Truth, Lies and the Unexpected on the Journey to Motherhood*, London, Chatto & Windus, 2001; Susan Kraemer, 'Betwixt the dark and the daylight of maternal subjectivity: meditations on the threshold', *Psychoanalytic Dialogues*, vol. 6, pp.765–91,1996.

47   Elizabeth Wilson, *Mirror Writing: An Autobiography*, London, Virago, 1982, p. 87 and p. 90.

48   This is the final poem in Robin Morgan's collection of poetry, *Monster*, which by 1974 could be found in the homes of most Women's Liberationists, as quoted in Carol Morrell, *Spare Rib*, no. 21, 1974, p. 42.

49   Sara Maitland, 'I Believe in Yesterday: An Introduction', in Sara Maitland (ed.), *Very Heaven: Looking Back at the 1960s*, London, Virago, 1988, p. 9–10.

50   It was Betty Friedan, in her groundbreaking call to arms, who most memorably analysed the ties between the advertising industry, the middle-class housewife and the challenge of post-war capitalism in *The Feminine Mystique*, New York, W. W. Norton, 1963.

51   Betty Friedan, *The Feminie Mystique*, New York, W. W. Norton, 1963, p. 228.

52   Carolyn Steedman, *Landscape for a Good Woman*, London, Virago, 1986, p. 39.

53   Sarah Benton, replying to my questions.

54   Audrey Battersby, p. 113 in Wandor, op. cit.; Sally Alexander, in Wandor,

op. cit. p. 91; Catherine Hall, in Wandor, op. cit. p. 178; Sally Belfridge, speaking in the article by the first Women's Liberation group in London, Belsize Women's Group, 'Nine Years Together', *Spare Rib*, no. 69, April 1978, reprinted in *Spare Rib Reader*, ed. Marsha Rowe, Harmondsworth, Penguin, 1982, p. 569; Janet Rée, in Wandor, op. cit. p.99.

55 Denise Riley, in response to my questions.

56 Sue O'Sullivan, 'From 1969', in *'68, '78, '88: From Women's Liberation to Feminism*, Dorset, Prism Press, 1988, p. 52.

57 The first flare of this new discussion around orgasm, indicting Freud and calling for female sexual emancipation, came from the USA, Anne Koedt, 'The Myth of the Vaginal Orgasm' (1968) in L. Tanner (ed.), *Voices from Women's Liberation*, New York, Mentor, 1970.

58 See Lillian Faderman, *Odd Girls and Twilight Lovers: A History of Lesbian Life in Twentieth-Century America*, New York, Columbia University Press, 1991.

59 Exemplified in Leeds Revolutionary Feminists (ed.) *Love Your Enemy? The Debate between Heterosexual Feminism and Political Lesbianism*, London, Onlywomen Press, 1981.

60 Personal communication, after reading a draft of this chapter.

61 Lynne Segal, 'Sensual Uncertainty or Why the Clitoris is Not Enough' in Sue Cartledge and Joanna Ryan, *Sex and Love*, London, The Woman's Press, 1983.

62 Michelene Wandor, 'London Airport', *Red Rag*, no. 4, 1973, p. 18.

63 Alison Fell, *Every Move You Make*, London, Virago, 1984, p. 22.

64 Ibid., pp. 24–25.

65 Noreen's older sister wrote about their childhood in her memoir, Nuala O'Faolain, *Are You Somebody? The Accidental Memoir of a Dublin Woman*, New York, Henry Holt & Co, 1998.

66 Liz Heron, *Changes of Heart: Reflections on Women's Independence*, London, Pandora, 1986, p. 123.

67 That friend is Ralph Edney.

68 The quotation is from Grace Paley, 'The Expensive Moment' in *Later the Same Day*, London, Virago, 1985, p. 180.

69 W. H. Auden, 'As I walked out one evening', in *As I Walked Out One Evening: Songs, Ballads, Limericks and Light Verse*, Faber, 1997.

70 I am relying on interviews with the children and adults I knew. I can find little published research on children raised in households with the sort of shared caring patterns we practised.

71 Virginia Haussegger, 'The sins of our feminist mothers', *The Age*, 23 July 2002; Zelda Grimshaw, 'Mothering: Feminism's Unfinished Business', *The*

Age, 1 August, 2002; Virginia Haussegger, 'Has feminism let us down?', *The Age*, 23 April, 2003.

72 Anne Roiphe, *Fruitful: A Real Mother in the Mother World*, New York, Penguin, 1997; Elizabeth Fox-Genovese, *Feminism is Not the Story of My Life: How Today's Feminist Elite Has Lost Touch with the Real Concerns of Women*, Doubleday, 1996.

73 Adrienne Rich, *Of Woman Born: Motherhood as Experience and Institution*, New York, W. H. Norton, 1976; Jane Lazarre, *The Mother Knot*, New York, McGraw Hill, 1976; Hélène Cixous, 'The Laugh of the Medusa', *Signs*, vol 1., no. 4, 875–93; Phyllis Chesler's more controversial *Sacred Bond: The Legacy Of Baby M*, New York, Times Books, 1988.

74 Stephanie Dowrick and Sybil Grundberg, *Why Children*, London, Women's Press, 1980.

75 See Rozsika Parker, *Torn in Two: the Experience of Maternal Ambivalence*, London, Virago, 1995; Wendy Hollway and Brid Featherstone, *Mothering and Ambivalence*, London, Routledge, 1997.

76 Ann Snitow, 'Feminism and Motherhood: An American Reading', *Feminist Review*, no. 40, Spring 1992, pp. 32–51.

77 Thanks to Eamonn McKeown for drawing my attention to this poem.

78 Lorna Sage, *Bad Blood: A Memoir*, London, Fourth Estate, 2000, pp. 261–3.

80 Sylvia Ann Hewlett, *A Lesser Life: The Myth of Women's Liberation in America*, 1986; Maureen Freely, *What About Us? An Open Letter to the Mothers Feminism Forgot*, London, Bloomsbury, 1996, p. 13.

81 In 1975, Child Benefit replaced Family Allowances in Britain; the following year the Domestic Violence Act came into effect, enabling women to obtain a court order against their violent husband or partner.

82 This is a story told to me (I assume in confidence) by a leading journalist on one of our top daily newspapers, *The Guardian*, about the secret bonds between working mothers, even those at odds with each other on other matters.

83 Personal response to my questions on the impact of the movement on feminist activists.

84 Polly Toynbee, 'The Myth of Women's Lib', *The Guardian*, 6 June 2002, p. 7.

85 Sheila Rowbotham, interviewed by Michelene Wandor, in op. cit., p. 41.

86 Vivian Gornick, *Approaching Eye Level*, New York, Beacon Books, 1996, p. 65.

Chapter 4

86 Barbara Taylor, 'Heroic Families and Utopian Histories' in *Historien: European Ego-histoires: Historiography and the Self, 1979–2000*, vol. 3, Nefeli Publishers, Athens, 2001, p. 60.

87 Tufnell Park Women's Group, 'Organizing Ourselves', *Shrew*, March, 1971; 'Manifesto on Motherhood', *Shrew*, September, 1970; 'Women on the Buses', *Women's Newspaper*, issue no. 2, 1971; Lis Kustow, 'Television and Women', in Michelene Wandor, *The Body Politic: Writings from the Women's Liberation Movement in Britain 1969–1972*, London, Spokesman, 1972.

88 Belsize Park Group, in Rowe, op. cit. p. 574.

89 From the discussion in my small feminist writers' group.

90 Sally Alexander, 'The Night Cleaners', in *Red Rag*, no. 6, 1973.

91 Personal communication.

92 Elizabeth Wilson, 'Libertarianism: Ideas in the Void', *Red Rag*, no. 4, 1973, pp. 6–7.

93 Terry Eagleton, *The Gatekeeper: A Memoir*, London, Allen Lane, 2002, p. 81.

94 Just one distressing example was the recent TV programme 'Lefties: Angry Wimmin', in which the tiny splinter group of 'revolutionary feminists' were presented in a slot which, more representatively, one would expect to have been filled by historical reflection on socialist feminism. BBC 4, 15 February 2006, 9–10 p.m.

95 See, for example, Wendy Brown, *States of Injury: Power and Freedom in Late Modernity*, New Jersey, Princeton University Press, 1995.

96 Ralph Edney, *Lazarus Lamb in The Riddle of the Sphincter*, London, Pluto Press, 1983, no page numbers.

97 Sheila Rowbotham, Lynne Segal, Hilary Wainwright, *Beyond the Fragments: Feminism and the Making of Socialism*, London, Merlin Press, 1980.

98 I am not one who accepts that it was the conflict between our radical idealism and the practicalities of winning elections that was responsible for the Thatcherite accommodations of New Labour, but that is a story I touched on at the close of my first chapter, to which I will return in my last chapter.

99 E-mail communication from Marsha Rowe, 23 November, 2005.

100 Michèle Roberts, personal communication, 24 Novemeber, 2005.

101 Jean Radford interviews Michèle Roberts, and Sara Maitland: 'Women Writing', *Spare Rib*, no 76, November 1978, reprinted in Feminist Anthology Collective (eds), *No Turning Back: Writings from Women's Liberation 1975–80*, London, The Women's Press, 1981, p. 261.

102 Ibid., p. 264.

103 Zoë Fairbairns et al., *Tales I Tell My Mother: A Collection of Feminist Short Stories*, London, Journeyman, 1978.

104 Ann Oosthuizen, 'Bulletins from the Front Line', in Alison Fell et al. *Licking the Bed Clean: Five Feminist Poets*, Teeth Imprints, London, 1978, p. 61.

105 See Rozsika Parker and Griselda Pollack (eds), *Framing Feminism: Art and the Women's Movement 1970–1985*, London and New York, Routledge, 1986.

106 Maria Isabel Barreno, Maria Teresa Horta, and Maria Velho da Costa, *The Three Marias: New Portuguese Letters*, trans. Helen R. Lane, New York, Doubleday, 1975 .

107 Nawaal El Saadawi, *The Hidden Face of Eve: Women in the Arab World*, trans. and ed. Sherif Hetata, London, The Women's Press, 1977.

108 Lisa Alther, *Kinflicks*, London, Virago Press, 1999; Marilyn French, *The Women's Room*, London, Andre Deutsch, 1978.

109 Anya Meulenbelt, *The Shame is Over*, first published 1976, London, Women's Press, 1980.

110 Alther, *Kinflicks*, p. 567.

111 Rita Mae Brown, *Ruby Fruit Jungle*, New York, Bantam Books, 1977.

112 Fay Weldon, *Down Among the Women*, London, Heinemann, 1971, p. 118.

113 Ibid., p. 187.

114 Ibid., p. 118, p. 217; p. 233.

115 Ibid., p.118.

116 Fay Weldon, 'On the dangers of turning men into an underclass', *Mail on Sunday*, 4 May, 1997, p. 41.

117 Marsha Rowe, reporting on a conversation with Margaret Drabble, 2005, personal communication, op. cit.

118 Buchi Emecheta, *In the Ditch*, London, Allison & Busby, 1972.

119 Toni Cade Bambara (ed.), *The Black Woman: An Anthology*, New York, Signet, 1970; Mary Helen Washington (ed), *Black-Eyed Susans: Classic Stories By and About Black Women*, New York, Anchor Books, Doubleday, 1975.

120 Toni Morrison, *The Bluest Eye*, New York, Pocket Books, 1970; Toni Morrison, *Sula*, New York, Knopf, 1974; Toni Morrison, *Song of Solomon*, New York, Knopf, 1977.

121 Ntozake Shange, *For Colored Girls Who Have Considered Suicide/When the Rainbow is Enuf*, New York, Macmillan, 1975; Paula Marshall, *Brown Girl, Brownstones* [first published 1959], Chatham, New Jersey, Chatham Bookseller, 1972; Alice Walker, *In Love and Trouble: Stories of Black Women*, New York, Harcourt Brace Jovanovich, 1973; Alice Walker, *Meridian*, New

York, Harcourt Brace Jovanovich, 1976.

122 Amrit Wilson, *Finding a Voice: Asian Women in Britain*, London, Virago, 1979.

123 Joan Riley, *The Unbelonging*, London, The Women's Press, 1985.

124 Maya Angelou, *I Know Why the Caged Bird Sings*, London, Virago, 1984; *Maya Angelou, Gather Together in My Name*, London, Virago, 1985; Maya Angelou, *Singin' and Swingin' and Getting Merry Like Christmas*, London, Virago, 1985; Maya Angelou, *The Heart of a Woman*, London, Virago, 1986.

125 Alice Walker, *The Color Purple*, London, Women's Press, 1983.

126 Suniti Namjoshi, *Feminist Fables*, London, Sheba, 1981; Audre Lorde, *Zami; A New Spelling of My Name*, London, Sheba, 1983, italics in original, p. 225, p. 226.

127 Zora Neale Hurston, [from *World Tomorrow*, 1928.] 'How it Feels like to be Colored me', accessed http://people.whitman.edu/~hashimiy/zora.htm.

128 Zora Neale Hurston, *Their Eyes Were Watching God* [first published 1937], London, Virago, 1986; Zora Neale Hurston, *Dust Tracks on the Road* [first published 1942], London, Virago, 1986.

129 Liz Heron, for one, had published nothing before contributing to *Spare Rib* in the mid-1970s, and would later teach literacy and writing with working-class women in Hackney, East London; see Heron, *Changes of Heart*, op. cit., p.14, pp. 18–20.

130 Personal communication, written as critical commentary on reading a draft of this chapter.

131 Sue O'Sullivan, 'Feminists and Flourbombs', written for the documentary of this title, first shown on Channel 4 on 13 January, 2002, accessed http://www.channel4.com/history/ microsites/F/flourbombs/essay.html.

132 See 'Sisters in Despair', *Jewish Chronicle*, 20 May, 1983.

133 Letty Cottin Pogrebin, 'Anti-Semitism in the Women's Movement', *Ms*, June, 1982.

134 Sheila Saunders, 'That's Funny. You Don't Look Anti-Semitic' in Hannah Kantor et. al. (eds) *Sweeping Statements: Writings from the Women's Liberation Movement 1981–3*, London, Women's Press, 1984, p. 100; Diane Hudson, 'That's Funny. You Don't Look Jewish', in Kantor, et.al., p. 103.

135 Ibid.

136 Response to my questions.

137 Peter Gowan, *The Global Gamble*, London, Verso, 1999; Leo Panitch, 'The New Imperial State', *New Left Review*, no. 2, March–April 2000.

138 Mark Mazower, *Dark Continent: Europe's Twentieth Century*, Penguin, London, 1998, p. 357.

139 Svetlana Boym, *The Future of Nostalgia*, New York, Basic Books, 2001.

140 Sheila Rowbotham, *The Past Is Before Us: Feminism in Action since the 1960s*, London, Pandora, 1989.

141 Slavoj Zizek, *The Ticklish Subject: The Absent Centre of Political Ontology*, London, Verso, 1999, p. 218.

142 See, for example, Lynne Segal, 'Theoretical Afflictions: Rich White Folk Sing the Blues' *Remembering the 1990s: New Formations*, no. 50, 2003, pp. 142–56.

143 See Bill Schwarz, 'Poetics: a Polemic', in Jose Pachero (ed), *Theory and Culture: Essays in the Sociology of Culture*, Lund, University of Lund Press, 2000.

144 Aijaz Ahmad, 'Postcolonialism: What's in a name?' in Roman De La Campa and E. Ann Kaplan, (eds), *Late Imperial Culture*, Verso, London, 1995, p. 1.

145 See Kevin Robbins, 'What in the World is Going On?', in Paul du Gay, (ed), *Production of Culture/Cultures of Production*, Sage, London, 1997; John Kraniauskas, 'Globalization is Ordinary: The Transnationalization of Cultural Studies', *Radical Philosophy*, July/August, 1998, pp. 9–20.

146 See Lynne Segal, *Why Feminism: Gender, Psychology, Politics*, Cambridge, Polity Press, 1999, especially chapter 2 and chapter 7.

147 Kate Soper, responding to my questions.

148 Elsa Ferri, John Bynner and Michael Wadsworth, *Changing Britain, Changing Lives*, London, Bedford Way Papers, Institute of Education, University of London, 2003, pp. 143–6.

149 The term, as we have seen before, is that of Eric Hobsbawm, *Age of Extremes: The Short Twentieth Century*, op. cit.

150 Reply to my questions.

151 Again sent in reply to my questions.

152 Conversation in my feminist writers group.

153 Ibid.

154 Response to questions.

155 Sue O'Sullivan, 'Introduction', *I used to be a nice girl*, London, Cassell, 1996, p. viii.

156 Response to my questions.

157 Ibid.

Chapter 5

158 Sheila Rowbotham, *Promise of a Dream*, Penguin, Allen Lane, London, 2000.

159 Ibid., p. xv.

160 Ibid., p. xvii.

161 Ibid., p. 48.

162 Sheila Rowbotham, *Women's Consciousness, Man's World*, Harmondsworth, Penguin, 1971, p. 17.

163 Rowbotham, *Promise of a Dream*, p. 89.

164 Sheila Rowbotham, Lynne Segal and Hilary Wainwright, *Beyond the Fragments*, Merlin, London, 1980.

165 Sheila Rowbotham, *Woman's Consciousness*, p. 20.

166 Rowbotham, *Promise of a Dream*, p. 188.

167 Ibid., p. 190.

168 Ibid., p. 209.

169 Ibid., p. 252.

170 Ibid., p. 247.

171 Michael Rosen, 'All in the Family', in Phil Cohen, ed, *Children of the Revolution: Communist Childhood in Cold War Britain*, Lawrence and Wishart, London, 1997, p. 61. Martin Kettle recalls his father, Arnold Kettle, making much the same point, matter-of-factly, of the Cambridge spies, whom he knew in the Thirties: 'We thought Chamberlain was the traitor', Martin Kettle, 'Asking the Questions', ibid., p. 185.

172 Eric Hobsbawm, *Interesting Times: A Twentieth-Century Life*, London, Penguin, Allen Lane, 2002, p. 41.

173 Ibid., p. 134.

174 Ibid., p. 413.

175 Ibid., p. 418.

176 Raphael Samuel, 'Faith, Hope and Struggle: The Lost World of British Communism, Part One', *New Left Review*, no. 154, Nov/Dec, 1985, p. 11.

177 Ibid., p. 12, p. 11, p. 46.

178 See E. P. Thompson, *The Making of the English Working Class*, Harmondsworth, Penguin, 1963; Raymond Williams, *The Long Revolution*, Harmondsworth, Penguin, 1961.

179 See Stuart Hall, 'The First New Left' in *Out of Apathy: Voices of the New Left 30 Years On* (ed) The Oxford University Socialist Discussion Group, London, Verso, 1989, p. 33.

180 Raphael Samuel, 'Class Politics: The Lost World of British Communism,

Part Three', *New Left Review*, no. 165, Sept/October, 1987, p. 55; Samuel, 'Staying Power: The Lost World of British Communism, Part Two', *New Left Review*, no. 156, March/April, 1986, p. 35.

181 Samuel, 'Class Politics', 1987, p. 52.

182 Stuart Hall, *New Left Review*, January/February, 1997, reprinted in Raphael Samuel – 1934 – 1996, p. 68.

183 Stuart Hall, 'The Formation of a Diasporic Intellectual: An Interview with Stuart Hall, by Kuan-Hsing Chen' in *Stuart Hall: Critical Dialogues in Cultural Studies*, ed. David Morley and Kuan-Hsing Chen, London, Routledge, 1996, p. 485.

184 Ibid., p. 489.

185 Stuart Hall, in Stuart Hall and Bill Schwarz, Conversations with Stuart Hall, unpublished.

186 Hall, in Morley and Chen, eds, op. cit. p. 489 and p. 488.

187 Hall, in *Out of Apathy*, op. cit. p. 36.

188 Ibid., p. 36, p. 38.

189 Hall, in Morley and Chen, eds, op. cit. p. 500.

190 Ibid.

191 Stuart Hall, 'The great moving right show', *Marxism Today*, January, 1979, pp. 14–29.

192 Hall, in Morley and Chen, eds, op. cit. p. 153.

193 The expression is that of Edward Thompson in E. P. Thompson, *The Poverty of Theory & Other Essays*, Merlin, London, 1978, p. 76.

194 Terry Eagleton, *The Gatekeeper: A Memoir*, London, Allen Lane, Penguin, 2001, p. 93.

195 Hobsbawm quoting Brecht, in *Interesting Times*, op. cit. speaks of the thrill of these lines for his generation of communists, p. 139.

196 See, for instance, Yvonne Kapp's *Time Will Tell*, London and New York, Verso, 2003.

197 Yvonne Kapp, ibid.

198 Doris Lessing 'Afterword' to Olive Schreiner's *The Story of an African Farm* (1968) in Paul Shlueter, ed., *Doris Lessing: A Small Personal Voice – Essays, Reviews, Interviews*, Flamingo, London, 1994, pp. 162–3.

199 Doris Lessing, *Under My Skin: Volume One of My Autobiography, to 1949*, London, Harper Collins, 1995, p. 269.

200 Ibid., p. 205 and pp. 230–2.

201 Ibid., Lessing, *Walking in the Shade: Volume Two of My Autobiography, 1949–1962*, Harper Collins, London, 1997.

202 Even in her activist phase, Lessing wonders what people fighting 'for

what they feel, at the time, to be justice [has] got to do with political attitudes?', as she writes in a letter to her friend Edward Thompson in 1957, in Lessing, *Walking in the Shade*, p. 196.

203   Lessing, *Walking in the Shade*, p. 196.

204   Lessing, *Under My Skin*, p. 248 and p. 410; Lessing, *Walking in the Shade*, p. 347.

205   Quoted in Barbara Ellen, *The Observer*, 9 September, 2001, p. 2.

206   Lessing, *Under My Skin*, p. 205.

207   Ibid., p. 206.

208   Lessing, *Walking in the Shade*, p. 130.

209   Lessing, ibid., p. 262.

210   Ibid., p. 206; p. 186.

211   Ibid., p. 364.

212   Doris Lessing, *The Sweetest Dream*, London, Flamingo, 2001.

213   In personal conversation with Sarah Benton.

214   Lessing, *Walking in the Shade*, p. 315.

215   Quoted in Deidre Bair, *Simone de Beauvoir: A Biography*, Jonathan Cape, London, 1990, p. 617.

216   Simone de Beauvoir, *The Second Sex*, trans. H. M. Parshley, Picador, London, 1988, pp. 295, 29, 643, 328.

217   The four directly autobiographical volumes are: *Memoirs of a Dutiful Daughter*, Harmondsworth, Penguin Books, 1973; *The Prime of Life*, trans. Peter Green, Penguin Books, Harmondsworth, 1968; *Force of Circumstance*, trans. Richard Howard, Penguin Books, Harmondsworth, 1978; *All Said and Done*, Paragon House, New York, 1993.

218   Lisa Appignanesi, *Simone de Beauvoir*, London, Penguin, 1988, p. 2; Sylvia Lawson, *How Simone de Beauvoir dies in Australia*, Sydney, Australia, UNSW Press, 2002, pp. 153–4; Ann Curthoys, 'Adventures of Feminism: Simone de Beauvoir's Autobiographies, Women's Liberation and Self-Fashioning', *Feminist Review*, no. 64, 2000, p. 11; Margaret Walters, 'The Rights and Wrongs of Woman: Mary Wollstonecraft, Harriet Martineau, Simone de Beauvoir' in *The Rights and Wrongs of Woman*, eds Juliet Mitchell and Ann Oakley, Harmondsworth, Penguin, 1976, p. 351; Kate Millett, in *Daughters of de Beauvoir*, Penny Forster and Imogen Sutton eds, London, Women's Press, 1989, p. 20; Sheila Rowbotham, *Women's Consciousness, Man's World*, Harmondsworth, Penguin, 1973, p. 10; Judith Okely, *Simone de Beauvoir*, London, Virago, 1986, p. ix.

219   Beauvoir, The Second Sex, p.295.

220   Discussed in yet another reflection fascinating reflection on Beauvoir's legacy, Toril Moi, *Simone de Beauvoir: The Making of an Intellectual Woman*,

Oxford, Blackwell, 1994, pp. 181–5; Fouque quoted in Bair, op. cit., p. 553.

221 Angela Carter, 'Colette' in *Nothing Sacred*, London, Virago, 1982, p. 176.

222 Beauvoir, *Force of Circumstance*, p. 6.

223 Simone de Beauvoir, *The Ethics of Ambiguity*, trans. Frechtman, New York, Citadel, 1976, p. 37; *Prime of Life*, p. 26.

224 Beauvoir, *Force of Circumstance*, p. 199.

225 See Margaret Walters, 'The Rights and Wrongs of Woman', p. 369; Mary Evans, 'Lies, All Lies: Auto/biography as Fiction', in *Missing Person: The Impossibility of Auto/biography*, London, Routledge, 1999, p. 40.

226 *Moi*, Simone de Beauvoir, op. cit. p. 187.

227 Simone de Beauvoir, *Force of Circumstance*, p. 187; Beauvoir, *Force of Circumstance*, p. 260.

228 *Force of Circumstance*, pp. 619–20.

229 A famous line from Sartre's play *No Exit*, first performed in 1944, Jean-Paul Sartre, *No Exit and Three Other Plays*, New York, Vintage International, 1976.

230 *Force of Circumstance*, p. 511.

231 Ibid., p. 673.

232 Simone de Beauvoir, 'Today I've changed – I've really become a feminist', *Seven Days*, 8 March 1972, p. 3.

233 Simone de Beauvoir, *Old Age*, trans. Patrick O'Brian, Harmondsworth, Penguin, 1977, p. 12.

234 Beauvoir, *Force of Circumstance*, p. 656.

235 Lessing, *The Sweetest Dream*, Harper Collins, London, 2002; Simone de Beauvoir, *The Woman Destroyed*, Fontana, London, 1971.

236 Beauvoir, *All Said and Done*, pp. 63–4.

237 Jenny Diski, 'A Long Forgotten War', *London Review of Books*, 6 July 2000, pp. 9–10.

238 Rowbotham, *Promise of a Dream*, pp. 252–3.

Chapter 6

239 Joan Bakewell, 'At 70', the *Guardian*, 3 October, 2003.

240 Simone de Beauvoir, *Old Age* [1970], Harmondsworth, Penguin, 1978, p. 7.

241 Margaret Morganroth Gullette, *Aged by Culture*, Chicago and London, University of Chicago Press, 2004, p. 137.

242 Susan Sontag, 'The Double Standard of Aging', *Saturday Review*, September 1972, p. 37.

243   Sidonie-Gabrielle Colette, *Chéri* [1920], pt. 2, trans Janet Flanner, p. 19.

244   See Judith Thurman, *Secrets of the Flesh: A Life of Colette*, London, Bloomsbury, 1999, p. 304.

245   See Alex Kuczynski, *Beauty Junkies: Inside Our $15 Billion Obsession with Cosmetic Surgery*, New York, Doubleday Books, 2006.

246   J.-B. Pontalis, *Windows*, Nebraska, University of Nebraska Press, 2003, p. 41.

247   Philip Roth, *The Dying Animal*, London, Jonathan Cape, 2001, p. 47, p. 32. This novel condenses Roth's account of the sexual lives and sexual politics of contemporary life in urban USA, which almost all his books have set out to explore.

248   Jeffrey Wells, 'Mirror, Mirror', quoted in Vivian Sobchack's excellent essay, 'Scary Women: Cinema, Surgery and Special Effects', in her book, *Carnal Thoughts*, Berkeley and London, University of California Press, 2004, p. 41.

249   Australian Demographic Statistics 2002 Population Special Article , 'Who'll be Home Alone in 2021', http://www.abs.gov.au/; Population Profile of the United States: 2000 US, Census Bureau (Internet Release) 5–1. http://www.census.gov/population/pop-profile/2000/chap05.pdf, p. 1.

250   From the British Census, 2001.

251   Kathleen Kiernan and Ganka Mueller, 'The Divorced and Who Divorces?' Centre for Analysis of Social Exclusion, website: http://sticerd.lse.ac.uk/case.htm.

252   Daniel Kahneman, Alan B. Krueger, David A. Schkade, Norbert Schwarz, Arthur A. Stone, 'Survey Method for Characterizing Daily Life Experience: The Day Reconstruction Method', *Science*, vol. 306, no. 5702, pp. 1776–80.

253   Daniel Kahneman, et al, ibid.

254   Research and conclusions reported in M. Willitts, M. Benzevaland, S. Stansfeld, 'Partnership history and mental health over time', *Journal of Epidemiology and Community Health*, 2004, vol. 58, pp. 53–8.

255   John Ermisch, *The Economics of the Family: Applications to Divorce and Remarriage*, Discussion Paper no. 140, Centre for Economic Policy Research, November, 1986.

256   Marilyn French, *The Women's Room* [1977], London, Abacus, 1993, back cover.

257   Ibid., p. 7.

258   Ibid., new introduction to 1993 edition, French, p. xv.

259   Ibid., p. xiii.

260   Angela Carter, *The Sadeian Woman*, London, Virago, 1979, p. 56.

261 Angela Carter, 'Notes from the Front Line'(1983), in *Shaking a Leg: Collected Journalism and Writing*, London, Vintage, 1998, p. 40, p. 38.

262 Reported in Grace Paley, *Just as I Thought*, London, Virago, 1999, p. 252.

263 Ibid., p. 285.

264 Ibid., pp. 286–8.

265 Ibid., Dedication and Thank Yous.

266 Anja Meulenbelt, *The Shame is Over: A Political Life Story*, London, The Women's Press, 1980, pp. 158–9.

267 Ibid., p. 13.

268 Anja Meulenbelt, *For Ourselves: Our Bodies and Sexuality – From Women's point of View*, London, Sheba Press, 1981, p. 7, p. 95.

269 Lynne Segal, 'Sensual uncertainty, or why the clitoris is not enough', in Sue Cartledge and Joanna Ryan (eds) *Sex and Love*, London, The Women's Press, 1983.

270 Alan Sinfield, 'Ideology and Commitment: A Personal Account', new introduction to *Cultural Politics – Queer Reading*, University of Pennsylvania Press and Routledge, 1994, 2004.

271 Janet Hobhouse, *The Furies*, London, Bloomsbury, 1992, p. 1, p. 5.

272 Barbara Ellen, 'Swing out spinster', the *Observer*, 6 January, 2002, p. 6. Statistics from US Census Bureau, 2003.

273 Quoted in Liz Heron, *Changes of Heart: Reflections on Women's Independence*, London, Pandora, p. 42.

274 Sue O'Sullivan, 'Menopause Waltz', in *I Used to be a Nice Girl*, London, Cassell, 1996, p. 62.

275 Alix Kates Shulman, *Burning Questions*, New York, Bantam 1979, p. vii.

276 Emily Dickinson, *Resurgam*, in *The Collected Poems of Emily Dickinson*, Part Four, Time and Eternity, New York, Barnes & Noble Books, 2004.

277 Alix Kates Shulman, *Drinking the Rain: a Memoir*, New York, Farrar Straus Giroux, 1995, pp. 5–7.

278 May Sarton, *Journal of a Solitude*, New York, W. W. Norton, 1973; *At Seventy: a Journal*, New York, W. W. Norton, 1984.

279 See Carl Gustav Jung, 'Youth and Age', in J. Jacobi and R. F. C. Hull (eds), C. G. Jung: *Psychological reflections*, Princeton, New Jersey, Bollingen, 1978.

280 Vivian Gornick, *Approaching Eye Level*, Boston, Mass., Beacon Press, p. 67.

281 Ibid., p. 138.

282 Denise Riley, 'Knowing in the real world', in *Denise Riley, Selected Poems*, London: Reality Street Editions, 2000, p. 54.

283 Gornick, op. cit., p. 140.

284 Liz Heron, op cit., p. 75.

285 Doris Lessing, *Under My Skin: Volume One of My Autobiography, to 1949*, London, Flamingo, 1995, p. 205.

286 All Anne Sexton's poems, including 'The Housewife', can be found in Anne Sexton *The Complete Poems*, with a foreword by Maxine Kumin, Boston, Houghton Mifflin, 1981.

287 Anne Sexton, 'Old', ibid.

288 Lillian S. Robinson, 'Doing what comes socio-culturally', *Women's Review Of Books*, vol. VXII, no. 7, April, 1995, p. 12, p. 11.

289 Lynne Segal, *Straight Sex: The Politics of Pleasure*, London, Virago, p. 68.

290 Ann E. Gerike, 'On Gray Hair and Oppressed Brains', in *Women, Aging and Ageism*, Evelyn Rosenthal (ed.) New York, Haworth, 1990, p. 35.

291 Vivian Sobchack, 'Cinema, Surgery, and Special Effects' in *Carnal Knowledge*, op. cit., p. 38.

292 Carol Ann Duffy, 'Medusa', *The World's Wife*, London, Picador, 1999, pp. 40–1.

293 Richard Dawkins, *The Selfish Gene*, London, Penguin, 1976; Wilson, *On Human Nature*, Cambridge, Mass., Harvard University Press, 1978; David Buss, *The Evolution of Desire: Strategies of Human Mating*, London, Harper Collins, 1994.

294 See, for example, Donna Haraway, *Primate Visions: Gender, Race and Nature in the World of Modern Science*, London and New York, Routledge, 1989.

295 Ernest Jones, Peter Gay, *Freud: A Life for Our Time*, London, Macmillan, Papermac, 1989, pp. 104; 134; 156; 218–9; 310; 369–70; 387.

296 Sigmund Freud, 'The Predisposition to Obsessional Neurosis', *Collected Papers*, Ernest Jones (ed.), trans. Joan Riviere, vol. 1, London, Hogarth, 1950, p. 130.

297 Dinora Pines, 'Sexuality and the Older Woman', talk given at the Freud Museum, London, 19 October, 1996, available online: http://www.freud.org.uk/aging.htm.

298 See, for example, Sonu Shamdasani and Michael Munchow (eds), *Speculations After Freud: Psychoanalysis, Philosophy and Culture*, London, Routledge, 1994; Susan Fairfield, Lynne Layton and Carolyn Stack (eds), *Bringing the Plague: Towards a* Postmodern Psychoanalysis, New York, Other Press, 2002.

299 Muriel Dimen, 'Perversion Is Us?: Eight Notes' in Muriel Dimen, *Sexuality, Intimacy, Power*, New Jersey, London, The Analytic Press, 2003, p. 257.

300 David L. Eng and Shinhee Han, 'A Dialogue of Racial Melancholia' in *Bringing the Plague: Towards a Postmodern Psychoanalysis*, Susan Fairfield, Lynne Layton and Carolyn Stack (eds), New York, Other Press, 2002, pp. 233–68.

301 Susan Fairfield, et. al. (eds), ibid.

302 Angela Carter, *Wise Children*, London, Chatto & Windus, 1991.

303 Ursula Owen, 'When the Machinery Stops Working', in Joanna Goldsworthy (ed.), *A Certain Age: Reflecting on the Menopause*, Virago, London, 1993, p. 88.

304 Germaine Greer, *The Change: Women, Ageing and the Menopause*, London, Hamish Hamilton, 1991, pp. 2–4; pp. 433–5.

305 Ibid., p. 62.

306 Eva Figes, 'Coming to terms', in Goldsworthy (ed.), op. cit. p. 145.

307 Betty Friedan, *Fountain of Age*, New York, Simon & Schuster, 1993.

308 Susan Sontag, 'The Double Standard of Aging', *Saturday Review*, September 1972, p. 36.

309 Quoted in 'Finding fact from fiction', the *Guardian*, 27 May, 2000, http://www.guardian.co.uk/Books/departments/generalfiction/story/0,283623,00.html as retrieved on 15 August 2006.

310 Sara Maitland, 'On becoming a fairy godmother: role models for the menopausal woman', in Goldsworthy (ed.) op. cit., p. 208.

311 See, for example, Doreen Asso, *The Real Menstrual Cycle*, New York, John Wiley, 1983.

312 'Germaine Greer: Feminist Icon', *Radio National*, features, downloaded from web, www.tv.cbc.ca/national/pgminfo/greer

313 Germaine Greer, *The Boy*, London, Thames & Hudson, 2003, p. 8.

314 Emma Brockes, interview with Hanif Kureishi, 'When you're writing, you look for conflict', the *Guardian*, 17 November, 2003, pp. 4–5.

315 Cherry Potter, 'Sex and the older woman' the *Guardian*, 23 February, 2004, p. 16.

316 Tara Brabazon, 'The Spectre of the Spinster: Bette Davis and the Epistemology of the Self', *Hecate*, January 2001; see also Linda Williams, 'When the Woman Looks', in *The Dread of Difference: Gender and the Horror Film*, Barry Keith Grant (ed.), Austin, University of Texas Press.

317 Jane Juska, *A Round-Heeled Woman*, London, Chatto & Windus, 2003, p. 120.

318 Joan Nestle, 'A Change of Life', *A Restricted Country: Essays and Short Stories*, London, Sheba, 1986, p. 131.

319 Joan Nestle, *A Fragile Union*, Cleis Press, San Francisco, California, 1998, p. 10.

320 Co-founding and for decades curating the Lesbian Herstory Archives in New York, Nestle fought not just for recognition of love between women as part of the historical imagination, but for the fullest appreciation of the

beauty and diversity of lesbian lives throughout the years.

321 Judith Butler, comment made in her talk, 'Forgotten Histories of Post-Zionism: Critical Jewish Approaches', 30 September 2004, at Birkbeck College, University of London.

322 Vivian Gornick, 'The House of Elder Artists: The Challenge of Making a Daydream into Reality', *Women's Review of Books*, July 2003: available www.wellesley.edu/WomensReview/backiss.html.

323 Personal communication.

324 Simone de Beauvoir, *Old Age*, Harmondsworth, Penguin Books, 1970, p. 601.

325 D. W. Winnicott, *Home is Where We Start From: Essays by a Psychoanalyst*, London, Penguin, 1986.

Chapter 7

326 'They have no roots, they are rootless cosmopolitans – there can be nothing worse than that', Ben-Gurion said of non-Zionist Jews, as quoted in Isaac Deutscher, 'Israel's Spiritual Climate' in *The Non-Jewish Jew and Other Essays*, London, Merlin, 1981, p. 92.

327 Jenny Bourne, 'Homelands of the Mind: Jewish Feminism and Identity Politics' in *Jewish Feminism and Identity Politics, Race & Class*, vol. xxxix, 1987, p. 4. Bourne is known primarily as a feminist anti-racist campaigner in Britain.

328 On the very first convict ship was the sixteen-year-old Esther Abrahams, later to became the unofficial first lady of New South Wales as the de facto convict wife of Lieutenant Johnston, after he overthrew Governor William Bligh in 1808.

329 See Suzanne D. Rutland, *Seventy Five Years: The History of a Jewish Newspaper*, Sydney, The Australian Jewish Historical Society, November 1970, pp. 9–10, Suzanne D. Rutland, *Pages of History: A Century of the Australian Jewish Press*, Sydney, Australian Jewish Press Ltd, 1995, p. 29; Hilary Rubinstein and W. D. Rubinstein, *The Jews in Australia: A Thematic History*, Melbourne, William Heinemann, 1991, pp. 81–9; pp. 181–2.

330 Paul R. Bartrop, 'Living Within the Frontier: Early Colonial Australia, Jews, and Aborigines', in *Jewries at the Frontier*, Sander Gilman and Milton Shain (eds), Urbana and Chicago, University of Illinois Press, p. 106.

331 Quoted in Bartrop, ibid., p. 97. Although the reasons for the destruction of Aboriginal people and culture have recently been disputed the careless contempt for their fate by the new settlers remains undeniable.

332 The Argos, 4 January 1962, quoted in Alan Crown, 'The Initiatives and Influences in the Development of Australian Zionism, 1850–1948',

Australian Jewish Historical Society, vol.viii, 1979, part 6, p. 330.

333 See for example Gil Anidjar (ed.) *Acts of Religion*, New York and London, Routledge, 2002, especially Jacques Derrida, 'Hospitality', pp. 356–420.

334 See Michael Liffman, *A Tradition of Giving: Seventy-Five years of Myer Family Philanthropy*, Melbourne, Melbourne University Press, 2004.

335 See Jon Stratton, 'The Color of Jews: Jews, Race, and the White Australia Policy', in Gilman and Shain (eds), op. cit.

336 Crown, op. cit., p. 320.

337 Bernard Gainer, *The Alien Invasion: The Origin of the Alien Act of 1905*, 1972, p. 116, as quoted in Brian Klug, 'The Collective Jew: Israel and the New Antisemitism', *Patterns of Prejudice*, June 2003, p. 127.

338 See Herzl's comment on the effect on him of the Dreyfus trial, which he covered as a journalist: 'In Paris, as I have noted, I achieved a freer attitude towards anti-Semitism, which I now began to understand historically and to pardon. Above all, I recognized the futility of trying to "combat" anti-Semitism.' Theodor Herzl, *The Diaries of Theodor Herzl*, London, Gollancz, 1958, p. 6. I am grateful to Moshé Machover for this reference.

339 Ibid., p.18.

340 All quotes taken from Rutland, 1970, op. cit. pp. 53–5.

341 Hélène Cixous, *Portrait of Derrida as a Young Jewish Saint*, New York, Columbia University Press, 2001, p. vii.

342 For a description of the 'whitening' of Jews in the USA, with certain parallels with Australia, see Karen Brodkin, *How Jews Became White Folks And What That Says About Race In America*, New Brunswick, Rutgers University Press, 1998.

343 See for example Peter Novick, *The Holocaust in American Life*, New York, Houghton Mifflin, 1999.

344 Fay Zwicky, *Hostages*, Fremantle, Fremantle Arts Centre Press, 1983.

345 Germaine Greer, *Daddy We Hardly Knew You*, London, Hamish Hamilton, 1989, pp. 7–8.

346 Personal communication.

347 See Breitman, R. and Kraut, A. M., *American Refugee Policy and European Jewry, 1933–1945*, Bloomington, Indiana University Press, 1987.

348 Dick van Galen and Rolf Wolfswinkel, *Anne Frank and After, Dutch Holocaust Literature in Historical Perspective*, Amsterdam, Amsterdam University Press, 1996, pp. 143–4; p. 10.

349 Paul Brickhill, *The Great Escape*, New York, Norton, 1950; Brickhill, *Reach for the Sky: The Story of Douglas Bader, Legless Ace of the Battle of Britain*, London, Collins, 1954.

350 Gillian Rose uses this term 'Holocaust piety' to point to the failings of the recent memorialization of the Holocaust, which does not wish to portray the inhumanity and complicity of the world at large, or its actual effects on the many who died and those few who survived the death camps. See Rose *Judaism and Modernity: Philosophical Essays*, Oxford, Blackwell, 1993. For a specific discussion of 'Holocaust piety' see 'Beginnings of the Day: Fascism and Representation' in Bryan Cheyette and Laura Marcus (eds), *Modernity, Culture and 'the Jew'*, Oxford, Polity Press, 1998, pp. 242–3.

351 See, especially, Andreas Huyssen, *Present Pasts: Urban Palimpsests and the Politics of Memory*, Stanford, Stanford University Press, 2003.

352 Ian Thomson, *Primo Levi*, London, Hutchinson, 2002; Carole Angier, *The Double Bond: Primo Levi, a Biography*, London, Viking, 2002.

353 Paul Steinberg, *Speak You Also: A Survivor's Reckoning*, London, Allen Lane, Penguin Books, 2001, p. 158.

354 Greet van Amstel, 'There was no Darkness on the Earth', quoted in van Galen and Wolfswinkel, op. cit. p. 128.

355 Isaac Deutscher, 'The Non-Jewish Jew' in *The Non-Jewish Jew and Other Essays*, London, Merlin Press, 1981, p. 37.

356 Tony Kushner, *The Holocaust and the Liberal Imagination*, Oxford, Basil Blackwell, 1994; see also Anton Gill, *The Journey Back from Hell*, London, Grafton, 1988, and James Young, *The Texture of Memory*, Newhaven, Connecticut, Yale University Press, 1993.

357 Anne Karpf, *The War After: Living with the Holocaust*, London, Heinemann, 1996, p. 149; see also Tony Kushner, *The Holocaust and the Liberal Imagination*, Oxford, Basil Blackwell, 1994.

358 'They have no roots, they are rootless cosmopolitans – there can be nothing worse than that,' Isaac Deutscher reports Ben-Gurion speaking these words when describing non-Zionist Jews. See Deutscher, 'Israel's Spiritual Climate' in *The Non-Jewish Jew and Other Essays*, London, Merlin, 1981, p. 92.

359 Tom Segev, *The Seventh Million: The Israelis and the Holocaust*, trans. Haim Watzman, New York, Henry Holt, 2000.

360 Grossman, quoted in Anne Karpf, *The War After: Living with the Holocaust*, London, Heinemann, 1996, p. 329.

361 Idith Zertal, *Israel's Holocaust and the Politics of Nationhood*, Cambridge, Cambridge University Press, 2005 (published in Hebrew the previous year as *Death and the Nation: History, Memory, Politics*).

362 Yosef Grodzinsky, *In the Shadow of the Holocaust: The Struggle Between Jews and the Zionists in the Aftermath of World War II*, San Francisco, California, Common Courage Press, 2004.

363 Anne Karpf, 'Mass emigration to that foreign country, the past', *Jewish*

Chronicle, 28 July 2000, p. 12.

364　Norman G. Finkelstein, *The Holocaust Industry*, London and New York, Verso. See also Peter Novick, *The Holocaust in American Life*, Boston, Houghton, Mufflin, 1999.

365　Eva Hoffman, *After Such Knowledge: Memory, History, and the Aftermath of the Holocaust*, London, Secker & Warburg, 2004, p. 177.

366　Stanley Cohen, *States of Denial: Knowing about Atrocities and Suffering*, Cambridge, Polity, 2001, p. 50.

367　See Susan Varga, 'The Gift of Tongues', *The Griffith Review, Our Global Face: Inside the Australian Diaspora*, Edition 6 , summer, 2004.

368　See for example Dan Cohn-Sherbok, *Modern Judaism*, London, Macmillan, 1996.

369　See for example Jon Stratton, *Coming Out Jewish: Constructing Ambivalent Identities*, London and New York, Routledge, 2000.

370　Esther Benbassa and Jean-Christophe Attias, *The Jews and Their Future: A Conversation on Jewishness and Jewish Identity*, London, Zed Books, 2004, p. 115.

371　Stratton, op. cit., p. 241; see also Jeremy Rosen and David Herman, 'What is Jewish culture?: a debate', *The Jewish Quarterly*, vol. 50, no. 2 (190), Summer 2003, pp. 35–9.

372　The statement is attributed to Ilya Ehrenburg, the strictly secular communist writer in mid-twentieth-century Russia who, despite his Popular Front humanism, mysteriously managed to escape the Soviet purges. See Sabby Sagall, 'Zionism and Anti-Semitism: The Jewish Question', *Socialist Review*, July 2002.

373　See Stephen Froth, *Hate and the Jewish Science: Anti-Semitism, Nazism and Psychoanalysis*, London, Palgrave, 2005, p. 211; Slavoj Zizek, *The Plague of Fantasies*, London, Verso, 1997, p. 76.

374　Quoted in Bernard Susser, 'The Ideology of Affliction', in *Diasporas and Exiles*, ed. Howard Wettstein, Berkeley, University of California Press, 2002, p. 222.

375　See Susser, ibid., pp. 221–2.

376　Jean-Paul Sartre, *Anti-Semite and Jew*, trans George Becker, New York, Schoken Books, 1965, p. 143. This was first published in France in 1946 as *Reflections on the Jewish Question*, and the year before, in a shorter essay in *Temps Modernes*, as 'Portrait of the Anti-Semite'.

377　Simone de Beauvoir, *The Second Sex*, trans. H. M. Parshley, Picador, London, 1988.

378　Sartre, op. cit., p. 153. The free man, Sartre continued, is the person who knows he is not free until every Jew in the world can 'enjoy the fullness of their rights'. Hannah Arendt, *The Jew as Pariah: Jewish Identity and Politics in the Modern Age*, ed. Ron Feldman, New York, Grove Press, 1978. Most recently, Lyotard expressed a contemporary (designated 'postmodern') version of much the same thesis, describing Jews as the inescapable 'other' of modernity. Jean-Francois Lyotard, *Heidegger and "the jews"*, Minneapolis, University of Minnesota Press, 1990, p. 22.

379   Landzmann, quoted in Pierre Vidal-Naquet, 'Remembrances of a 1946 reader', *October*, vol. 87, Winter, 1999, p. 7.

380   Robert Misrahi, trans. Carol Marks, 'Sartre and the Jews: a Felicitous Misunderstanding' in *October*, ibid., p .62.

381   Buhle, Paul, 'The Hollywood Blacklist and the Jew: An Exploration of Popular Culture', *Tikkun* 1995 vol. 10, no. 5; Clancy Sigal, 'Hollywood During The Great Fear', *Present Tense*, 1982, vol. 9 (3), pp. 45–8; Marjorie Garber and Rebecca L. Walkowitz (eds), *Secret Agents, The Rosenberg Case, McCarthyism and Fifties America*, Routledge, New York and London, 1995.

382   See Arthur Liebman, 'The Ties that Bind: Jewish Support for the Left in the United States' in Ezra Mendelsohn (ed.) *Essential Papers on Jews and the Left*, New York, New York University Press, 1995.

383   Anthony Lerman, 'Sense on Antisemitism', *Prospect*, August 2000, p. 16.

384   See, for example, Leslie Fiedler, *To the Gentiles*, New York, Stein & Day, 1972; Michael Rogin, *Blackface, White Noise: Jewish Immigrants in the Hollywood Melting Pot*, Berkeley, University of California Press, 1998; Buhle, Paul, *From the Lower East Side to Hollywood: Jews in American Popular Culture*, New York, Verso, 2004; J. Hoberman, *The Dream Life: Movies, Media and the Mythology of the Sixties*, New Press, 2003.

385   Leslie Fiedler, Preface to *Fiedler on the Roof, Essays on Literature and Jewish Identity*, Boston, Godine, 1991.

386   See Daniel Snowman, *The Hitler Emigrés: The Cultural Impact on Britain of Refugees from Nazism*, London, Chatto & Windus, 2002; Snowman, 'The Hitler émigrés: the cultural impact on Britain of refugees from Nazism', *Historical Research*, vol. 77, issue 197, August 2004; Malachi Haim Hacohen, *Karl Popper – The Formative Years, 1902–1945: Politics and Philosophy in Interwar Vienna*, North Carolina, Duke University, 2002. See also Perry Anderson, 'Components of the National Culture', *New Left Review*, no. 50, July–August 1968, pp. 18-20.

387   See Michael Staub, *Torn at the Roots: The Crisis of Jewish Liberalism in Postwar America*, New York, Columbia University Press, 2002, p. 2.

388   Naomi Schor, 'Anti-Semitism, Jews and the Universal', *October*, vol. 87, Winter 1999, p. 116.

389   Until the 1950s Jews were the only significant non-Christian community, whereas today the Muslim population is seven times larger than the estimated Jewish presence. See David Cesarani, 'Anti-Zionist Politics and

Political Anti-Semitism in England, 1920–1924', *Patterns of Prejudice*, vol. 23:1, 1989, pp. 28–45.

390   New EU Monitoring Centre Report 'Manifestations of Anti-Semitism in the EU 2002-2003', http://eumc.eu.int/eumc/ index.php.

391   Rabbi Naftali Schiff said of the attack on a synagogue in North London, 'the destruction recalled Germany's Kristallnacht in 1938'; Lord Janner, president of the Parliamentary committee against anti-Semitism said it reminded him of what he 'had seen years ago as a war crimes investigator in Germany', as reported in Elizabeth Hopkirk, 'Priceless books ruined by arson at synagogue', *Evening Standard*, 21 June, 2004, p. 19.

392   D. D. Guttenplan, 'Letter From London', *The Nation*, 13 June, 2002, p.14.

393   These figures are collected annually by The Community Security Trust National Press Office, http://www.thecst.org.uk/docs/Incidents_Report_05.pdf.

394   See Hugh Muir, 'Report reveals hierarchy of hate', the *Guardian*, 7 March, 2005, p. 8.

395   Jamie Doward, 'Jews predict record level of hate attacks … Jewish groups … accuse the government of inaction', the *Observer*, 8 August, 2004, p. 7; Richard Jinman, 'Anti-Semitic attacks rise to a record level', the *Guardian*, 11 February, 2005, p. 9.

396   Cohn-Sherbok, for an interesting account by an Orthodox Jew, see Stephen Frosh, 'Fundamentalism, Gender and Family Therapy', *After Words: The Personal in Gender, Culture and Psychotherapy*, London, Palgrave, 2002.

397   David Cesarani, 'Anti-Zionist Politics and Political Anti-Semitism in England, 1920–1924', *Patterns of Prejudice*, vol. 23:1, 1989, pp. 28–45.

398   Persecution was not such a significant phenomenon for the Jews of the Ottoman Empire, but Sephardic history and culture, with its links to the Arab-Islamic universe, has been till now largely obliterated by the European Ashkenazi narrative of of anti-Semitism and the Holocaust. See Ella Shohat, 'Rupture and Return: Zionist Discourse and the Study of Arab Jews', *Social Text*, vol. 21, no 2, Summer 2003.

399   Quoted in Antony Lerman, 'Sense on Anti-Semitism', *Prospect*, August 2002, p. 9. Emphasis added.

400   Phyllis Chesler, *The New Anti-Semitism: The Current Crisis and What We Must Do About It*, San Francisco, Jossey-Bass, 2003, p. 3.

401   Abraham Foxman, *Never Again? The Threat of the New Anti-Semitism*, New York, Harper Collins, 2003, quoted in Brian Klug, 'The Myth of the New Anti-Semitism', *The Nation*, 2 February, 2004. See also Alan Dershowitz, *The Case for Israel*, New York, John Wiley & Sons, 2003.

402   See Klug, ibid.

403   See almost all the essays in Paul Iganski and Barry Kosmin, (eds) *A New Antisemitism? Debating Judeophobia in 21st Century Britain*, London, Profile Books, 2003.

404   This in-depth survey of thousands of British Jews was undertaken by Steven Cohen and Keith Kahn-Harris, reported in Simon Rocker, 'Minority support for Sharon among British Jews' *Jewish Chronicle*, 18 June, 2004. I am grateful to Irene Bruegel and Richard Kuper for drawing my attention to it.

405   Greg Philo and Mike Berry, *Bad News from Israel*, London, Pluto Press, 2004. See also Graham Usher, *Dispatches from Palestine: the Rise and Fall of the Oslo Peace Process*, London, Pluto Press, 1999.

406   Egon Mayer, Barry Kosmin and Ariela Keysar, *American Jewish Identity Survey, 2001*, New York, The Graduate Center of the City University of New York, available http://www.gc.cuny.edu/studies/ajis.pdf.

407   Jennifer Senior, 'Columbia's Own Middle East War', *New York Magazine* 17 January, 2005, p. 12.

408   See Dan Cohn-Sherbok, *Modern Judaism*, op. cit. pp. 178–81.

409   See Brian Klug, 'The Collective Jew: Israel and the new anti-Semitism', *Patterns of Prejudice*, vol. 37, no. 2, June 2003.

410   Peter Loewenberg, 'Theodor Herzl: Nationalism and Politics' in *Decoding the Past: The Psychohistorical Approach*, New York, Alfred A. Knopf, 1983, p. 120.

411   George Mosse, *Confronting the Nation: Jewish and Western Nationalism*, New England, Brandeis University Press, 1993; also Daniel Boyarin, 'The Colonial Drag: Zionism, Gender, and Mimicry' in *Unheroic Conduct: The Rise of Heterosexuality and the Invention of the Jewish Man*, Berkeley, University of California Press, 1997; Jonathan Boyarin, *Palestine and Jewish History: Criticism at the Borders of Ethnography*, Minneapolis, London, University of Minnesota Press, 1996.

412   Jacqueline Rose, *The Question of Zion*, Princeton and Oxford, Princeton University Press, 2005.

413   See Avi Schlaim, 'Collusion across the Jordan and the Debate about 1948', *International Journal of Middle East Studies*, vol. 27, no. 3, August 1995; Simha Flapan, *The Birth of Israel: Myths and Realities*, New York, Pantheon Books, 1987; Zeev Sternhell, *The Founding Myths of Israel: Nationalism, Socialism and the Making of the Jewish State*, Princeton, Princeton University Press, 1998; Ilan Pappé, *The Making of the Arab–Israeli Conflict, 1948–1951*, London, Routledge, 1992; Ilan Pappé, *The Israel/Palestine Question*, London, Routledge, 1999. Although he is today a passionate Zionist, these arguments were also supported in the historical work of Benny Morris, for example, his *The Birth of the Palestinian Refugee Problem 1947–1949*, Cambridge, Cambridge University Press, 1987. In a hideous twist of fate,

the worst massacre, at Deir Yassin, now sits alongside the present site of Yad Vashem, the Holocaust Museum, commemorating not the massacre of Palestinians, by Jews, nearby, but of Jews slaughtered in a distant land.

414 Jacqueline Rose, *The Question of Zion*, New Jersey, Princeton University Press, 2005.

415 See Oren Yiftachel, '"Ethnocracy": The Politics of Judaizing Israel/Palestine', *Constellations*, vol. 6, September 1999; Gershon Shafir and Yoav Peled, *Being Israeli: The Dynamics of Multiple Citizenship*, Cambridge, Cambridge University Press, 2002; Nadim N. Rouhana, *Palestinian Citizens in an Ethnic Jewish State: Identities in Conflict*, New Haven,1997; Baruch Kimmerling, 'Religion, Nationalism, and Democracy in Israel', *Constellations*, vol. 6, September 1999; Avi Schlaim, *The Iron Wall: Israel and the Arab World*, London, Allen Lane, Penguin, 2000.

416 Shulamit Aloni, 'Pre-Messianic Pangs', trans. Sol Salbe from Ynet (29/07/04), the website associated with *Yediot Acharonot*, Israel's largest circulating daily. http://www.ynet.co.il/home/0,7340,L-392,00.html.

417 See Zertal, op. cit.

418 Oren Yiftachel, 'Contradictions and Dialectics: Reshaping Political Space in Israel/Palestine: An Indirect Response to Lina Jamoul', *Antipode*, vol. 36, no. 4, September 2004, p. 607.

419 Eyad Sarraj, 'Bombs and madness: understanding terror', *Index on Censorship*, vol. 4, 2001, p. 7.

420 Deutscher, 'Israel's Tenth Birthday', in *The Non-Jewish Jew*, op. cit., p. 12.

421 See, for example, Avi Shlaim, *The Iron Wall*, op. cit.

422 Mitchell Pitnick, 'Reclaiming the Struggle Against Anti-Semitism' in *Reframing Anti-Semitism*, Jewish Voice for Peace Publication, pp. 8–9. While it is the Left that gets attacked nowadays for its 'unholy alliance' with radical Islam over its support for Palestinian rights, it was the US state department and corporate capital that for decades propped up the ultra reactionary Wahabi sect in Saudi Arabia, funded Islamic fundamentalist forces in Afghanistan, for years tolerating, if not encouraging, Osama bin Laden. Meanwhile, it is the US-led intervention in Iraq that has brought an Islamicist government to power there and contributed to the rise of Mahmud Ahmadinejad in Iran. See Ahmed Rashid, *Taliban: Militant Islam, Oil and Fundamentalism in Central Asia*, New Haven, Yale University Press, 2000; Graham Usher, 'The Sadr Revolt', *Red Pepper*, 1 May, 2004, p. 6.

423 See, for example, Oren Yiftachel, 'Ethnocracy and its discontents: Minority Protest in Israel', *Critical Inquiry*, vol. 26, pp. 725–56.

424 Mirjam Hadar, 'On having a voice', talk delivered in Jerusalem, October 2005.

425   See Nachman Ben-Yehuda, *The Masada Myth*, Amherst, New York,
      Humanity Books (imprint of Prometheus Books), 2002.

426   Akiva Eldar, 'From refuge for Jews to danger for Jews', *Ha'aretz Daily*, 3
      November, 2003, http://www.geocities.com/munichseptember1972/
      from_refuge_for_jews.htm, accessed 29 July, 2004.

427   See Mazin Qumsiyeh, *Sharing the Land of Canaan*, London, Pluto Press,
      2004; Catherine Cook, Adam Hanieh and Adah Kay, *Stolen Youth*, London,
      Pluto Press, 2004.

428   Joel Kovel, 'Zionism's Bad Conscience', *Tikkun* Magazine, vol 17, no. 5,
      Sept/Oct, 2002, www.tikkun.org/Magazine/index.cfm.

429   Afif Safieh, then Director of the Office of Representation of the PLO in
      London, in a letter to the Pope, written on 7 October, 1997,
      http://www.al-bushra.org/vatican/safieh.htm, accessed 12 August, 2004.

430   Edward Said, 'New History, Old Ideas' (1998), reprinted in *The Challenge
      of Post-Zionism: Alternatives to Israeli Fundamentalist Politics*, ed. Ephraim
      Nimni, Zed Books, London and New York, 2003, p. 202.

431   Zygmunt Baumann, *Liquid Modernity*, Cambridge, Polity Press, 2000.

432   Benbassa and Attias, op. cit., p. 51.

433   For an interesting survey of Jews in the USA, see Anna Greenberg and
      Kenneth D. Wald, 'Still liberal after all these years? The contemporary
      political behavior of American Jewry', in *Jews in American Politics*, Sandy
      Maisel and Ira N. Forman (eds), p. 163.

434   See, for example, Shawn Twing, 'A Comprehensive Guide to US Aid to
      Israel,' *Washington Report on Middle East Affairs*, April 1996.

435   Bruce Robbins, 'On Solidarity at a Distance', A talk delivered at the
      Franklin Humanties Institute at Duke University, 1 March, 2004.

436   Judith Butler, 'No, it's not Anti-Semitic', *London Review of Books*, 21 August
      2003, p. 5.

Chapter 8

437   As Walter Benjamin famously wrote, in his essay on photography, 'The
      beholder feels an irresistible urge to search ... to find the inconspicuous
      spot where in the immediacy of that long forgotten moment the future
      subsists so eloquently that we, looking back, may rediscover it', 'A Small
      History of Photography', in *One-way Street and Other Essays*, London, New
      Left Books, 1979, p. 243.

438   Simone de Beauvoir, *Force of Circumstance*, p. 276.

439   Eric Hobsbawm, *Interesting Times*, p. 57.

440 Eric Hobsbawm, *Age of Extremes: The Short Twentieth Century*, London, Abacus, 1995, pp. 257–344.

441 See Susan J. Creighton, 'Prevalence and incidence of child abuse: international comparisons', NSPCC Research Department, April 2004.

442 K. Shook, 'Does the Loss of Welfare Income Increase the Risk of Involvement with the Child Welfare System?' *Children and Youth Services Review*, vol. 21, 1999, pp. 781–814; A. Sherman et al., 'Welfare to what? Early findings on family hardship and well-being.' Washington, DC, Children's Defense Fund, 1998.

443 Sarah Benton, 'Critical Intellectuals in the post-socialist world', *Soundings*, issue 27, Autumn 2004, p. 14, pp.10–11.

444 Edmund Burke, *Reflections on the Revolution in France and on the Proceedings in Certain Societies in London Relative to That Event* [first pub. 1790], Harmondsworth, Penguin, 1968, p. 211.

445 Ibid., pp. 194–5; see also David Musselwhite, 'Reflections on Burke's Reflections' in *The Enlightenment and its Shadows*, Peter Hulme and Ludmilla Jordanova (eds), London, Routledge, 1990.

446 John Laughland, 'The Chechen's American friends', the *Guardian*, 8 September 2004, p. 23.

447 Adrienne Rich, *The Art of the Possible*, New York, Norton, 2001, p. 153, p. 2, p. 75.

448 See Lynne Segal, 'Theoretical Afflictions: Poor Rich Folk Play the Blues' in *Remembering the 1990s: New Formations*, no. 50, Autumn 2003.

449 Judith Butler, 'No, it's not Anti-Semitic', *London Review of Books*, 21 August, 2005.

450 Judith Butler, 'Violence, Mourning, Politics', *Studies in Gender and Sexuality*, vol. 4, no. 1, Winter 2003, p. 19.

451 Barbara Ehrenreich, *Nickel and Dimed: Undercover in Low-Wage USA*, London, Granta Books, 2002.

452 Barbara Ehrenreich and Arlie Russell Hochschild (eds), *Global Woman: Nannies, Maids and Sex Workers in the New Economy*, London, Granta Books, 2003.

453 Alan Sinfield, 'Middle-class Dissidence', *Ideas and Production*, 1999, nos ix and x, p. 25.

454 Julian Barnes, 'The silence', in *The Lemon Table*, London, Jonathan Cape, p. 203.

455 The latest appeal of Hardt and Negri's highly abstract notion of 'multitude' in the current 'anti-capitalist movement' is conceptualized as an ever-present immanent force of resistance inside the new global capitalist 'empire', but provides no specific sites or methods of resistance,

disdainful of any cosy accommodations to either capital or the state; see Michael Hardt and Antonio Negri, *Empire*, Cambridge, Mass., Harvard University Press, 2000.

456 Gillian Slovo, *Every Secret Thing*, London, Little Brown, 1997.

457 See Human Rights Watch World Report, 2006, http://hrw.org/podcast/wr2k6pod.xml.

Index